WALT DISNEY

Fodor's

Author: Kim Wright Wiley
Editor: Laura M. Kidder
Editorial Production: Evangelos Vasilakis
Production/Manufacturing: Amanda Bullock
Design: Guido Caroti
Cover Photo: © Disney

**To my children,
Leigh and Jordan,
the best ride-testers in the business.**

Published by Fodor's Travel, a division of Random House, Inc.

Fodor's is a registered trademark of Random House, Inc.

www.fodors.com

Every effort has been made to make this book complete and accurate as of the date of publication. In a time of rapid change, however, it is difficult to ensure that all information is entirely up-to-date. Although the publisher and authors cannot be liable for any inaccuracies or omissions in this book, they are always grateful for corrections and suggestions for improvement.

All products mentioned in this book are trademarks of their respective companies.

This book is available for special discounts for bulk purchases for sales promotions or premiums. Special editions, including personalized covers, excerpts of existing books, and corporate imprints, can be created in large quantities for special needs. For more information, write to Special Markets/Premium Sales, 1745 Broadway, MD 6-2, New York, New York 10019, or e-mail specialmarkets@randomhouse.com.

Twentieth Edition

ISBN: 978–1–4000–0830–8

PRINTED IN THE UNITED STATES OF AMERICA

10 9 8 7 6 5 4 3 2 1

Contents

Chapter 3 Once You Get There   99

Chapter 4 Touring Tips and Plans   115

Chapter 5 The Magic Kingdom   149

Chapter 6   Epcot 195

Chapter 7   Disney's Hollywood Studios 225

Chapter 8   The Animal Kingdom   253

Chapter 9   The Disney World Water Parks   275

Chapter 10   The Rest of the World   291

Chapter 11   Dining at Disney   323

Chapter 15 Islands of Adventure   427

Chapter 16 SeaWorld and Discovery Cove   469

Index   485

HELPFUL PHONE NUMBERS

All Orlando numbers have a 407 area code. Be sure to make all
Disney hotel reservations by calling 934–7639 (W–DISNEY),

and use the resorts' direct lines only to report a delayed check-in, to call Guest Services (a.k.a. Guest Relations), or to reach a registered guest.

General Walt Disney World Information Phone Numbers

General Information	824–4321
WDW Resort Information	934–7639 (W–DISNEY)
WDW Dining Information and Advance Reservations	939–3463 (WDW–DINE)
WDW Recreational Information	939–7529 (WDW–PLAY)
WDW Golf Information	939–4653 (WDW–GOLF)
WDW Tour Information	939–8687 (WDW–TOUR)
Disney Cruise Line	800/951–3532
Disney Travel Company	828–8101

Walt Disney World Resort Phone Numbers

All-Star Movies	939–7000
All-Star Music	939–6000
All-Star Sports	939–5000
Animal Kingdom Lodge	938–3000
Beach Club Resort	934–8000
BoardWalk Inn and Villas	939–5100
Caribbean Beach Resort	934–3400
Contemporary Resort	824–1000
Coronado Springs Resort	939–1000
Dolphin Resort	934–4000
Fort Wilderness Campground	824–2900
Grand Floridian Resort	824–3000
Old Key West Resort	827–7700
Polynesian Resort	824–2000
Pop Century Resort	938–4000
Port Orleans Resort	934–5000
Saratoga Springs Resort and Spa	827–1100
Swan Resort	934–3000
Wilderness Lodge and Villas	824–3200
Yacht Club Resort	934–7000

Universal Orlando Phone Numbers

General Information	363–8000
Universal Orlando Resort Information	888/273–1311

SeaWorld, Discovery Cove, and Aquatica Phone Numbers

SeaWorld	351–3600
Discovery Cove	877/434–7268
Aquatica	800/327–2420

Other Helpful Phone Numbers

Alamo Car Rental	800/462–5266
American Airlines	800/433–7300
Avis Car Rental	800/331–1212
Budget Car Rental	800/527–0700
Delta Airlines	800/221–1212
Dollar Car Rental	800/800–4000
Hertz Car Rental	800/654–3131
Mears Shuttle Service	423–5566
National Car Rental	800/227–7368
Orlando Visitors Bureau	800/255–5786
US Airways	800/428–4322

HELPFUL WEB SITES

Walt Disney World	www.disneyworld.com
The Disney Corporation	www.disney.com
The Disney Cruise Line	www.disneycruise.com
Universal Orlando	www.universalorlando.com
SeaWorld	www.seaworld.com
Discovery Cove	www.discoverycove.com

LIST OF MAPS

LIST OF QUICK-GUIDE REFERENCE TABLES

ABBREVIATIONS, TERMS, AND ICONS

Abbreviations and Terms

Downtown Disney	A shopping, dining, and entertainment complex
Hollywood	The Disney's Hollywood Studios Theme Park
Water parks	Typhoon Lagoon and Blizzard Beach
Major parks	The Magic Kingdom, Epcot, Disney's Hollywood Studios, and Disney's Animal Kingdom
Off-season	The less crowded times of the year—specifically those weeks between September and May that do not flank major holidays
On-season	The most crowded times of the year—specifically summers, holidays, and spring break
Off-site	Any resort or hotel not owned by Disney
On-site	A Disney-owned resort
TTC	Ticket and Transportation Center: The monorail version of a train station, where you can transfer to monorails bound for Epcot, the Magic Kingdom, or monorail-line hotels. You can also catch buses at the TTC bound for the parks, the on-site hotels, and Downtown Disney.

Icons

 Helpful Hint

 Hidden Mickey

 Insider's Secret

 Money-Saving Tip

 The Scare Factor

 Time-Saving Tip

PREFACE

How Has Walt Disney World Changed?

The simple answer is, it's gotten bigger. And they're still building.

In the 21 years since I first began researching this guide, Disney has added one major park, three minor ones, seven hotels, a cruise line, and more attractions and restaurants than I can count. It was once possible for a fleet-footed and well-prepared family to see most of Walt Disney World during a four-day stay. But that's no longer true. As the Disney complex expands, it's more vital than ever that you target what you want to see, work these priorities into your schedule, and then relax. Anything beyond that is pure gravy.

Sometimes I'm asked if the prevalence of travel guides makes them less useful to their readers. After all, if everyone knows about a "secret tip," is it still a secret?

Good question, but even with all those books on the market, a relatively small number of WDW visitors actually make advance preparations. Most people still show up late and wander around aimlessly, so anyone with any sort of touring plan at all is automatically a step ahead of the crowd.

It's tempting to treat Orlando as if it were a kiddie version of Las Vegas—you go there to play the numbers, and a family that hits 24 attractions in a day must, by definition, be having twice as much fun as a family that sees 12. Not so.

You'll find a lot of crying kids and exasperated parents by mid-afternoon, largely because everyone is frantic with the idea that this trip is so expensive they darn well better squeeze the most out of every minute. Actually, the most successful touring plans boil down to a few simple guidelines:

1. Plan your trip for those times of year when the parks are less crowded. When people write to me about having had bad experiences at Disney World, it seems that about 90% of the disasters happen either over spring break or in July.

2. Order maps and tickets and arrange all hotel and dining reservations well in advance. Every phone call you make from home is a line you won't have to stand in later.

3. Read up on attractions and let each family member choose three or four must-see attractions per park. An amazing number of parents plan this trip for their kids without really consulting them about what they'd most like to do.

4. Accept your differences and be willing to split up occasionally. Forcing a sullen 13-year-old onto It's a Small World or strapping a terrified 5-year-old into Rock 'n' Roller Coaster in the interest of family togetherness will guarantee at least one tantrum per hour.

5. Arrive at the parks early, rest in the afternoon, and return to the parks at night. Walt Disney World can be very tiring and regular rest stops are key.

Those five tips are always in fashion, but in the past three years there have been a few other changes worth noting:

1. The popularity of the Disney Dining Plan has changed the face of Disney restaurants—even for families who don't opt to purchase the plan. The reason? Families who once would never have considered herding the kids into top on-site

restaurants are now deciding it's cost-effective to give fine dining a try. So suddenly you're seeing even toddlers in restaurants like the Brown Derby, Citricos, Flying Fish, or California Grill. Although they're still great places to eat, the Dining Plan is indirectly taking a little of the adult feel and glamour out of these top restaurants. And the fact that so many more visitors are vying for seats inside the restaurants means that making reservations before you leave home is more important than ever. I've gotten tons of mail from families who waited until they got to Orlando to make dining reservations and found themselves closed out of the restaurants they most wanted to visit.

2. Spring and fall are becoming slightly more crowded, especially during the two weeks flanking Easter and the fall weekends in which the Mickey's Not-So-Scary Halloween parties are offered. The off-season is still a better choice than visiting in summer or at Christmas, but be aware that it's not quite as "off" as it used to be.

3. Princess power reigns supreme. The character breakfasts have always been popular, but those featuring the princess characters are so hot that they require more planning than a NASA launch. Little girls can also get styled like their favorite princess at the Bibbidi Bobbidi Boutiques, and you see more little girls than ever walking around the parks in full princess regalia. There's some effort to counterbalance this girl-power invasion with activities that boys will enjoy, such as the Jedi Training Academy at Hollywood and the Pirate Tutorial featuring Captain Jack Sparrow at Adventureland in the Magic Kingdom. But for now, at least, the prevalence of the princesses is undeniable and most little girls come under its spell. Bring costumes from home if you have them. If not, prepare to purchase.

What hasn't changed in 21 years is my belief that Walt Disney World is the best family travel destination on the planet. There's truly something for everyone within these gates, and the spectacular, awe-inspiring rides are juxtaposed with sweet, small moments of joy. As one father shared: "My best-of-all moment was my 23-month-old daughter standing on the seat of Disney's Magical Express as we entered the gates of Walt Disney World yelling 'Mickey . . . don't worry . . . I coming!' That made it worth all the trouble and expense before we'd even arrived."

Throughout this book I've included such comments as the one above from Disney visitors who've written to me to share their best tales, tips, and "never again" stories. I'd love to hear how your trip went and any feedback you have about this book. If you'd like to share your travel experiences with me, please take a few minutes to respond to my survey online at www.fodors.com/disneysurvey, e-mail me at kwwiley @fodors.com, or write to me at Fodor's, 1745 Broadway, New York, NY 10019. Thanks for your time, and have a great trip!

—Kim

CHAPTER

1

Before You Leave Home

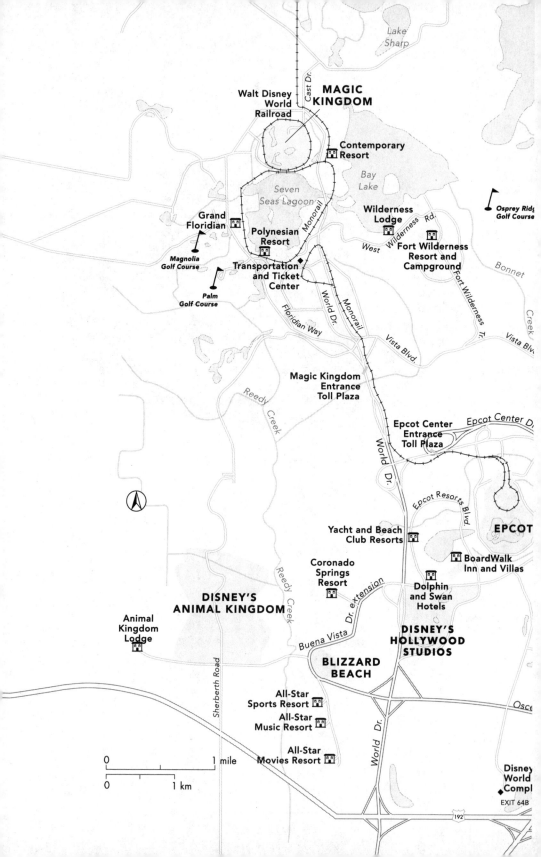

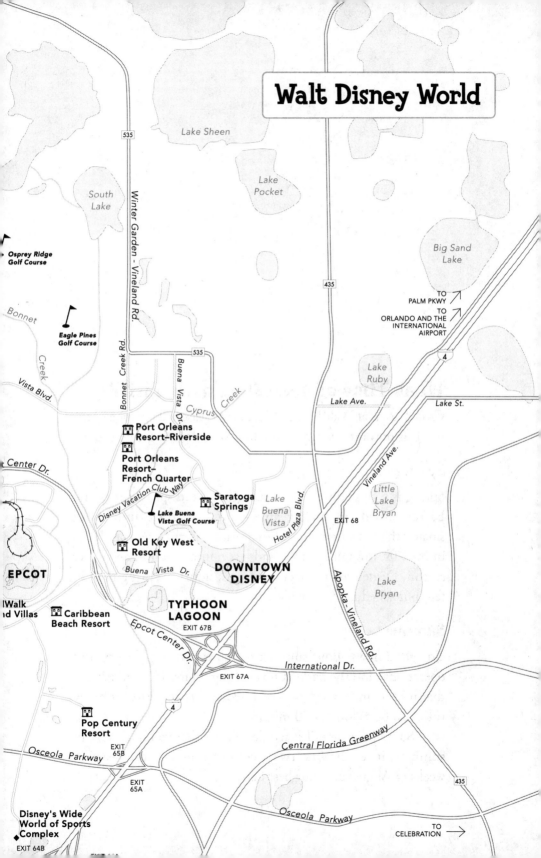

What Time of Year Should We Visit?

Crowd levels at Walt Disney World vary seasonally, so one of the most important decisions you'll make is deciding when to go.

Spring

Spring is a great time to visit. Except around spring break and Easter, crowds are manageable—not as sparse as in fall, but smaller than in summer. And the weather is sublime, with highs in the 70s, lows in the 60s, and less rainfall than in any other season. Disney maintains longer park hours in spring than in fall, but schedules vary widely.

Summer

The good news about summer is that everything is open and operational and the parks run very long hours. The bad news is that it's hot and crowded—so crowded that the wait for many rides can be as long as 90 minutes.

Sometimes school schedules dictate that you must visit in summer; if so, the first two weeks of June and the last two weeks of August are your best bets.

Insider's Secret

To check projected hours of operation during the weeks you're considering, visit www.disneyworld. com. Park hours generally remain as projected but can change; to be safe, revisit the site a couple of weeks before you leave home to reconfirm theme park hours.

Fall

Fall has lighter crowds than summer and the weather is usually great. There are, however, disadvantages to a fall visit. You have to work around the fact that older children are in school. The parks run shorter hours in fall; the Magic Kingdom, Animal Kingdom, and Hollywood may close as early as 5 PM, although Epcot always remains open later. Earlier closings mean that some of the special evening presentations, such as the evening parade in the Magic Kingdom, are scheduled only on the weekends.

Helpful Hint

If you have preschoolers, babies, or senior citizens in the party, avoid summers like the plague.

Fall is the season for two of Walt Disney World's most popular events: Mickey's Not-So-Scary Halloween Party at the

Helpful Hint

The size of the crowds corresponds with the school schedule. Any time the kids are out of school (i.e., summers, spring break, and major holidays) is the "on-season." Any time children are traditionally in school is the "off-season."

Magic Kingdom (with selected dates beginning just after Labor Day) and the Epcot Food & Wine Festival. These events are doing exactly what Disney designed them to do—drawing people in during slower times. Consult www.disneyworld.com to buy tickets early, or to note the party dates if you want to avoid them.

Insider's Secret

One of the major changes since we began doing this book 20 years ago is that the number of fall visitors has steadily grown. It's still less crowded than summers and holidays but the special events (especially the über-popular Halloween parties) have influenced crowd flow. If you want to go to the Halloween parties, great. The fun is worth the extra effort. But even if you don't, be aware of the dates. The Magic Kingdom closes early on evenings the parties are scheduled to run, so you can't go there, but with so much of the crowd clustered at the Magic Kingdom, it's the perfect time to visit the other parks.

Late summer and early fall make up hurricane season in Florida, so there is some risk that you'll schedule your trip for the exact week that Hurricane Laluna pounds the coast. Fortunately, Orlando is an hour inland, meaning that coastal storms usually only yield rain and, should worst come to worst, Disney has "ride out" plans (i.e., a hurricane policy) to ensure your safety. Furthermore, there are more rainy days in summer than there are in the fall, so, in general, the advantages of autumn touring far outweigh the disadvantages.

Winter

Winter is a mixed bag. The absolute worst times are holidays. Christmas and New Year's can pull in as many as 90,000 visi-

Helpful Hint

Don't underestimate the holiday crowds. In the weeks flanking Christmas, Disney World is mobbed, and any holiday when the kids are out of school—such as Presidents' Day weekend—will draw larger-than-average crowds.

tors per day, and even extended hours can't compensate for crowds of this size. But if you avoid the holiday weeks, winter can be an ideal time to visit. With the exception of the weekends around Martin Luther King Jr. Day and Presidents' Day, January and February aren't crowded—and they're pleasantly

Insider's Secret

Mickey's Very Merry Christmas Party, held each year on several evenings throughout December, is madly popular. If you want to attend the party, get tickets early—they sell out months in advance. Dates for each year's parties are listed on www.disneyworld.com.

cool. The first two weeks of December, when the Christmas decorations are already up but the crowds have not yet arrived, are wonderful options. The parks run the same shortened hours in winter that they run in fall, but since the crowds are so much lighter, you'll still have time to see everything you want.

Off-Season Touring Caveat

Some parents have written in to say that they like taking the kids to Orlando during the off-season, but that they've heard this is when Disney is most apt to close attractions for refurbishing. It's a valid point. On a recent trip in January, I found five attractions closed for refurbishing, including Big Thunder Mountain in the Magic Kingdom and Star Tours at Holly-

Insider's Secret

Water babies take note: pools may be closed for refurbishing in January and February. Generally, only one water park is open at a time in winter, and both may shut down if the temperature dips below 55 degrees.

wood. But I still believe it's better to tour during the off-season. Here's why: during that same January week, the most popular Magic Kingdom attractions, such as the Many Adventures of Winnie the Pooh and Splash Mountain, were posting wait times as short as 20 minutes, about a third of what they normally are, so even taking closings into account, you'll still ride more and wait less during the off-season. If your kids have their hearts set on a certain attraction, you can avoid last-minute disappointments by checking www.disneyworld.com to see what's scheduled to be closed during your trip.

Insider's Secret

Certain annual events—most notably the marathon in January, College Week in April, Gay Day in June, and various press events throughout the year—bring large groups into the parks. Ask about events or groups before you book, so you'll know what to expect.

How Long Should We Stay?

It will take at least four days for a family to tour the major parks. If you also want to visit the water parks and Downtown Disney, make that five days. Six days are best for families who'd like to work in sporting options like boating or golf, or those who would like to tour at a more leisurely pace.

If you plan on visiting other area attractions, such as Sea-World or Universal Orlando, allow a week.

Insider's Secret

In 2009 Walt Disney World began inviting guests to visit a theme park free on their birthday. As Disney is loathe to discontinue popular programs, this option is likely to continue beyond 2009. You can start the process by registering at www.disneyparks.com.

Should We Take the Kids out of School?

Even if you're sold on the advantages of off-season touring, you may be reluctant to take your children out of school. However, there are ways to highlight the educational aspects of a trip to Disney World. Work together with your child's teacher to create a plan that keeps him from falling behind. Ideally, half of the make up work should be done before you leave—the post-trip blues are bad enough without facing three hours of homework each night. Also, timing is everything. Don't plan your trip for the week the school is administering exams or standardized testing.

In addition, help your child create a project that's related to the trip—perhaps something like a scrapbook. The mother of one first-grader helped him design an "ABC" book before he left home, and he spent his week at Disney World collecting

Epcot Projects

• The greenhouse tour in the Land is full of information on space-age farming.

• Marine biology is the theme of the Living Seas pavilion.

• Missing health class? The Wonders of Life pavilion is devoted to that greatest of all machines, the human body.

• The World Showcase demonstrates the culture—including music, architecture, food, and history—of several foreign countries.

• Innoventions offers a hands-on preview of technological advances.

souvenirs for each page—Goofy's autograph on the "G" page, a postcard of a Japanese pagoda on the "P" page, and so on. An older child might gather leaves from the various trees and shrubs that were imported to landscape the countries in the World Showcase. Or a young photographer could demonstrate her proficiency with various lighting techniques by photographing Cinderella Castle in early morning, high noon, sunset, and after dark.

You can even work on math. If a car containing six people departs from the Test Track loading area every 20 seconds, how many riders go through in an hour? A day? If the monorail averages 32 mph, how long does it take it to travel the 7 miles from the Magic Kingdom to Epcot? Once you get going on these sorts of questions, they're addictive. Or give your kids a set amount of mythical money to spend, such as $1,000. Then let them keep track of expenses, deducting purchases from their starting total and making decisions about what they can and cannot afford on their budget.

Animal Kingdom Projects

- The Cretaceous Trail—a path filled with plants that have survived from the Cretaceous period—is an excellent introduction to botanical evolution.

- Rafiki's Planet Watch is the park's research and education hub, where kids can tour veterinary labs and watch interactive videos about endangered animals.

- It's always fun to do a report on one of the animals you see on Kilimanjaro Safaris or along one of the exploration trails.

Other Orlando Educational Programs

Disney World isn't the only place in Orlando that can be educational. Consider the following:

SeaWorld

SeaWorld offers daily tours, as well as weeklong classes and overnight programs in summer and during holidays. Call 800/406–2244 for information on the extended Adventure Camps or visit www.seaworld.org. If your kids aren't up for a full program or you're visiting at a time of year when they're not offered, it's easy to work in one of SeaWorld's behind-the-scenes tours. See Chapter 16 for details on touring SeaWorld.

Orlando Science Center

This impressive facility has oodles of hands-on exhibits and programs for kids of all ages. Something is happening all the time—especially in spring and summer when most of the camps are held—and the prices are reasonable.

Admission to the center is $23 for adults and $18 for kids ages 3 to 11. Classes are individually priced. To see what's happening during your visit call 888/OSC–4Fun or 407/514–2000 or visit www.osc.org.

Kennedy Space Center

Orlando is only about an hour's drive from the Kennedy Space Center so it's an easy day trip. Kids will enjoy seeing the rockets and the IMAX films about space exploration. You can even plan your visit to coincide with a launch. (It's a strange but cool fact that space launches are also visible from Orlando.)

Crew passes, which include a bus tour of the space center as well as the IMAX film, are $38 for adults and $28 for kids ages 3 to 11. Call 321/867–5000 or visit www.kennedyspace center.com for details on launch dates and tours.

Insider's Secret

The Kennedy Space Center's Astronaut Training Experience (ATX) is ideal for science-crazed kids aged 8 and up. This is a full-immersion experience—you ride in flight simulators, build and launch rockets, and play crew in a mock-up of a shuttle mission. The cost is $250 per person for the one-day program; there's also a two-day family package (including overnight stay) beginning at $625, which covers one adult and one child ($275 per each additional child or adult). Make reservations in advance at www.kennedyspace center.com.

Should We Buy a Package?

This is a toughie. There are advantages to package trips, most notably that if you play your cards right, you can, indeed, save money. It's also helpful to know up front exactly what your vacation will cost. Packages often require hefty prepayments, which are painful at the time, but at least you don't return home with your credit card utterly maxed out. And with the mega-popular Disney Dining Plan package, there's the convenience of having one card serve as your room key, theme park ticket, and dining ticket. It eliminates the hassles of carrying cash and tracking how much you're spending.

Package trips can have drawbacks. Like buying a fully loaded car off a dealer's lot, you may find yourself paying for options you don't want and don't need. Packages are sometimes padded with perks such as reduced golf-course greens fees, which interest only a few families, or free rental cars, which you may not need if you're staying on-site. Unless you're certain you'll use most of the features contained in the package, you'll probably end up losing money on the deal. At the other end of the spectrum are deeply discounted packages that place you in run-down or out-of-the-way hotels.

Money-Saving Tips

- AAA and travel agents can provide genuine bargains, especially if you don't need to stay on Disney property.
- Want to stay on-site? Travel agents can be a helpful resource. Check with an agency for prices and then call Disney directly to compare.
- Look for deals online. Disney's own Web site has added a special page highlighting cost-saving options at www.disneyworld.com/affordable. Or check out www.expedia.com, www.hotels.com, www.wdwvacations.com, or www.vacationoutlet. com for deals on off-site rooms and packages.
- If you're calling to book your room, whether on-site or off-site, always ask, "Are there any discounts or special offers available?" Sometimes you'll learn about deals over the phone that aren't listed on the resort Web site.

Money-Saving Tip

Don't automatically assume that a package will save you big bucks. Unless you're sure you'll use every feature—or almost every feature—that the package includes, you may end up losing money on the deal. Run the numbers.

Airline Packages

If you're flying, check out the airline's own packages, which include airfare, theme park tickets for Disney and other Orlando attractions, and lodging at either on-site or off-site hotels. Again there's a huge range of amenities—you can have valet parking and bottles of champagne if you're willing to pay for them. And again the packages can be fine-tuned to meet your needs.

Cruise Packages

Some of the most popular Disney packages are those that combine a cruise with a vacation in the parks. Check out www.disneycruise.com, call 800/370–0097, or contact your travel agent. See Chapter 13 for more information.

Disney Package Vacations

By far the most popular packages are those offered by Disney itself. The basic Magic Your Way package includes a hotel room on Disney property and theme park tickets. You can choose any resort in any price range as well as the ticket options that suit your family's needs. Magic Your Way allows you to customize your package to the nth degree, fine-tuning the time of year, length of stay, resort, type of ticket, and type of dining. The good news is, it gives you lots of options. The bad news is . . . it gives you lots of options.

So how do you know what to choose? Let's start with tickets. The rule of thumb is, if your kids are young or this is your first trip to Disney World, you'll probably be spending most of your time in the four major theme parks, so choose a package with base tickets. If your kids are 8 and up, consider upgrading to the Park Hopper option since it gives you the flexibility to move from one park to another in the course of the day. The more expensive premium and platinum options are really only helpful for families who've been to Disney World before and want to explore beyond the basic parks and those whose kids are old enough to enjoy the water parks, sporting options, tours, and Cirque du Soleil. For most families, the base ticket or the base ticket with the Park Hopper option works fine.

How does the ticket type affect the cost of the trip? Let's take a mythical family of four and walk them through the process. If they're traveling during the off-season, let's say in October, a five-night package at a value resort with base tickets will cost them approximately $1,400. Pretty reasonable, huh? If they add the Park Hopper option to their tickets, the price will rise to $1,600.

The resort category—from value to moderate to deluxe to deluxe villa—and the season also affect the price of a package. (Chapter 2 outlines the pluses and minuses of each on-site resort; for now, you just need to consider how much this choice affects costs.) So, let's go back to our mythical family of four who can get five nights at a value resort for $1,400. In peak season that same package will cost them approximately $1,700.

Still pretty reasonable. But what if they upgrade their hotel? A stay at a deluxe hotel for five days during value season will cost them approximately $3,000. The same five-night package in the same deluxe hotel during peak season is closer to $4,200. So by making two changes—the type of resort and the time of year—our family has literally tripled their vacation price.

Going through the exercise above has probably done two things: given you sticker shock and overwhelmed you. Still, it's a good introduction to the Disney vacation experience, which involves an almost staggering number of choices. Your best bet is to go to www.disneyworld.com, click on "Vacation Booking Guide" and punch in all your dream options. Then start tweaking, eliminating or downgrading options, changing the dates of your visit, etc., until you arrive at a price you can live with.

Before you go to the site, however, you also need to decide whether or not to add a dining plan, which ups the package price by about $100 a day for a family of four. Since there's so much controversy on the dining plan issue, it deserves its own section.

Should You Add a Dining Plan?

The Magic Your Way dining plans start at about $40 per day for adults and $12 per day for kids ages 3 to 9. The basic plan includes, for each day of your trip, one full-service meal, one counter-service meal, and a snack from a list of the 100-plus participating Disney restaurants, which are scattered throughout the four theme parks and on-site hotels.

Is it worth it? If you have big eaters in the party, the plan can save you an estimated 32% over the individual cost of meals. But, if 6-year-old Katie eats nothing but cereal and 3-year-old Danny grows so restless that sit-down dinners are a nightmare, it's unlikely they'll eat enough food to justify the cost of the dining plan.

One other thing to consider: Certain experiences, like the dinner shows, character meals, and meals in most of the "signature" (i.e., most upscale) restaurants, are worth more than your daily full-service meal allowance. For one of these exceptional dining experiences, you must swap out two of your regular full-service meals. But the swap can still save you a bundle on what would otherwise be a very expensive dinner. One mother wrote, "By eating at counter-service places for a couple of days beforehand we saved enough credits for dinner at California Grill and it was superb."

Another mom wrote that, "the Disney Dining Plan makes a lot of sense if you like character meals. We were able to attend three: at Crystal Palace, Chef Mickey's, and 1900 Park Fare, and we could not have afforded all this without the plan."

A father from Texas added, "I'm a little compulsive, at least according to my wife, and I ran a tally of what we would have paid if we'd ordered menu items on our own versus going with the dining plan. Trust me, the dining plan is a great value."

One family of foodies from New York opted to upgrade to the Deluxe Dining Plan, which allows sit-down dining at every meal and further added the "Wine and Dine" option. "For us, it was worth it," said the mother. "We had some terrific meals which were, thanks to the plan, reasonably priced. And our kids are old enough to enjoy the ambience of the restaurants, which are actually as full of Disney atmosphere as the resorts and parks."

On the other hand, a couple from Georgia with three children under age 10 said that even the basic meal plans weren't for them: "In our opinion," said the father, "adding meals to

Theme Park Ticket
Price Chart

TICKET OPTIONS								
TICKET	**10-DAY**	**7-DAY**	**6-DAY**	**5-DAY**	**4-DAY**	**3-DAY**	**2-DAY**	**1-DAY**
BASE TICKET								
Ages 10–up	$237	$228	$225	$220	$219	$212	$149	$75
Ages 3–9	$202	$193	$190	$187	$184	$179	$125	$63

Base Ticket admits guest to one of the four major theme parks per day's use.
Park choices are: Magic Kingdom, Epcot, Disney Hollywood Studios, Disney's Animal Kingdom.
8-day and **9-day** tickets are also available

ADD: Park Hopper	$50	$50	$50	$50	$50	$50	$50	$50

Park Hopper option entitles guest to visit more than one theme park per day's use. Park choices are any combination of Magic Kingdom, Epcot, Disney Hollywood Studios, Disney's Animal Kingdom.

ADD: Water Park Fun	$50	$50	$50	$50	$50	$50	$50	$50
	5 visits	7 visits	6 visits	5 visits	4 visits	3 visits	2 visits	2 visits

Water Park Fun option entitles guest to a specified number of visits (between 2 and 10) to a choice of entertainment and recreation venues. Choices are Blizzard Beach, Typhoon Lagoon, DisneyQuest, and Wide World of Sports.

ADD: No Expiration	$200	$110	$80	$70	$50	$23	$17	n/a

No expiration means that unused admissions on a ticket may be used any time in the future.
Without this option, tickets expire 14 days after first use.

MINOR PARKS AND ATTRACTIONS		
TICKET	**AGES 10-UP**	**AGES 3-9**
TYPHOON LAGOON OR BLIZZARD BEACH 1-Day 1-Park	$40	$34
DISNEYQUEST 1-Day	$40	$34
DISNEY'S WIDE WORLD OF SPORTS	$10.98	$8.41
CIRQUE DU SOLEIL'S *LA NOUBA*	$67–$117	$54–$94

*All prices are subject to Florida sales tax.

your package only makes sense if you're prepared to eat 6,000 calories a day and spend three hours a day in restaurants." A mom from New York added, "We considered it a hassle to have to plan all our full-service meals in advance and make reservations. Normally we're pretty flexible on vacations—but not this time."

Helpful Hint
You must add the dining plan before you arrive in Orlando. You can't tack it on once you're there.

Not participating in the dining plan can impact your vacation. Most families on the plan make reservations for all their full-service meals, which means that peak dining times for popular restaurants are often booked months in advance. Families who don't jump on the early reservation bandwagon may arrive in Orlando to find themselves with few dining options, especially if they're traveling during the on-season.

What Kind of Tickets Do We Need?

Under Disney's flexible Magic Your Way ticketing system, you can customize your tickets to reflect your family's priorities and length of stay.

Let's say you have a long weekend to visit and want a three-day ticket. The base price is $212 for ages 10 and up, which comes to $71 a day, a slight savings over the one-day ticket price of $75. However, this base price lets you into only one park per day. From there, you can add the Park Hopper option, which allows you to move from park to park within a day. This will bring the price of your three-day ticket to $262. If you add on Blizzard Beach, Typhoon Lagoon, and Disney-

Quest—called the Water Park Fun & More option—your ticket price rises to $262. If you want both the Park Hopper and the Water Fun option, the price rises to $312.

Confused yet? Hang on, it gets even more complicated. Although your tickets won't expire if you don't go to the parks, say, every day (indeed, most families like to space out their park visits), there's the matter of the No Expiration option. Without it, Magic Your Way tickets expire 14 days after their first use. Adding it to a three-day adult ticket the price will raise the price to $235.

If you want the Park Hopper option and the Water Park Fun & More option and the No Expiration option—in other words, the whole ticketing enchilada—the cost of your three-day ticket leaps all the way to $335.

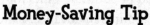

Money-Saving Tip

If you know for sure that you'll be returning to Orlando in the future it could make real sense to buy a ticket with multiple days and the No Expiration option. For example, an eight-day adult ticket with a No Expiration option is $376, which breaks down to $47 a day, a significant savings over the present one-day ticket price of $75 and an even more significant savings if (and when) Disney raises the prices again. Just make sure to hang on to your tickets. I've received letters from several families who paid for the No Expiration option and then managed to lose their pricey tickets sometime during that relocation to Omaha.

So, how do you know what ticketing options to buy? If this is your first trip to Disney World, keep it simple. If you have young kids, you'll likely spend most of your time in the four major parks, so a base ticket is fine. As a mom with three preschoolers said, "We bought the Park Hopper option but the logistics of moving around with that many strollers and backpacks was just overwhelming. After one day of trying to park-hop we decided it would be less stressful to stay in a single park every day. So we basically paid extra for nothing."

Money-Saving Tip

The more days you buy, the less your per-day cost. If you're staying for a week, your ticket price per day drops significantly. An adult buying a seven-day basic ticket ends up paying around $32 per day, a significant savings over the one-day ticket price of $75.

But if your kids are older and able to withstand a long day, the Park Hopper option is worthwhile. The Park Hopper also comes in handy if you're traveling during the off-season when the Magic Kingdom and Hollywood Studios close earlier; without it you may find yourself with little to do after 6 PM. And it's also good for people who've been to Disney World before and know exactly what attractions they want to see or who know they like to move around swiftly, revisiting these favorites. (Many of the touring tips in this book assume that you have the ability to move from one park to another in the course of the day.) If any of these conditions apply to you, the vote on the Park Hopper option should be "yes."

Money-Saving Tip

Disney "adjusts"—that is, raises—prices regularly, so you should always confirm the numbers by calling 407/824–4321 or visiting www.disneyworld.com. Also note that children under age 3 are admitted free.

Finally, the Water Park Fun & More option makes sense if you have older kids who would enjoy the water parks and DisneyQuest, or if you've been to Disney World before and are looking to venture outside the four major parks. On the other hand, if this is your first trip to Disney World you'll have all you can handle just visiting the four major parks. And if your kids are very young, you may find your hotel pool is a far more practical way to cool off than trekking to a water park. So, it's a "yes" on Water Park Fun & More only for families with kids over 8 or who are visiting Disney World for the second time. For first-time visitors or families with kids under 8, the answer is usually "no."

And if you get to Orlando and change your mind, not to worry. You can add the Water Park Fun & More option at any time during your vacation.

There's one other thing to keep in mind about theme park tickets, which are also your room keys if you're staying on-site. They demagnetize easily, so keep them in a separate pocket away from your credit cards and cell phone. If your ticket does become demagnetized and won't swipe at the entrance turnstiles, Disney will gladly replace it. But this involves a trip to Guest Services (a.k.a. Guest Relations) and it's exasperating to have to make this detour when you're itching to get to the rides or exhausted after a day in the parks.

Disney uses a biometric identification system to keep track of exactly who is using those multiday tickets. The first time you enter a Disney park, you'll be asked to do a hand scan, and the minute measurements of your individual fingers will be recorded. You'll be re-scanned each time you use the same ticket to enter another Disney park. It's a high-tech way to cut down on ticket swapping and the black-market sales of multiday tickets.

Transportation

If you're flying to Orlando, another major decision is whether or not you need to rent a car. For families staying on-site and focusing primarily on Disney attractions, the answer is probably "no," especially since Disney offers free bus transportation between the airport and your Disney hotel. Quite a few families have reported that they used their rental car less than they

Insider's Secret

At times it may make more sense to use a taxi than a rental car or Disney's transportation. Taxi rides around Disney property average $15, and parking is $12—not a big difference. If you plan to drive around a lot it makes sense to have your own car, but if you only need direct transportation occasionally, a cab is a perfectly fine option. Consider taking a cab if:

- You'd like quick, direct transportation from the airport to your hotel.
- You'd like quick, direct transportation from one resort to another.
- You're headed to a minor park like Downtown Disney or the water parks and don't want a lengthy shuttle commute.
- You're staying at a Disney hotel but heading to Universal Orlando or SeaWorld for the day.
- Everyone's absolutely exhausted. If you've pushed too far and the kids are in a meltdown, cabs are the fastest way to get back to your room. They're always waiting near the theme park exits and, at times, this is $15 well worth spending.

anticipated. "We paid $350 for the privilege of driving from the airport to our hotel and back," wrote one father.

But for families staying off-site or anyone planning to visit both Disney and non-Disney attractions, the answer is often "yes." "We got a great hotel rate but it was about 15 miles from Disney World," one mother reported. "We also spent a day at Universal and a day at SeaWorld, so we would have been sunk if we hadn't had our own transportation."

Another mother added, "Our kids get so excited at Disney that they go full-out the whole time, running around in a frenzy. But when they collapse, they really collapse. There were a couple of times when even having to wait 15 minutes for a bus would have been a disaster. Every time we left a theme park, they'd be asleep in the car before we were even out of the parking lot."

Transportation with a Rental Car

Some rental car companies, such as Avis, Budget, Dollar, and National, have desks at the Orlando airport, with cars in the adjacent lot. Others, including Hertz and Alamo, are away from the airport and require a separate shuttle ride.

Alamo	800/462–5266	www.alamo.com
Avis	800/331–1212	www.avis.com
Budget	800/527–0700	www.budget.com
Dollar	800/800–4000	www.dollar.com
Hertz	800/654–3131	www.hertz.com
National	800/227–7368	www.nationalcar.com

An average weekly rental fee for a midsize car is around $350. Don't be fooled by the quoted rate of $30 a day; by the time you add on taxes and insurance it's closer to $50.

Transportation without a Rental Car

If you're staying at a Disney resort, the Magical Express Service makes transport from the airport to your hotel room less costly, and, if all goes according to plan, more convenient. Here's how it works:

Check your bags at your hometown airport. This is the last time you'll see them until you're in your Orlando hotel room, so be sure to put anything you may need in the meantime, such as medication or summer-weather clothing, into your carry-on. When your plane arrives, you don't have to go to baggage claim to pick up your bags—instead, follow the directions of the Disney representative waiting on the baggage claim level. You'll board a motor coach and head for your resort to start having fun, and—if all goes smoothly—your bags will arrive in your room about three hours after you do. You don't have to be on-site to sign for your luggage; if you want to go straight to the theme parks, the bags will be waiting for you when you get back.

The Magical Express Service not only saves you the hassle of tracking and dragging your bags every step of the way but it also means free airport-to-resort transport for all Disney hotel guests, which will save a minimum of roughly $120.

Insider's Secret

The Magical Express airport buses usually stop at several hotels and this can add up to a long commute time. If you're really eager to get your vacation going fast, take a cab. Also, some families have reported significant wait times for their luggage, so do pack essentials in a carry-on. "It took seven hours to get our luggage," said one mother from Wisconsin. "We couldn't take the kids swimming, we didn't have our camera, and we ended up spending the whole first day walking around in 90-degree weather in long sleeves and jeans."

If you're not staying at a Disney resort and not renting a car, you have two options for airport transfers. The fastest and easiest is a cab; prices average about $50 to the Universal–SeaWorld area and $60 to the Disney area, plus tip. Alternatively, you can take the Mears Shuttle Service, which costs $32 round-trip for adults and $24 for kids. You can reserve your shuttle before leaving home by calling 407/423–5566. If there are more than two people in your party, it's cheaper to take a cab.

Insider's Secret

You just got to Orlando, so of course you're not thinking about going home yet. But, as a sadder-but-wiser mother from Ohio advises, "If you use the Magical Express for your return service to the airport, don't book your return flight before noon. They require you to be on the bus three hours before your flight time, which for us basically involved getting up and checking out in the middle of the night."

Countdown to Disney World

Okay, let's summarize. Here's what needs to be done—and when.

As Soon as Possible

- Choose your resort. To help find the best on-site hotel for you, consult Chapter 2, and once you've narrowed your options, make reservations via www.disneyworld.com or 407/934–7639 (407/W–DISNEY).

- Book your room. Even if you're staying off-site, booking early is smart. A great way to get discounts on off-site lodging is to go to the Orlando Travel Bureau Web site at www.orlandoinfo.com to request an Orlando Vacation Planning Kit Magicard. It takes three to four weeks to get the package, but the card qualifies you for significant discounts at many off-site hotels.

- Buy your theme park tickets. You can either buy online at www.disneyworld.com, which sometimes offers a slight discount, or call 407/934–7639 (407/W–DISNEY).

- Get maps. When you purchase your tickets, request maps of the theme parks to aid in your planning. If you need a "Guidebook for Guests with Disabilities," request that, too.

Money-Saving Tip

The Magicard, offered through the Orlando Travel Bureau, is a great source of savings for families staying at off-site hotels, and you can download the card, as well as get lots of general Orlando information, by visiting www.orlandoinfo.com. Another way to cut your costs is to buy an entertainment discount coupon book for your hometown. The books are best known for their local restaurant coupons, but few people realize that a nationwide directory of hotels offering discounts can be found in the back. Several off-site Orlando hotels—including several in the well-located Disney Hotel Plaza area—are listed, and a discount can make an upscale resort as inexpensive as an interstate cheapie. But only a few rooms per hotel are earmarked for the discount, so your chances of cashing in improve if you're willing to book early.

Six Months in Advance

@ Flying? Book now.

@ If you need a rental car, reserve it now.

@ You can arrange for dining reservations, including character meals and dinner shows, 180 days in advance by calling 407/939–3463 (407/WDW–DINE).

@ Does your little princess want to be styled at the Bibbidi Bobbidi Boutique? Sign her up 180 days in advance by dialing 407/939–3463 (407/WDW–STYLE).

@ Families who would like to take a behind-the-scenes tour or enroll their kids in one of the Grand Floridian programs—such as the pirate-theme scavenger hunt or tea with Alice and the other Wonderland characters—should book at this stage. Call 407/939–8687 (407/WDW–TOUR) for the tours and 407/939–3463 (407/WDW–DINE) for the Grand Floridian programs. Kid-friendly tours and programs are explained in Chapter 10.

Four Months in Advance

@ To book a fireworks cruise call 407/939–7529 (407/WDW–PLAY). See Chapter 10 for more information.

@ Interested in golf, parasailing, surfing, or some other sport? Book your time by calling 407/939–7529 (407/WDW–PLAY). See Chapter 10 for details.

@ Want a spa treatment? Call Saratoga Springs Resort & Spa at 407/827–4455 or the Grand Floridian Resort at 407/824–2332 for a reservation.

@ For Cirque du Soleil tickets, call 407/939–7600.

Two Weeks in Advance

@ You should be good to go. Just reconfirm theme park hours at www.disneyworld.com and check over reservations, so when you get to Orlando all you'll have to focus on is having fun.

Helpful Hint

Numerous Web sites provide information and advice on Walt Disney World. Disney's official site, www.disneyworld.com, is definitely the place to start but for no-holds-barred reviews, check out www.mousesavers.com, www.disboards.com, and www.fodors.com/forums.

Things to Discuss with Your Kids Before You Leave Home

It's important to include the kids in the vacation planning, so discuss the following topics before you leave home.

The Trip Itself

There are two schools of thought on just how far in advance you should tell the kids you're headed to Disney World. Because many families make reservations as much as a year in advance, it's easy to fall into a "waiting for Christmas" syndrome, with the kids nearly in a lather of anticipation weeks before you leave. To avoid the agony of a long countdown, one couple packed in secret and then woke the kids up at 5 AM and announced, "Get in the car, we're going to Disney World." The best method is probably somewhere between these two extremes. Tell your kids at the time you make the reservations and solicit their opinions about what activities to book in advance, but don't begin poring over the brochures in earnest until about a month before the trip.

The Layout of the Parks

Testimonies from the more than 1,000 families surveyed or interviewed for this book have shown that the amount of advance research you do directly correlates with how much you enjoy your trip. Don't get me wrong—visitors who show up at Disney World without any preparation can still have fun, but their comment sheets are peppered with "Next time I'll know . . ." and "If only we had . . ."

If you're letting preteens and teens roam around on their own, brief them on the locations of major attractions. But the pleasures of being prepared can extend even to preschoolers. If you purchase a few Disney World coloring books or a kids' touring guide, even the youngest child will arrive able to identify Spaceship Earth and Splash Mountain. A little knowledge before entering the gates is essential to helping you spend your time in the parks wisely.

The Classic Stories of Disney

If your kids are under 8, another good pre-trip purchase is a set of Disney books with CDs or tapes. Even though parental eyes may glaze over when Dumbo starts over for the 34th time, these recordings and books help to familiarize kids with the characters and rides they'll be seeing once they arrive. "I made sure my 1-year-old was familiar with the Disney characters, but what really helped was buying the Disney Classics CD before the trip," wrote one mom. "We listened to it in the car every day and when we were at Disney, we would get so excited when he heard a song; we knew that he would jump around and try to sing along."

Some families rent Disney movies before the trip. For example, viewing *Honey, I Shrunk the Kids* before you leave will vastly improve your children's appreciation of Epcot's Honey, I Shrunk the Audience as well as the Honey, I Shrunk the Kids Movie Set Adventure at Hollywood. Even watching an old favorite like *The Little Mermaid* or *Aladdin* can refresh your child's memory and make it doubly exciting when, a few weeks later, he comes face to face with the characters in the park.

Special Academic Projects

See the section "Should We Take the Kids Out of School?" earlier in this chapter for ideas. Whatever project you decide upon, it's essential you get the kids on board before you arrive in Orlando. Once there, they'll be too distracted for your lectures on academic responsibility.

Souvenirs and Money

Will you save all souvenir purchases for the last day? Buy one small souvenir every day? Are the children expected to spend their own money, or will you spring for the T-shirts? Whatever you decide, set the rules before you're in the park. Otherwise the selection of goodies will lure you into spending far more than you anticipated.

One excellent technique for limiting impulse buys is to purchase Disney Dollars the first day you're in WDW. (You can get them at any on-site hotel or at Guest Services in any park.) Disney Dollars come in denominations of $1, $5, and $10 (with pictures of Disney characters where presidents would be) and are accepted throughout Disney World. You can give your kids an age-appropriate number of Disney Dollars at the beginning of the trip, explaining that this money alone is for souvenirs.

The Scare Factor

Finally, give some thought to the scare factor. A disappointing meal or boring show can ruin an hour, but if misjudging a ride leaves you with a terrified or nauseated child, that can ruin the whole day.

How frightening a ride is can be tough to gauge because Disney World scariness comes in two forms. First there are atmospheric rides, ranging from the shadows and cardboard witch of Snow White's Scary Adventures to the creepy, cobwebbed old hotel in the Tower of Terror. The other kind of fear factor is motion related: while Space Mountain and Expedition Everest are obviously risky, some guests can lose their lunch on sweet little charmers like the Mad Tea Party.

Disney's guidance comes in the form of height requirements, but saying that a 41-inch-tall 5-year-old can ride Big Thunder Mountain is no indication that he should ride Big Thunder Mountain. As we all know, some 6-year-olds are fearless and some 11-year-olds easily unnerved. Read the ride descriptions and scare-factor ratings in this book to find out what you're dealing with.

Height Requirements

The Magic Kingdom

Barnstormer	35 inches
Big Thunder Mountain	40 inches
Splash Mountain	40 inches
Space Mountain	44 inches
Stitch's Great Escape	40 inches
Tomororowland Speedway	32 inches

Epcot

Mission: SPACE	44 inches
Soarin'	40 inches
Test Track	40 inches

Hollywood Studios

Rock 'n' Roller Coaster   48 inches
Star Tours   40 inches
Tower of Terror   40 inches

The Animal Kingdom

Dinosaur   40 inches
Expedition Everest   44 inches
Kali River Rapids   38 inches
Primeval Whirl   48 inches

If you're still unsure, employ these strategies:

- *Do a Baby Swap.* (No, this does not mean you can trade your shrieking toddler for that angelic napping infant behind you!) If you have doubts about whether a ride is appropriate for your child, inform the attendant that you may need to do a Baby Swap. As you approach the attraction, one parent rides and returns with the verdict. If the first parent thinks the child will do okay, the second parent immediately boards and rides with the child. If the first parent thinks the ride is too wild, the second (yet-to-ride) parent passes the child through to the first parent and then rides him- or herself. It sounds confusing, but the attendants help you and it actually works smoothly.

- *Slowly increase ride intensity throughout the day.* This advice runs counter to the touring tips you'll find later in this book that recommend you ride the big-deal attractions first thing in the morning, but if you're not sure your 7-year-old is up for a roller coaster, start her off slowly. Kids who begin with something relatively mild like Pirates of the Caribbean often build up their nerve throughout the day and close out the night on Space Mountain.

- *Avoid motion sickness.* Obviously, steer clear of bumpy rides after eating. If you feel queasy on a motion-simulation ride like Star Tours, stare at something inside the cabin, like the seat in front of you, instead of the screen.

Don't Leave Home Without . . .

✔ *Comfortable shoes.* Forget about wearing sandals or slides in the parks—stick to sneakers. And this is no time to be breaking in new shoes.

✔ *Minimal clothing.* Many hotels have laundry facilities and you can always wash out clothes in the sink. Most families over-pack, not figuring on all the souvenirs they'll bring back. Disney T-shirts are not only great for touring but can serve as swimsuit cover-ups and pajamas as well. And unless you're planning a special evening out at Victoria & Albert's, casual clothing is acceptable everywhere.

✔ *Lightweight jackets.* It rains in Orlando year-round, so jackets should be water-resistant.

✔ *Basic necessities.* These include disposable diapers, baby formula, camera, memory cards or film, and blank camcorder tapes. All these are available within Disney World, but at premium prices.

✔ *Sunscreen.* Keep a tube with you, and reapply it often. Sunburn is the number-one complaint at the first-aid clinic in the Magic Kingdom. You need sun protection all through the year in Orlando, not just in summer.

✔ *A waist pack.* Unlike a purse, a waist pack frees up your hands for boarding rides, pushing strollers, and holding on to your kids. A backpack is another option and good for carrying snacks and water, but even a light one can start to hurt your shoulders after a while. Plus, some rides don't allow backpacks, so you may have to keep putting yours in a locker.

✓ *Ziploc bags.* Disney serves such large dining portions, even on kiddie meals, that some parents report they save some of the fruit or chips for a later snack.

✓ *Sunglasses.* The Florida sun is so blinding that more than once I've reached into my bag for my sunglasses only to realize I already had them on. Kids too young for sunglasses need wide-billed caps to cut down the glare.

✓ *Strollers.* Most Orlando hotels are huge, so if you have an infant or toddler, you'll need your own stroller just to get around your hotel.

Helpful Hint

One thing you probably don't want to bring with you is the family pet. If you do, board it at one of the kennels and be prepared to both show proof of vaccinations and to return to the kennel to exercise the animal up to twice a day. Call 407/824–6568 for reservations at the Magic Kingdom, 407/560–6229 at Epcot, 407/560–4282 at Hollywood Studios, 407/938–2100 at the Animal Kingdom, and 407/825–2735 at Fort Wilderness. Never, repeat, never leave an animal locked in a car, no matter what time of year you're visiting. The Florida heat and humidity are far too dangerous.

The Frantic Factor

Although I rate rides throughout this book according to their "scare factor," I've often thought that I should include ratings on the "frantic factor" as well, measuring how hysterical the average parent is apt to become in any given situation.

I'm often asked to speak to parent groups on the topic of family travel. Almost inevitably, someone asks me how to make a Disney vacation relaxing. These people are very earnest, but they might as well be asking me to recommend a nice ski lodge for their upcoming trip to Hawaii. The only honest response is, "If you want to relax, you're going to the wrong place." Disney World is a high-stimulation environment, a total assault on all five senses mixed in with a constant and mind-boggling array of choices. This is not the week to take your kids off Ritalin or discuss marital issues with your spouse. It helps to keep a sense of humor and to go in with a full understanding that, vacation or not, this is unlikely to be the most relaxing week of your life. As one French mother of three sagely points out, "You can sleep later, when Mickey is done with you."

Actually, high stimulation and a lively pace may be the reason most people go to Disney World in the first place. Families who slip over the line from happily stimulated to unhappily frantic often do so because:

1) they forget to build in adequate rest breaks

2) they've planned their trips for the busiest times of the year

3) they're confused about the logistics of touring

4) they're hell-bent on taking it all in because "We're paying through the nose for this!" and "Who knows when we'll get back?"

This book is full of tips to help you avoid the first three mistakes, but your attitude is pretty much up to you. Just remember that doing it all is not synonymous with having the most fun, and if time is tight, limit your touring to those attractions that have the most appeal for your particular group. As for when you'll get back, who knows? But using this as a rationale for pushing everyone in the family past his personal exhaustion limit only guarantees that you'll never want to come back. The way for parents to really relax at Disney (besides spending time in hotel hot tubs with adjacent bars) is to do a little less, and enjoy it a little more.

One wise-beyond-his-years 14-year-old admits, "I was really obsessive-compulsive about getting everything done, seeing every ride, parade, and show. This led to a couple of breakdowns halfway through the trip, but we pulled it together and the last few days focused more on having fun in the moment than planning what we would do next."

CHAPTER 2

Choosing a Hotel

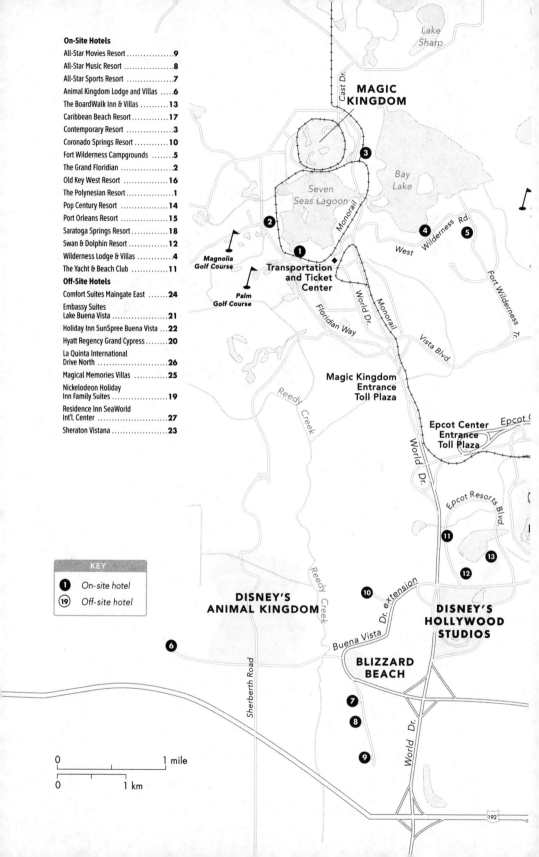

On-Site Hotels

Off-Site Hotels

KEY

❶ On-site hotel

⑲ Off-site hotel

MAGIC KINGDOM

Lake Sharp

Cast Dr.

Bay Lake

Seven Seas Lagoon

West Wilderness Rd.

Fort Wilderness Tr.

Magnolia Golf Course

Palm Golf Course

Transportation and Ticket Center

Monorail

Floridian Way

World Dr.

Vista Blvd.

Magic Kingdom Entrance Toll Plaza

Epcot Center Entrance Toll Plaza

World Dr.

Epcot Resorts Blvd.

Reedy Creek

DISNEY'S ANIMAL KINGDOM

DISNEY'S HOLLYWOOD STUDIOS

Dr. extension

Buena Vista

BLIZZARD BEACH

Sherberth Road

World Dr.

0 _____ 1 mile

0 _____ 1 km

192

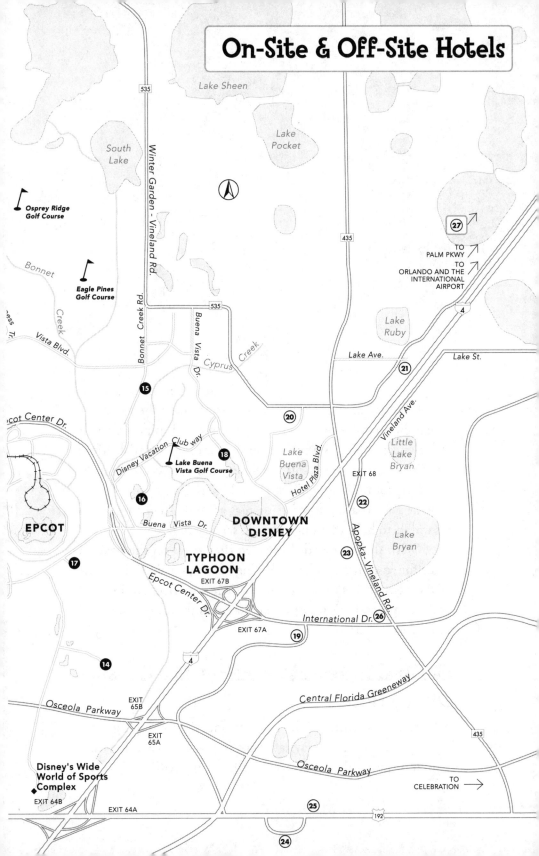

Lake Sheen

Lake Pocket

535

Winter Garden - Vineland Rd.

South Lake

Osprey Ridge Golf Course

Bonnet

Eagle Pines Golf Course

Bonnet Creek Rd.

Creek

Vista Blvd.

ess Tr.

535

Buena Vista Dr.

Cyprus Creek

435

27

TO PALM PKWY

TO ORLANDO AND THE INTERNATIONAL AIRPORT

4

Lake Ruby

Lake Ave.

Lake St.

21

15

20

Vineland Ave.

cot Center Dr.

Disney Vacation Club way

Lake Buena Vista Golf Course

18

Lake Buena Vista

Hotel Plaza Blvd

Little Lake Bryan

EXIT 68

EPCOT

16

Buena Vista Dr.

DOWNTOWN DISNEY

22

Lake Bryan

17

TYPHOON LAGOON

EXIT 67B

23

Apopka - Vineland Rd.

Epcot Center Dr.

EXIT 67A

International Dr. 26

19

4

14

Central Florida Greeneway

EXIT 65B

Osceola Parkway

EXIT 65A

435

Disney's Wide World of Sports Complex

EXIT 64B

Osceola Parkway

TO CELEBRATION

EXIT 64A

25

192

24

he ratings for the hotels discussed in this chapter are based on three factors: the responses of families surveyed; the percentage of repeat business a resort experiences, which is a reliable indicator of guest satisfaction; and the quality of the resort in relation to the price. Obviously, you'd expect more amenities and a higher employee-to-guest ratio at a $300-a-night resort than at a $100-a-night resort, so it's unfair to hold them both to the same standard.

With that in mind, I've rated the hotels on the basis of value for cost; that is, are you getting what you paid for? Do the advantages of this resort make it worth the price? And would you recommend this resort to families with the same amount of money to spend?

General Information About the On-Site Disney Hotels

@ A deposit equal to the price of one night's lodging is required within 14 days after making your reservation. You may pay with cash, traveler's checks, or credit card. If you cancel at least five days in advance, your deposit will be fully refunded.

@ Disney hotels operate under the family plan, meaning that kids under 18 stay free with parents.

@ Check-in time is 3 PM at most Disney hotels. If you arrive before your room is ready, you can check in, store your bags, pick up your tickets and resort IDs, and go ahead to the parks.

@ Checkout time is 11 AM, but, once again, you need not let this interfere with your touring. Check out early in the morning, store your bags, then go on to enjoy your last day in the parks.

@ When you check in, you'll be issued a room key/resort ID that allows you to charge meals, drinks, tickets, and souvenirs to your room and also gives you access to all Disney World transportation. If you have chosen the dining plan, your resort ID also serves as your meal pass.

Time-Saving Tip

If you pay with a credit card, you can arrange for automatic checkout—a definite time-saver. An itemized statement is hung on your doorknob early on the morning of your departure. If it's correct, you can keep it as your receipt and leave immediately.

Is It Worth the Expense to Stay On-Site?

Staying at one of the Disney-owned hotels is very convenient, and with rates as low as $82 a night at the All-Star resorts and Pop Century Resort, it's more affordable than you might think.

Off-site hotels fight back with special promotions and perks of their own, arguing that the Disney hotels still cost more and bring you only slightly closer to the action. On-site or off-site? Ask yourself the following questions to help you decide:

@ *What time of year are you going?*

If you're visiting Disney World in summer or during a major holiday, you'll need every extra minute, so it's worth the cost to stay on-site.

@ *How old are your kids?*

In the Florida heat and humidity it's nearly a medical necessity to keep young kids out of the sun in the middle of the afternoon, and an on-site hotel room makes it easier to return for a nap. If your kids are preteens or teens who can handle a whole day in the parks, commute time is less of a factor.

@ *Are you flying or driving?*

If you're flying and doing only Disney World, it may make more economic sense to stay on-site and use Disney World's transportation system in lieu of a rental car. But if you're driving to Orlando, it's just as easy to stay off-site. You'll be able to drive into the parks at hours that suit you without having to rely on shuttles.

@ *What's your budget?*

If money isn't a major issue, stay on-site. If money is a primary consideration, you'll find your best deals at the budget hotels along Interstate 4. Exits 62 and 68, the exits that flank Disney World, are chock-full of chain hotels and restaurants.

@ *How much do your kids eat?*

Food is expensive at Disney World, both in the parks and at the on-site hotels. If you're staying off-site, you can

Money-Saving Tip

Disney isn't exactly known for deep discounts, but when times are slow they're as eager to fill their rooms as any other hotel chain. The trouble is they don't always announce these discounts to people who seem ready and willing to pay the full price. When you call in to make your resort reservations always ask, "Are there any special offers available during the times I'll be visiting?"

always eat in the numerous fast-food and family-style restaurants along Interstate 4, Route 192, and International Drive. Many off-site hotels have complimentary breakfast buffets, while the all-suites properties have in-room kitchenettes where you can fix your own meals.

Do you plan to visit other attractions?

If you'll be spending half your time at SeaWorld, Universal Orlando, or the other non–Disney World attractions, stay off-site—at least during those days. There's no need to pay top dollar for proximity to Disney if you're headed for Islands of Adventure.

Will your party be splitting up at times?

Does Dad want to golf one afternoon? Do you have teenagers who can spend a day at Blizzard Beach on their own? Will there be times when it would make sense for Dad to take the younger kids back to the hotel while Mom stays in the park with the older ones? Is your 5-year-old raring to go at dawn, whereas your 15-year-old sleeps until noon? If so stay on-site, where the use of the Disney World transportation system makes it easy for all of you to go your own way.

@ *What's your tolerance level for hassles?*

If you don't want to deal with interstate traffic, big parking lots, toting luggage, and carrying cash, stay on-site.

The Advantages of Staying On-Site

Extra Magic Hours

Extra Magic Hour works like this: Each day year-round, one of the four major theme parks opens for Disney resort guests an hour early or stays open an extra hour or two after the regular closing time. This gives resort guests the chance to ride some featured attractions and greet the characters in a relatively uncrowded park. (Note the word "relatively." There are so many Disney resort guests that there are still plenty of people around, just not as many as usual.)

Generally only a few attractions per park are open for the Extra Magic Hour, but this is your chance to ride them easily. Just as important—in the morning you'll be deep inside the theme park when it officially opens so you can dash to other big-deal attractions before the rest of the crowd gets there.

For evening Extra Magic Hours, you'll need to show your resort ID/room key card in order to get a special wristband pass.

When you check into your hotel you'll receive a brochure printed with the Extra Magic Hours schedule for the week; if you'd like this information in advance to help with your planning, visit www.disneyworld.com, where you'll find "Park Hours" under "Plan."

Magical Express Service

The Magical Express Service allows you to check your bags at your hometown airport and not see them again until you walk into your hotel room in Walt Disney World. You also get free shuttle service from the Orlando airport to your resort.

When it's time to go home, the system works in reverse. You check your bags and receive your boarding passes before departing your Disney resort. Take another complimentary shuttle back to the airport and go directly to your flight. Your luggage will be waiting for you at baggage claim in your hometown. This also saves you the inconvenience of having to store your bags on the last day of your trip.

Transportation

On-site guests have unlimited use of the monorails, buses, and boats of the WDW transportation system.

Use of Other On-Site Hotel Facilities

If you want to use the child-care or sports facilities of other Disney hotels or dine at their restaurants, you can receive preferential treatment over off-site visitors. (Each hotel, reasonably enough, allows its own guests first shot at its services.) This means that even if you're staying at the mid-price Port Orleans,

Insider's Secret

The Magical Express Service is supposed to save you time and money, but in reality it doesn't always work seamlessly. Quite a few readers have complained of long delays. Comments range from: "We stopped at three hotels, and it took over an hour to get to ours from the airport" to "Thanks to this so-called benefit we began the whole trip with confusion and irritation." The general consensus seems to be that the system works well at times when it's not too crowded, but during peak travel times slow service is common. If you're traveling at such a time, consider handling your own bags and arranging for your own transportation between the airport and your hotel.

Helpful Hint

While anyone staying on-site can use the Magical Express buses for transport between the airport and their hotel, not all airlines participate in the baggage handling part of the deal. US Airways and Southwest, for example, are two major carriers who are presently not on the list—although Disney is in negotiations to add more airlines to the program. When you book your on-site room, you'll automatically receive information about the Magical Express Service that includes a list of participating airlines. If you're flying on a carrier that isn't included, you'll have to check and claim your bags in the usual way.

you can use the kids' club at the Polynesian or take a tennis lesson at the Contemporary.

Free Parking at the Theme Parks

You don't have to pay the $12 daily fee to park. The attendant will wave you through when she sees the resort parking ID on your dashboard.

Package Delivery

Don't lug your souvenirs around while touring. When you make a purchase, you can fill out a form and Disney will deliver the package to your hotel gift shop for free. It's generally the next day before your purchases show up so don't use the package delivery service on the last day of your visit.

Charging Privileges

If you're staying on-site, everyone in your party will be issued a resort ID the day you arrive. The ID allows adults (or kids, if you opt to give them a card with privileges) to charge tickets, food, and souvenirs back to their hotel room. It's certainly easier not to have to carry huge amounts of cash around, especially at the pool, water parks, and marinas.

It's up to you whether older kids have charging privileges. Giving them this privilege makes it easier to send Johnny to the snack bar for a round of Cokes, but be sure to impress upon kids that these IDs work like credit cards. They're not an open invitation to order pizza for all the kids at the arcade, purchase all seven dwarfs from the hotel gift shop, or, heaven forbid, obtain cash advances.

Dining Plans

Many families swear by the Disney dining plan, which can be added to any on-site package. The plan saves you from having to carry around cash and—at least on the surface—masks the sting of coughing up nine bucks for a cheeseburger.

Family Atmosphere

All of the on-site hotels are designed with families in mind. The ambience is casual, security is tight, and there are always other children around to play with. The on-site hotels have laundry facilities, generally near the pools and arcades, so that you can run a quick load while the youngsters play;

Helpful Hint

If an ID with charging privileges is lost, it should be reported to the front desk immediately to avoid unauthorized charges.

Insider's Secret

The on-site resorts, especially the luxury ones, often have fun little activities for kids such as scavenger hunts, pool races, or "unbirthday" parties. Activity schedules are usually posted around the pool areas or child-care centers.

there's late-night pizza delivery to your room; and if there's not a child-care facility at your particular hotel, Guest Services (a.k.a. Guest Relations) can help you arrange for an in-room sitter. The emphasis at the Disney hotels is on making life more convenient for parents.

Cool Themes

All the on-site hotels have themes that are carried out in mega-detail. At the Polynesian, the staff greets you with "Aloha"; at the Port Orleans, jazz music plays all day; and at the All-Star Sports, the dressers in the rooms look like gym lockers. This makes staying at an on-site hotel almost as exciting for kids as being inside the parks.

In fact, because the on-site hotels are all so different from each other, it's fun to visit other hotels. Many families surveyed told us they enjoyed eating dinner at a different resort from their own.

Rating the On-Site Disney Hotels

The Orlando area has more than 140,000 hotel rooms and a fair percentage of these are Disney owned. In other words, a family that has decided to stay on-site faces a bewildering number of choices. Does the convenience of being on the monorail line justify the increase in price? Do you want to stay amid Victorian splendor, or is a fort more your style? At which park do you plan to spend most of your time? As with all of WDW, making the best choice hinges on your awareness of what your family really needs.

On-Site Luxury Hotels

Luxury hotels are full-scale resorts with fine dining, health clubs and spas, valet parking, on-site child-care facilities, full room service, and lots of sporting options. There's a price attached—

Helpful Hint

Disneyworld.com is a great planning tool, allowing you to compare the prices of different on-site hotels during the week you'll be visiting. You can comparison shop at leisure without a travel agent or phone reservation agent nudging you into a quick decision.

the Disney luxury hotels cost, on average, twice as much a night as the mid-price hotels. Luxury hotels include the Board-Walk, Yacht and Beach Clubs, Contemporary, Grand Floridian, Polynesian, Swan, Dolphin, Wilderness Lodge, and Animal Kingdom Lodge. (Note: The Wilderness Lodge and Animal Kingdom Lodge are at the lowest price point in the luxury category.)

On-Site Mid-Price Hotels

"Mid-price" is something of a misnomer because both the price and the quality are higher than what you'd find in an off-site chain hotel in Orlando. You may pay a little more but the hotels are beautifully maintained and landscaped, with their themes carried out to the nth degree. Resorts that fall into this category include the Caribbean Beach, Port Orleans, and Coronado Springs.

On-Site Budget Hotels

The on-site budget hotels include the All-Star Music, All-Star Movies, All-Star Sports, and Pop Century resorts.

Again, the resorts are well maintained and have eye-popping catchy graphics that dazzle the kids. You can find a food court but no sit-down dining; a swimming pool but no other sporting options; a lengthier check-in line and smaller staff but rates that more than compensate for the minor inconveniences.

Quick Guide to

Hotel	Description
All-Star Resorts	Very popular, great price
Animal Kingdom Lodge	An exotic African theme
Beach Club Resort	Homey, lovely, and not one bit fancy
Beach Club Villas	Big suites in a great location
BoardWalk Inn	Rooms are spacious, modern, and attractive
BoardWalk Villas	Great location for both Epcot and Hollywood Studios
Caribbean Beach Resort	Tropical theme and the price is right
Contemporary Resort	Convenient and lively
Coronado Springs Resort	Elaborate pool with pyramid slide
Dolphin Resort	Adult atmosphere, great restaurant selection
Fort Wilderness Campground	Great for families who like to camp
Grand Floridian	Expensive, but luxurious
Old Key West Resort	Lots of room, quiet
Polynesian Resort	Relaxed and casual with a loyal, repeat clientele
Pop Century Resort	5,760 budget rooms, lively theme
Port Orleans Resort	With French Quarter or Riverside options
Saratoga Springs Resort and Spa	Amazing grotto pool, spacious
Swan Resort	Adult-oriented, great water areas
Wilderness Lodge	Rustic looking, with an intimate feel
Wilderness Lodge Villas	Great setting, a bit more space
Yacht Club Resort	At the door of the World Showcase

NOTE: The central reservations number for on-site hotels is 407/W–DISNEY.

On-Site Hotels

Location	Rating	Price Range
Animal Kingdom	★★	$82–$141
Animal Kingdom	★★★	$240–$635
Epcot	★★★	$335–$710
Epcot	★★★	$335–$1105
Epcot	★★★	$335–$750
Epcot	★★★	$335–$2090
Epcot	★★	$149–$225
Magic Kingdom	★★	$280–$755
Animal Kingdom	★★	$149–$225
Epcot	★	$249–$525
Magic Kingdom	★★	$43–$96
Magic Kingdom	★★	$375–$910
Downtown Disney	★★	$279–$1595
Magic Kingdom	★★★	$335–$815
Animal Kingdom	★	$82–$141
Downtown Disney	★★★	$149–$225
Downtown Disney	★★	$295–$1595
Epcot	★	$249–$525
Magic Kingdom	★★★	$240–$675
Magic Kingdom	★★★	$325–$1075
Epcot	★★★	$335–$710

The most important on-site benefits—transportation to the parks, help with tickets and priority-seating reservations, Extra Magic Hours, and charging privileges—are just as available to those paying $82 a night at All-Star Sports as to those paying $335 a night at the BoardWalk. And, hey, the housekeepers still leave your kids' stuffed animals in the window to greet them in the evening, so who can complain?

Villa-Style Accommodations

Larger families or those who like to prepare their own meals may want to rent a villa. Resorts included in this category are the Wilderness Lodge Villas, Saratoga Springs Resort, Board-Walk Villas, Beach Club Villas, Animal Kingdom Lodge Villas, and Old Key West Resort. (The Contemporary Villas will shortly join the line-up.) Although these properties are all part of the Disney Vacation Club, they can be rented by any family seeking villa-style accommodations.

On-Site Camping

The Fort Wilderness Campground is a great choice for families who love to camp and is by far the cheapest way to stay on-site and get on-site privileges.

Definition of Star Ratings for Hotels

★★★ This resort was a favorite among families surveyed and offers solid value for the money.

★★ Surveyed families were satisfied with this resort and felt they got what they paid for.

★ This resort is either more adult-oriented, with fewer amenities designed to appeal to families, or is more expensive than you'd expect considering the location or level of service.

Best On-Site Choices at a Glance

BEST MAGIC KINGDOM RESORT: WILDERNESS LODGE

A full $100 per night cheaper than the other
Magic Kingdom resorts with a casual, outdoorsy
feel, the Wilderness Lodge has always been a
favorite among our readers.

BEST EPCOT RESORT: THE YACHT AND BEACH CLUBS

You like Epcot and MGM? They're both easy to get to
from this prime location—and the pool is to die for.

BEST MID-PRICED RESORT: PORT ORLEANS

Relaxed and homey, the Port Orleans resorts have
the charm of the luxury resorts for less.
The French Quarter, smaller and quieter than its
sister, Riverside, is easier for families with young kids.

BEST BUDGET RESORT: THE ALL-STAR RESORTS

Kids love the wacky themes at these simple but
totally adequate hotels.

BEST VILLAS: VILLAS AT WILDERNESS LODGE

Families stay loyal to the Wilderness Lodge in any
form. The BoardWalk Villas also gets many votes.

Magic Kingdom Hotels

If Magic Kingdom is your focus and you're willing to pay up,
consider these resorts.

★★

Contemporary Resort   407/824–1000

You'll either love or hate Disney's original, always-hopping resort, which has 1,050 rooms surrounding a mammoth, high-
tech lobby full of shops and restaurants. The glamorous new

Contemporary Villas, part of the Disney Vacation Club, are some of the sleekest, most user-friendly rooms at this property. They also afford great Magic Kingdom views.

Proximity to the Magic Kingdom:	Excellent, via monorail
Proximity to Epcot:	Good, via monorail with a change at the TTC
Proximity to Hollywood:	Fair, via bus
Proximity to the Animal Kingdom:	Fair, via bus

Pluses

+ On the monorail line.

+ The easiest Magic Kingdom resort to book; discounts are sometimes available.

+ Exceptional sporting options, including WDW's largest tennis center and a full marina, with parasailing and waterskiing options.

+ Outstanding dining choices, including the California Grill, Disney's premiere restaurant, and Chef Mickey's, a great place to meet the characters for breakfast and dinner.

Minuses

− It's loud with a big-city feel, which is exactly what some families come to Florida to escape. "Like sleeping in the middle of Space Mountain," wrote one mother. Note that the rooms in the Garden Wings are quieter, cheaper, and more spacious than those in the main building.

− The futuristic ambience strikes some guests as sterile and ugly. "The pool area reminded me of a scene from a 1970s B-movie that would depict future decay," wrote one disgruntled Canadian dad. "I expected Charlton Heston to come around the corner any minute, being chased by apes."

− Like all the other hotels on the monorail line, the Contemporary is expensive, with prices starting at $280 a night.

Insider's Secret

When the luxurious Contemporary Villas open, they're bound to be a hit with families: You have a great location vis-à-vis the Magic Kingdom and even your own viewing platform to watch the evening fireworks.

Overall Grade: ★★ Convenient and lively. Perhaps a little too lively.

★★
Fort Wilderness Campground   407/824–2900

Fort Wilderness, which has campsites for tents and oversized concrete parking pads for RVs as well as air-conditioned cabins, got a major face-lift in 2009. The cabins, which sleep six, rent for approximately the same nightly rate as a luxury hotel. As part of the campground refurbishment the cabins received new furniture, carpeting, linens, and fixtures, and each has a private patio deck with a charcoal grill and picnic table. The wide-open spaces of the campground are perfect for volley-

Helpful Hint

Fort Wilderness Campground is so sprawling that many families rent a golf cart to make it easier to get around.

ball, biking, and exploring, making the resort a good choice for families with kids old enough to enjoy all the outdoor options. "Fort Wilderness lights two campfires every night for marshmallow roastings and sing-alongs," reports one mom from Maine. "The s'mores packages, which are $7 and include toasting sticks, are a real bargain, and after the singing a Disney movie is shown in the amphitheater under the stars. Perfect!"

Proximity to the Magic Kingdom:	Good, via bus or launch
Proximity to Epcot:	Fair, via bus
Proximity to Hollywood:	Fair, via bus
Proximity to the Animal Kingdom:	Fair, via bus

Pluses

+ Fort Wilderness offers tons of activities for kids: wagon rides, horseback and pony riding, and a petting zoo.

+ Hookups and tent sites, starting at $43, are your cheapest lodging options. The upgraded campsites start at $62 a night. Fort Wilderness Cabins start at $265 a night.

+ Groceries are available at the on-site trading post.

+ Fort Wilderness is pet friendly; dogs have a playground at the "Waggin' Trails," an off-leash play area.

Minuses

— Camping may not seem like a vacation to you.

— A large number of people are sharing relatively few facilities; the pools and the beach can get very crowded.

— This place is so spread out that it requires its own in-resort bus system to get you from one area to another. You can rent golf carts or bikes, but make no mistake: Fort Wilderness is huge and hard to navigate.

Overall Grade: ★★ If you like to camp and can put up with a little inconvenience for great savings, this is a good option.

★★
The Grand Floridian   407/824–3000

Modeled after the famed Florida beach resorts of the 1800s, the Grand Floridian is possibly the prettiest of all Disney hotels, with 900 rooms ensconced among its gabled roofs, soaring ceilings, and broad white verandas. This elegant and stately lady is also the hub of many activities, including a variety of programs for children.

Proximity to the Magic Kingdom: Excellent, via monorail or launch

Proximity to Epcot: Good, via monorail with a change at the TTC

Proximity to Hollywood: Fair, via bus

Proximity to Animal Kingdom: Fair, via bus

Pluses

+ Convenient location on monorail line.

+ A private beach and marina on the Seven Seas Lagoon and numerous boating options.

+ On-site child-care center.

+ Two programs for children: Disney's Pirate Adventure, and the Wonderland Tea Party.

+ On-site health club and full-service spa.

+ Exceptional dining. Citricos and Victoria & Albert's are among the finest restaurants in all of WDW. If you have the kids along, check out 1900 Park Fare, which hosts breakfast and dinner character buffets.

+ Lots of special little touches, such as afternoon tea and live music in the lobby each night.

Minuses

− Starting at $399, these are the most expensive rooms on Disney property.

− The elegance puts off some families who feel funny trooping past a grand piano with squalling babies in their arms.

Overall Grade: ★★ Luxurious but expensive.

The Polynesian Resort

★★★

407/824–2000

Designed to emulate an island village, the Polynesian is relaxed and casual. Activities take place at the Great Ceremonial House, where all the shops and restaurants encircle a beautiful garden with orchids, parrots, and fountains. Guests stay in one of the sprawling "long houses" along the lagoon. "The Polynesian was worth every penny," wrote one satisfied mom from Connecticut: "The rooms were gorgeous and we sat on the beach two magical nights in a row to catch the Magic Kingdom fireworks."

Proximity to the Magic Kingdom:	Excellent, via direct monorail, boat launch, or ferry
Proximity to Epcot:	Good, via monorail with one change at the TTC
Proximity to Hollywood:	Fair, via bus
Proximity to the Animal Kingdom:	Fair, via bus

Pluses

+ The Polynesian offers the most options for transport to the Magic Kingdom. You have monorail, ferry, and launch service.

+ There's a private beach with an attractive pool, plus numerous boating options. Canvas shells shade napping babies and toddlers digging in the sand.

+ The Kona Café is one of the best places for desserts in all of Disney World.

+ Excellent on-site child-care center.

+ The recently refurbished rooms are some of the prettiest on Disney property.

Minuses

− Without a discount, expect to pay $355 a night and up.

— The pool area is too small, considering the capacity of the property, though this may change as the resort continues its ongoing refurbishment. As of this writing there's no hot tub.

Overall grade: ★★★ The Polynesian enjoys a loyal repeat clientele, and that says it all.

★★★
Wilderness Lodge and Villas   407/824–3200

Starting at $240 a night, the Western-spirited Wilderness Lodge is aimed at filling the gap between the mid-price and luxury resorts. The theme of the Wilderness Lodge extends into every aspect of the hotel's design. The pool begins indoors as a hot spring and then flows through the lobby into a waterfall that tumbles over rocky caverns and culminates in the outdoor pool. The awe-inspiring lobby, which looks like a Lincoln Log project run amok, centers on an 82-foot fireplace that blazes all year round. The Native American–theme wallpaper, the staff dressed like park rangers, and even the stick ponies children ride to their tables in the Whispering Canyon Café all combine to evoke the feel of a National Park Service lodge built in the early 1900s.

Proximity to the Magic Kingdom:	Good, via launch
Proximity to Epcot:	Fair, via bus
Proximity to Hollywood:	Fair, via bus
Proximity to the Animal Kingdom:	Fair, via bus

Pluses
+ The lodge is heavily themed and the pool area, with its erupting geyser and stone hot tubs, is especially dramatic.

+ On-site child-care facilities.

+ Tons of happy quasi-campers here. Families return to the Wilderness Lodge again and again.

+ The Wilderness Lodge villas, starting at $325 a night, provide all the great amenities and a little more space.

Minuses

— Although it's one of the least expensive luxury options, at $240 a night and up it still isn't cheap.

— This is the only Magic Kingdom resort without monorail service. The boat takes slightly longer than the bus.

— The rooms are small and sleep only four people; the other luxury resorts sleep five. "It's a great resort once you get outside of your room," said a mom from Indiana. "But while inside the room we were practically on top of each other."

Overall Grade: ★★★ A great family-pleasing setting and a favorite with many of our readers.

Epcot Hotels

The Epcot resorts share their own "back-door" entrance into Epcot's World Showcase, accessed by water taxis and walkways. Unfortunately—and somewhat ironically considering these properties are marketed as "Epcot resorts"—it can be tricky to get to Epcot's front gates. The Future World section of Epcot usually opens at 9 AM, but Epcot resort guests enter through the World Showcase, where the rides, shops, and restaurants don't open until 11 AM. That means Epcot hotel guests have to walk through the World Showcase and enter Future World at a special rope-drop area. (Many people assume the Epcot hotels offer bus service to the main entrance of Epcot. They don't.) The bad news is that this stroll through the World Showcase adds 10 minutes to your commute. The good news is that there are fewer people at this entrance point so you can still get a jump on the crowds, a key factor if you're heading to a popular attraction like Soarin'.

In contrast, getting to Hollywood is a breeze. Water taxis leaving from the Epcot resort marinas will have you at the Hollywood gates within minutes. In addition, there are plenty of restaurants, clubs, and entertainment options around the lagoon. "We never left the Epcot resort area," wrote one mom from Texas. "Everything we wanted to do was right there."

★★★

The BoardWalk Inn and Villas   407/939–5100

The BoardWalk Inn and Villas form the hub of a large complex with convention space, several restaurants and shops, the ESPN sports club, and a dance club and piano bar. The mood is turn-of-the-20th-century Atlantic City. Bright, attractive rooms are clustered above an old-fashioned boardwalk and the action on the waterfront goes on until late at night.

"Once you stay at the BoardWalk, nothing else is good enough," wrote one enthusiastic grandmother of two in Ohio. "The location is perfect for both Epcot and Hollywood, and there's always free entertainment, like jugglers or comedians, to keep the kids happy."

Proximity to the Magic Kingdom:	Fair, via bus
Proximity to Epcot:	Excellent, via a short stroll or water taxi
Proximity to Hollywood:	Excellent, via water taxi
Proximity to the Animal Kingdom:	Fair, via bus

Pluses

+ Lots of entertainment: surrey bikes for rent, midway games, and a wider variety of restaurants and bars than you'd find at most resorts.

+ On-site health club.

+ On-site child-care facilities.

+ Great location for both Epcot and Hollywood.

+ Great restaurant choices, including the excellent Flying Fish Café.

Minuses

— Expensive, at $335 and up per night.

— Maybe too lively and hopping for families with very young kids. The boardwalk can get loud at night, and you can hear the revelers from some rooms.

Overall grade: ★★★ You'll feel like you're right in the middle of the action—because you are.

★

Caribbean Beach Resort   407/934–3400

This family-priced, 2,112-room resort is on 200 acres with a private lake surrounded by beaches. Each section of this mammoth hotel is painted a different tropical color and named for a different Caribbean island, and each "island" has its own shuttle bus stop, beach, and pool with waterslide. The rooms, although small, are attractively decorated.

Proximity to the Magic Kingdom:	Fair, via bus
Proximity to Epcot:	Fair, via bus
Proximity to Hollywood:	Fair, via bus
Proximity to the Animal Kingdom:	Fair, via bus

Pluses

+ The price is right, starting at $149 a night.

+ The Pirate and Nemo rooms are absolutely adorable and themed to the max—for example, some of the furniture looks like cargo chests. These quarters are well worth the extra $25 a night!

+ Caribbean Cay, an artificial island with a playground, climbing fort, and small aviary, is fun for young kids.

+ The pirate-themed water play area, which offers small slides and fountains, is a hit with young kids.

+ A marina with watercraft is available.

Minuses

— Although the buses are regular, they must stop at all of the resort's many "islands." Expect a longer commute time to the parks.

— The place is huge. It may be a major hike from your hotel room to the food plaza or marina. If you have young kids, bring your own stroller.

Overall Grade: ★★ All the moderate-priced resorts offer solid value for the money, but due to its size, Caribbean Beach is overwhelming. Try the others first.

★
Swan and Dolphin Resorts   407/934–4000
407/934–3000

This convention–resort complex made up of two side-by-side hotels is connected to Epcot and Hollywood by water taxi and bridges. The Swan and Dolphin are the only hotels not owned by Disney that are on Disney property and whose guests qualify for on-site perks. Sometimes called "twin" hotels (like the nearby Yacht and Beach Clubs), the Swan and Dolphin have separate check-ins but are alike in architecture and mood.

Proximity to the Magic Kingdom:	Fair, via bus
Proximity to Epcot:	Excellent, via a moderate walk or water taxi
Proximity to Hollywood:	Excellent, via water taxi
Proximity to the Animal Kingdom:	Fair, via bus

Pluses

+ On-site child-care facilities.

+ The beach area has a playground, kiddie pools, water-slides, and a small marina with paddleboats.

+ Bike rentals, tennis courts, and a health club.

Minuses

– Expensive, with rates beginning at $249 per night.

– Conventioneers can erode the family feel.

– Since these resorts aren't owned by Disney, they don't qualify for the Magical Express Service and they don't have their own airport shuttles. In other words, you'll have to arrange for transportation from the airport to you.

Overall grade: ★ A great place to go if the company is picking up the tab. Otherwise, try the Yacht and Beach Clubs first.

The Yacht and Beach Clubs

★★★
407/934–7000
407/934–8000

Designed to resemble a turn-of-the-20th-century Nantucket seaside resort, the Yacht and Beach Clubs are side-by-side resorts that share many facilities. Both hotels are charming yet casual (think Polo Ralph Lauren), with sunny, airy rooms overlooking a freshwater lake, and a wide variety of restaurants and sporting options.

Proximity to the Magic Kingdom:	Fair, via bus
Proximity to Epcot:	Excellent, via a short stroll or water taxi
Proximity to Hollywood:	Excellent, via water taxi
Proximity to the Animal Kingdom:	Fair, via bus

Pluses

+ Stormalong Bay, the water recreation area shared by the two resorts, is like a private water park. The sand-bottom "bay" contains pools of varying depths, whirlpools, water-slides, and a wrecked ship for atmosphere. This is by far the best resort pool in all of WDW.

+ The Yacht and Beach Clubs are perfectly situated for easy travel to both Epcot and Hollywood.

+ On-site child-care facilities.

+ Disney characters are on hand for breakfast at the Cape May Café in the Beach Club.

+ The two resorts share an on-site health club.

Minuses

— Price is the only real drawback. Rates begin at $335 per night.

Overall Grade: ★★★ These hotels enjoy a lot of repeat business from satisfied families.

Downtown Disney Hotels

These hotels are the first ones you encounter when you enter Disney property and are a good choice for families who'll also be visiting Universal Studios, SeaWorld, or other Orlando attractions. Also, proximity to the action of Downtown Disney vastly increases your restaurant options.

★★
Old Key West Resort   407/827–7700

At the villas of Old Key West you'll get all the standard amenities of a Disney resort, plus a lot more room. The setting is pleasant, casual, and very Floridian in spirit. "We love the quieter atmosphere of Old Key West," wrote a mother of three from Maryland. "Our kids are young (ages 2, 5, and 7), so even with naps they're often too exhausted at night for us to take them to a restaurant and expect them to behave. We like being able to go 'home' to a villa and order pizza or make sandwiches. The villas are more like an apartment than a hotel room."

Proximity to the Magic Kingdom: Fair, via bus
Proximity to Epcot: Fair, via bus
Proximity to Hollywood: Fair, via bus
Proximity to the Animal Kingdom: Fair, via bus

Pluses

+ If you have more than two children and need to spread out or you'd like a kitchen to prepare your own meals, Old Key West is a good on-site option.

+ A water taxi provides swift transit to Downtown Disney.

+ Tennis courts, pools, bike rentals, shuffleboard, basketball, a marina, a sand play area, an arcade, and a fitness room are all on-site.

+ Prices run from $295 for a studio with kitchenette to $1,595 for a Grand Villa that can accommodate up to 12 people. If you're willing to swap proximity to the parks for more space, Old Key West may be just what you need.

Minuses

− Still pricier than off-site villas such as the Embassy Suites on Hotel Plaza Boulevard.

− Quieter, with less going on than at other resorts.

− No on-site child-care facilities, which is unusual in a resort at this price point.

− A longer than average commute to the theme parks. "We were impressed with the accommodations at Old Key West," reported a mom from Toronto, "but transport to the parks involved surprisingly lengthy trips."

Overall Grade: ★★ Very homey, with nice touches, and a great option for families seeking peace and quiet at the end of the day. But if you want lots of amenities and food choices, look elsewhere.

★★★

Port Orleans Resort   407/934–5000

This mid-price resort called Port Orleans has two sections. The French Quarter has manicured gardens, wrought-iron railings, and streets with cute names like Rue d'Baga. The Mardi Gras mood extends to the pool area, where alligators play jazz while King Triton sits atop a funky-looking waterslide, regally surveying his domain.

The Riverside section is a bit more down-home, with a steamboat-shaped lobby, general stores run by gingham-clad girls, and a swimming area themed on Song of the South. Schizophrenic in architecture, with white-column buildings encircling fishing holes and cotton mills, Riverside manages to mix in a variety of Southern clichés without losing its ditzy charm. If Huck Finn ever married Scarlett O'Hara, this is where they'd come on their honeymoon.

Since the French Quarter is only half the size of Riverside, it's a shorter walk to the lobby, pool, food court, and shuttle bus station; at Riverside, getting around is a bit more of a headache. Both resorts have a fast-food court and a bar that offers live entertainment; Riverside also has a full-service restaurant called Boatwright's.

Proximity to the Magic Kingdom:	Fair, via bus
Proximity to Epcot:	Fair, via bus
Proximity to Hollywood:	Fair, via bus
Proximity to the Animal Kingdom:	Fair, via bus

Insider's Secret

If you can't decide which section of Port Orleans is best for your family, keep in mind that the French Quarter is smaller and quieter. There's more activity at Riverside. A mom from Illinois wrote to us that "the Port Orleans French Quarter is amazing, especially the pool. We stay there every time and request building 2 or 5 so we'll be close to the action."

Pluses

+ Affordable, starting at $149 a night.

+ Great pool areas (especially at the French Quarter), which can easily keep the kids entertained for an afternoon. Riverside also offers on-site fishing.

+ Well designed and maintained; you won't believe you're staying on-site for half the price of the luxury resorts.

+ Both hotels have marinas with a selection of watercraft as well as bike rentals.

+ Horse-and-carriage tours are available around the resort and are especially romantic at night.

+ The Sassagoula Steamboat offers easy water transport from both resorts to Downtown Disney.

Minuses

– The two resorts share a bus to all major theme parks, which means a slightly longer commuting time.

Overall Grade: ★★★ You get a good deal here in more ways than one.

Saratoga Springs Resort and Spa   407/827–1100

Saratoga Springs recalls the posh upstate–New York retreats of the 1890s, complete with a horse-racing theme. Villas here are numerous and roomy. The recently updated and very attractive Treehouse Villas, for instance, have raised decks and enough space to accommodate large families. They're truly a home away from home.

Proximity to the Magic Kingdom:	Fair, via bus
Proximity to Epcot:	Fair, via bus
Proximity to Hollywood:	Fair, via bus
Proximity to the Animal Kingdom:	Fair, via bus

Pluses

+ Proximity to the restaurants and entertainment of Downtown Disney via water taxi.

+ Access to the biggest and best health club in WDW and a full-service spa.

+ The location is great for golfers—Saratoga Springs is adjacent to the Lake Buena Vista course.

+ A good choice for family reunion groups seeking larger accommodations and a relaxed atmosphere with plenty of space for the kids to play.

+ The grotto pool, complete with man-made hot springs, is one of the most dramatic hotel pools in WDW. Even the auxiliary pools are beautifully themed with great play areas for the kids.

Minuses

− With villas starting at $295, Saratoga Springs is more expensive than off-site villa accommodations.

— Saratoga Springs is often used by corporations for retreats and conferences so you may find yourself in the middle of a group of businesspeople.

— Limited dining options on-site, although you do have the option to prepare your own meals or head over to the restaurants of nearby Downtown Disney.

— Since you're pretty far out of the Disney loop, expect a longer commute time via bus to any of the major parks.

— At 65 acres, Saratoga Springs is so spread out that you might find yourself in a room far from the food court and main pool. Request to be as close as possible to the main building when you make your reservation.

Overall Grade: ★★ Roomy and close to Downtown Disney. The trouble is it's not particularly close to anything else.

Animal Kingdom Hotels

These hotels are in a surprisingly central location vis-à-vis the four theme parks and Downtown Disney.

	★★
All-Star Sports, All-Star Music, and All-Star Movies Resorts	407/939–5000, 407/939–6000, and 407/939–7000

The All-Star resorts have built such a loyal following that, despite having about 6,000 rooms, they fill up quickly. There are three reasons for this success—price, price, and price. The All-Star resorts make staying on-site possible for families who previously could only dream of such a splurge.

All-Star Sports has five sections, each decorated with a tennis, football, surfing, basketball, or baseball theme. At All-Star Music, you can choose between jazz, rock and roll, country, calypso, and Broadway tunes. All-Star Movies offers The

Love Bug, Toy Story, Fantasia, 101 Dalmatians, and The Mighty Ducks.

Insider's Secret

If your child adores *101 Dalmatians* or is a big football buff, you can indeed ask to be lodged in that section of the hotel when you make your reservation. Disney won't guarantee you'll get your request, but they'll try.

The in-your-face graphics of the brightly colored buildings and the resort's general zaniness appeal to kids. There are giant tennis-ball cans and cowboy boots, a walk-through jukebox, and footballs the size of houses. At the diamond-shaped baseball pool at All-Star Sports, you'll find Goofy as pitcher; Mickey conducts sprays of water in the Fantasia pool of All-Star Movies; and show tunes play all day under the marquee in the Broadway district of All-Star Music. It may be budget, but it ain't boring.

Time-Saving Tip

The All-Star resorts are enormous and check-in time is a madhouse. If you arrive before 3 PM, try to check in early. If your room isn't available, you can store your bags and return later, when you'll only have to wait in the shorter, swifter-moving "key pickup" line.

Proximity to the Magic Kingdom: Fair, via bus
Proximity to Epcot: Fair, via bus
Proximity to Hollywood: Fair, via bus
Proximity to the Animal Kingdom: Good, via a short bus ride

Helpful Hint

If you don't care what All-Star section you're in, request a room near the lobby when you make your reservation. This can save you lots of walking each time you leave your room to catch a bus or eat a meal.

Pluses

+ In a word, cost. Rooms start at $82.

+ The 214 new suites at All-Star Music are the most afford-able on-site suite options. Units that sleep six cost as little as $184 a night.

+ All the All-Stars have special rooms for people with dis-abilities. For $109 a night, you can have a slightly larger ground-floor suite with roll-in showers.

+ The free shuttle buses are a good transportation option, considering the price. When you get into this price range at off-site hotels, you often have to pay for a shuttle.

+ Proximity to Blizzard Beach and the Animal Kingdom.

Minuses

— Food options are limited to fast-food courts and pool bars only, with no restaurants or indoor bars.

— Sports options are limited; swimming is it.

— The rooms are very small. They sleep four, but you'll be bunched.

— Long check-in lines.

— By breaking each resort into five separate sections, Disney is striving to eliminate that sleeping-in-the-middle-of-Penn-Station feel. But the bottom line is, it takes more ef-fort to get around a huge hotel than a small one.

Overall Grade: ★★ Lots of bang for the buck here. Just don't expect too many amenities.

★★★
Animal Kingdom Lodge and Villas   407/938–3000

Step inside the massive lobby of the Animal Kingdom Lodge and you'll be transported . . . outdoors. From the thatch roof to the enormous mud fireplace, and from the rope bridges to the tribal art to the lighting that's designed to simulate sunrise to sunset, the resort creates the feel of a game lodge in the middle of a wildlife preserve.

The Animal Kingdom Lodge is in the middle of a 33-acre savanna where more than 200 animals freely roam. Thirty-six species of mammals, including giraffes, zebras, and gazelles, and 26 species of birds, such as the sacred ibis and African spoonbill, live within the working wildlife preserve. The kopje, a series of rock outcroppings, serves as a natural barrier but is also an elevated walkway that offers panoramas of the landscape and the chance for you to come within 15 feet of the animals. If you'd rather engage in animal viewing from the comfort of your own balcony, many of the guest rooms have a savanna view.

Proximity to the Magic Kingdom:	Fair, via bus
Proximity to Epcot:	Fair, via bus
Proximity to Hollywood:	Fair, via bus
Proximity to the Animal Kingdom:	Excellent, via a short bus ride

Pluses

+ A dramatic and exotic setting.

+ The Animal Kingdom Lodge has truly fantastic restaurants, including Boma, a buffet restaurant with especially good breakfasts, and Jiko, which serves excellent and authentic African food and an exclusively South African wine list.

+ Lots of extras for the kids, including tours that tell about the animals and "bush camp activities" such as African crafts, games, and folktales. You can even track the animals with night vision goggles!

+ On-site child-care facilities, spa, and health club.

+ Proximity to the Animal Kingdom and Blizzard Beach.

+ Some Animal Kingdom Lodge rooms have bunk beds, a good choice if your kids are older, different genders, or for some other reason balk at sleeping together.

+ The Animal Kingdom Lodge villas are relatively new and very attractive.

Minuses

— Although not as expensive as many of the other luxury hotels, the Lodge can be pricey, with rates beginning at $240 a night. Villas begin at $269.

— The out-of-the-way location means a longer-than-average bus ride to the Magic Kingdom, Epcot, and Hollywood.

— They save the architectural drama for the public spaces. Rooms are small and basic, and if the animals aren't right outside, the views are pretty dull.

Overall Grade: ★★★ The most unique resort on Disney property.

★★
Coronado Springs Resort   407/939–1000

Disney's only moderately priced convention hotel—rooms begin at $149—has a Mexican theme with Spanish-tile roofs, adobe walls, and a pool area that is dominated by an imposing Mayan temple. The rooms are scattered around a 15-acre lake. There's a full-service restaurant called Maya Grill and also an adult-oriented club called RIX with a bar and small dance floor.

Proximity to the Magic Kingdom:	Fair, via bus
Proximity to Epcot:	Fair, via bus
Proximity to Hollywood:	Fair, via bus
Proximity to the Animal Kingdom:	Good, via a short bus ride

Pluses

+ Dramatic pool area with waterslide, arcade, bar, fast-food stand, and theme playground.

+ Marina with standard boat and bike rentals.

+ On-site health club—a rarity in this price range.

+ Proximity to the Animal Kingdom and Blizzard Beach.

Minuses

— Coronado Springs is a convention hotel, meaning it has more businesspeople and fewer families than is typical for a Disney resort.

— The fast-food court is too small to accommodate 2,000 rooms and can get very crowded, especially in the morning.

— The resort is quite spread out, even by Disney standards. If you're in one of the more far-flung rooms, you face a 15-minute walk to the food court and shuttle bus stop.

Overall Grade: ★★ Because of the convention trade, Coronado Springs has more amenities than are typical in this price range. But the conventioneer vibe can also be a turnoff.

★

Pop Century Resort   407/938–4000

Disney's newest resort is also in the budget category, bringing 5,760 more affordable rooms into the mix. At Pop Century, each pair of buildings is themed to a different decade, from the 1900s to the 1990s. Expect the same larger-than-life icons that earmark the All-Stars. Cultural touchstones from each decade—including giant yo-yos, Big Wheel bikes, and Rubik's Cubes—mark the entrances, and the roofs are lined with catch-phrases from each era.

Insider's Secret

Request placement in the '60s section when you make your reservation. It's a bit louder, but you're close to the bus stops, food court, and the fun Hippie Dippy pool. The '80s and '90s sections are a long walk from most of the hotel services and some of the buildings also overlook a construction site.

Proximity to the Magic Kingdom:	Fair, via bus
Proximity to Epcot:	Fair, via bus
Proximity to Hollywood:	Fair, via bus
Proximity to the Animal Kingdom:	Fair, via bus

Pluses

+ The price is affordable, starting at $82 a night.

+ Free transportation, a rarity in this price range.

Minuses

— Food options are limited to a fast-food court.

— The retro music is relentless and sometimes overwhelming. Doo-wop and disco aren't dead at Pop Century.

— Sporting options are limited to swimming.

— The rooms are small; they sleep four but you'll be crowded.

— Longer check-in than is typical for Disney resorts.

— The out-of-the-way location means a slightly longer commute by bus to all of the theme parks.

Overall Grade: ★ As Disney's second value resort, Pop Century brings a lot more affordable rooms into the mix. But, due to the location, try the All-Stars first.

Off-Site Hotels: Which Location Is Best?

Here's the scoop on the three main off-site areas that tourists frequent: Exits 62 and 68 off Interstate 4, and International Drive.

Exits 62 and 68 are within a 10-minute drive of the theme parks. Exit 68 (U.S. 535) has a vast number of chain hotels and eateries, and the area underwent some major development and expansion in the last few years, so many of the hotels are relatively new. It's your best bet if you want to get close to Disney without paying Disney prices.

Exit 62, which leads to U.S. 192, has similar chains represented but the rates are about $20 less per night. Why? The hotels are, in general, older and a bit farther off I–4 than the hotels of Exit 68. The whole area is a little less spiffy but still safe and still close to Disney property.

International Drive is farther out, about 20 minutes from the Disney theme parks, but it's modern and well kept. This area has representatives from every chain restaurant and hotel you've ever heard of, as well as entertainment options like malls, ice-skating, and miniature golf. International Drive is the conduit that runs between SeaWorld and Universal Orlando, so it's a smart central location if you're planning to visit those parks as well as Disney.

How to Get the Best Deals on Off-Site Hotels

Orlando has more hotel rooms than any other U.S. city besides Las Vegas, so there are plenty of beds out there for the taking. Here are a few tips to make sure you're getting the most for your money.

Money-Saving Tip

Try calling both the hotel chain's 800 number and the direct line to the particular hotel. You may be quoted different rates.

The Orlando Magicard is free and offers 20% to 30% discounts on area hotels, as well as restaurants and non-Disney attractions. You can download a card by visiting www.orlando info.com/magicard.

Buying an Entertainment Book is another source of major discounts; dozens of hotels in the greater Orlando area offer price breaks to cardholders. For more information, visit www.entertainment.com.

If you especially like a particular hotel chain, you can simply call their 800 number and ask for the hotel nearest Disney World. This eliminates the element of surprise, because one Hampton Inn looks pretty much like another. Big chains have multiple Orlando locations, so stress that you'd like to be as close as possible to the Disney gates, preferably near Exit 62 or 68. Proximity to Disney raises the rate about 20%, but location is important; if you end up in a hotel near the airport or downtown, that means a major daily commute, and Orlando traffic can be brutal.

Helpful Hint

One note of caution: An extremely cheap hotel rate, say $55 or less, generally means that the hotel is in a less desirable part of town than those I've listed, both in terms of theme park proximity and general security.

Time-Saving Tip

Many off-site hotels claim to run shuttles to the theme parks, but beware. Relying on off-site transportation can sometimes make for a long commute. The worst situations are when two or three hotels share a shuttle and you have to make stops at all of them. Even if a resort has its own shuttle, it may make stops at all of the major parks on each run, meaning commutes of up to an hour just to get from your hotel to the theme park of your choice. A lengthy bus ride is maddening in the morning when the kids are eager to get to the rides, and at night, when you're all exhausted, it can be disastrous.

To make matters worse, some off-site hotels charge you for shuttle rides. They may tell you that by buying shuttle tickets you'll save the "horrendous" cost of Disney parking, but the truth is Disney parking is $12 for the whole car and the shuttle bus tickets can be from $5 to $12 per person. And it still may take you an hour to get there!

This is why I suggest that families staying off-site either drive to Orlando or get a rental car. If you do decide to use an off-site resort shuttle be sure to ask if it's a private shuttle and if service to theme parks is direct. If you don't like what you hear, rent a car or call a cab.

Finally, six magic words can save you major bucks. When talking to a reservation clerk always ask, "Do you have any discounts available?" Remember that the reservation clerk works for the hotel, so if he can sell you a room at $95 a night there's no incentive for him to tell you how you can drop the rate to

Quick Guide to

Hotels	Description
Comfort Suites at Maingate East	Inexpensive but close to Disney
Embassy Suites Lake Buena Vista	Good location, solid value
Holiday Inn SunSpree	Child-oriented activities all day long
Hyatt Regency Grand Cypress	Luxury hotel with lots of activities for adults and kids
La Quinta International Drive North	Convenient location for all three parks
Magical Memories Villas	Private homes and condos for rent
Nickelodeon Holiday Inn Family Suites	Nonstop Nick-theme action for the kids
Residence Inn SeaWorld Int'l. Center	Quiet and homelike suites
Royal Pacific Resort	Elegant, upscale resort on Universal grounds
Sheraton Vistana	A favorite with our readers

Off-Site Hotels

Phone #	Nearest Theme Park	Price Range
407/397–7848	Walt Disney World	Budget: $99 and up
407/239–1144	Walt Disney World	Moderate: $119 and up
407/239–4500	Walt Disney World	Budget: $99 and up
407/239–1234	Walt Disney World	Luxury: $179 and up
407/351–4100	Universal Studios, SeaWorld	Budget: $70 and up
407/390–8200	Depends on location	Moderate: $99 and up most $169 and up
407/387–5437	Walt Disney World	Moderate: $169 and up
407/313–3611	SeaWorld	Moderate: $109 and up
407/503–3000	Universal Studios	Luxury: $219 and up
407/238–5000	Equidistant from all	Moderate: $149 and up

Money-Saving Tip

If you're staying off-site and thus will be eating at least some of your meals outside of Disney property, pick up a few of those free tourist magazines that are available in the airport and all around Orlando. They're full of dining discount coupons, some of them for family-oriented restaurants near the theme parks.

$79. But if you specifically inquire about discounts, he has to tell you.

Things to Ask When Booking a Room at an Off-Site Hotel

There's a wide range of amenities and perks among the hundreds of hotels in the Orlando area. To make sure you're getting top value for your dollar, take nothing for granted. Some $250-a-night hotels charge you for shuttle service to the parks; some $75 ones do not. Some hotels count 12-year-olds as adults, others consider 19-year-olds to be children. Some relatively inexpensive hotels have kids' clubs; some larger and more costly ones are geared to convention and business travelers and don't even have an arcade. The moral is, always ask.

The following questions should help you ferret out the best deal.

- Does the hotel provide in-room babysitters? Is there an on-site child-care center or kids' club? What's the cost? How far in advance do you have to make reservations?

- Does the hotel provide direct shuttle service to the theme parks? How often do the buses run? How early do they begin and how late do they run? How many stops do they make? Is there a fee?

@ Do kids stay free? Up to what age?

@ Do you have any suites with kitchens? If not, can we rent refrigerators or microwaves?

@ Does the hotel provide a free buffet breakfast?

@ What fast-food or family-style restaurants are nearby?

@ Are laundry facilities on the premises?

@ Can I buy tickets to area attractions through the hotels? Are the tickets discounted? (Note: Disney tickets are rarely discounted but sometimes off-site hotels offer discounts to Universal Orlando, SeaWorld, and area dinner shows.)

Great Off-Site Hotels for Families

Orlando has plenty of hotel rooms, so how is a family to choose? The listed properties that follow are tried-and-true family favorites based on proximity to Disney World, amenities, and value. For descriptions of the Universal Orlando resorts, see Chapter 14.

Two notes: Since the hotels listed are all recommended as good family choices we did not provide star ratings. And since Walt Disney World is so huge and spread out, our "proximity to Disney" rating is based on the distance between the hotel and Disney's main entrance gate.

Off-Site Luxury Hotels

Hyatt Regency Grand Cypress   **407/239–1234**
www.hyattgrandcypress.com

This beautiful hotel—so close to Disney that it's almost on-site—has expansive grounds, lush landscaping, an elegant lobby, and numerous sporting options. It's a serene oasis and a great choice for families who want the option to escape from Disney in the evenings and yet remain conveniently close to the parks. Prices range from $179–$279 during the off-season and $199–$299 during the on-season. The variation in prices is mostly due to the view; standard rooms are the same size throughout the hotel.

Proximity to Disney World:	Excellent, via a 5-minute drive
Proximity to Universal:	Good, via a 15-minute drive
Proximity to SeaWorld:	Good, via a 15-minute drive

Pluses

+ The pool area is gorgeous, with 12 waterfalls and several very secluded whirlpools.

+ You can golf, play tennis, and ride horses at the equestrian center. Pleasant trails wind through the grounds for walkers and runners.

+ Camp Hyatt has great activities for kids, such as pool games, nature walks, poolside movies, canoeing, tennis lessons, and pitch-and-putt golf. It runs daily during the summer and weekends throughout the off-season. Prices are $75 a day and $50 for evenings and include meals.

+ Sophisticated dining options include Hemingway's, dramatically perched atop one of the pool waterfalls, and La Coquina's Chef's Table which offers a seven-course tasting menu served in a luxurious nook tucked back in the restaurant kitchen. (Yes, it's actually in the kitchen.)

+ The Hyatt basically backs up to Disney World grounds and offers an easy commute to any Disney theme park.

Minuses

— Price: both the rooms and restaurants are expensive. The standard-room rates here can get you a suite with a kitchen at a mid-range or budget property.

— The Hyatt sometimes hosts conventions and attracts a more adult crowd than other area hotels.

— The property is undergoing a significant renovation in late 2009 and early 2010. If you book during that time request a room located away from construction.

Residence Inn SeaWorld International Center
www.residenceinn.com   **407/313–3611**

The suites at the Residence Inn are especially homelike and you can choose among one- to three-room units, all with separate areas for eating and relaxing. Plus the hotel is practically at the back door of SeaWorld and Discovery Cove. Disney World and Universal Studios are each about 5 miles away. Prices begin at $109 for a studio, $159 for a one-room suite with sofa bed and go up to $249 for a three-room (two bedrooms and a living room with sofa bed) suite. During peak times the prices rise about $20 a night. The property features a heated outdoor pool, a games room, a sports court with basketball and tennis, a health club, and a children's playground. "My husband hates crowds and noise and was very skeptical about taking a vacation in Orlando," a woman wrote to us. "But even he had to admit that the Residence Inn was very relaxing and that SeaWorld was a wonderful theme park."

Proximity to Disney World:	Good, via a 10-minute drive
Proximity to Universal:	Good, via a 10-minute drive
Proximity to SeaWorld:	Excellent, via a 5-minute drive or shuttle ride

Pluses

+ Suites are spacious and the kitchens are well equipped.

+ Complimentary hot breakfast buffet.

+ The hotel is relatively new so everything looks crisp and well maintained.

+ Packages including SeaWorld tickets are available.

+ Complimentary theme park transportation.

Minuses

— The bigger the suite, the higher the price.

— The hotel is a bit off the main drag of International Drive. For families seeking peace and privacy, that actually may be a plus, but you'll have to drive for every meal unless you're eating in your own kitchen.

Off-Site Mid-Price Hotels

Embassy Suites Lake Buena Vista   407/239–1144
www.embassysuites.com

The Embassy Suites chain is very popular with our readers, especially this location. The suites include kitchenettes, the hotels are generally exceptionally well maintained, and a bountiful breakfast is included in the price. There are four Embassy Suites in Orlando; rates at the Lake Buena Vista location, which is the closest to Disney World, range from $119–$149 during the off-season and $129–$159 during the on-season. (The two International Drive locations—Embassy Suites International Drive South and Embassy Suites International Drive Jamaican Court—are also convenient to area theme parks, being reasonably close to Disney World, Universal, and SeaWorld.)

Proximity to Disney World:	Good, via a 10-minute drive

| Proximity to Universal: | Fair, via a 15-minute drive |
| Proximity to SeaWorld: | Good, via a 10-minute drive |

Pluses

+ There are many all-suites hotels in Orlando but this is one of the closest to Disney. You can access Disney property through the Downtown Disney gate without the hassle of getting on I–4.

+ Complimentary breakfast buffet with made-to-order pancakes and an omelet station.

+ Kitchenettes make it easy to keep snacks and sandwich supplies on hand.

+ A shopping center with a grocery and fast-food restaurants is nearby.

+ The heated indoor-outdoor pool is an asset in the off-season.

+ Lots of sports options: a gym, tennis courts, basketball, shuffleboard, and volleyball.

Minuses

− Proximity to I–4 means a consistently high noise level.

− This Embassy Suites is on Palm Parkway surrounded by many other hotels, which means you may hit traffic getting to the parks—another reason to start early.

Magical Memories Villas   407/390–8200
www.magicalmemories.com

One can only imagine how thrilled Disney is that this independent rental agency has adopted the word "magical"—perhaps the most frequently employed word in Disney promotional materials. But Magical Memories, while having no affiliation with Disney, can offer good deals for families. The company handles both condo and house rentals in nine different neighborhoods throughout Orlando. If you want to pay for a home with a private pool in a gated community, that's certainly available, but most of the rentals are clean, simply furnished, safe apartments in condo complexes. Rates start surprisingly low: During the off-season you'll pay $99 for a two-bedroom condo and $169 for a five-bedroom house with a private pool. During the on-season condos begin at $169 a night and houses at $229 a night. Be sure to browse the Web site to see all your options. There's a substantial range of amenities and prices.

But the benefits can be substantial as well, as outlined by a mother from Canada. "Because we have a family of six we would have had to rent two hotel rooms, so renting a house was ideal for our situation—not to mention that we split the cost with another family. We ended up with a five-bedroom, five-bath house with all the perks. They said it was minutes from Disney, and it really was."

Proximity to Disney:	Minimum 5 miles, maximum 8 miles
Proximity to Universal:	Maximum 16 miles
Proximity to SeaWorld:	Maximum 13 miles

Pluses

+ Good choice for large families and groups, since you can get a multi-bedroom house or condo with a well-equipped kitchen and all the conveniences of a hotel.

+ If you're staying at one of the condo-style Magical Memories villas, you'll also have use of the villa clubhouse. Some have amenities such as Wi-Fi, exercise rooms, larger pools, etc. The Magical Memories Villas encompass 15 different villa sites, and each clubhouse is different, so if you're seeking a specific amenity, be sure to ask when reserving.

Minuses

— This isn't like a familiar hotel chain where you know what to expect. There's a range in the quality of accommodations.

— For rentals of four nights or fewer you'll be charged a cleaning fee based on the size of your unit.

— A stay of three nights is required for the villas and five nights for the houses.

— There's a very strict reservations and payment policy. You have to pay a $100 deposit when you reserve, and $50 of that is nonrefundable no matter when you cancel. The full balance is due 15 days in advance of your arrival, and if you cancel within a week after that date, you only get 50% of that balance back. If you must cancel less than seven days before your arrival date, or if you depart early for any reason, you get no refund at all.

Nickelodeon Holiday Inn Family Suites
www.nickhotel.com 407/387–5437

Okay, you say you're totally doing this trip for the kids? You'll never find a hotel any more kid-oriented than this one. First of all, you're not going to miss it while driving in from the airport—the lime green and hot orange facade of the building looks like it's been slimed. Once there, you'll find an array of Nick-theme activities, including a character breakfast with SpongeBob SquarePants, nightly live stage shows, and poolside games. There are two separate water park–style pools. One is oriented toward older kids with big-deal slides and a 400-gallon "dump tank" that periodically, without warning, splashes gigantic waves of water down the slides and flumes. The other pool is geared to younger kids, with preschooler-size slides, climbing areas, and games. Other types of recreation include basketball, miniature golf, and one of Orlando's largest arcades. There's even a kids' spa offering manicures, pedicures, hair braiding and wraps, and airbrush tattoos. Whew! While several hotels in Orlando offer a limited number of so-called kid-suites—multi-room suites in which one of the rooms is decorated to please children, with amenities like video-game consoles and bunk beds, as well as a private master bedroom for parents and kitchenette with a mini-refrigerator and microwave—the Nickelodeon Holiday Inn has plenty of them. Rates begin as low as $169 in the off-season, rising to $259 for peak season. If you don't want a kidsuite, rates begin at $123.

Proximity to Disney World:	Good, via a 10-minute drive
Proximity to Universal:	Fair, via a 20-minute drive
Proximity to SeaWorld:	Good, via a 15-minute drive

Pluses

+ Entertainment options for kids are practically unlimited. The newest offering is the 4-D Experience, a 3-D theater offering shows such as SpongeBob Squarepants and The Animal Adventure along with special effects.

+ This is the ultimate family-focused hotel; you'll find virtually nothing but parents with kids here.

+ If your kids are into Nick characters like SpongeBob, this place will be heaven to them.

+ Some effort is made—such as having two separate pool areas—to keep the hyperexcited older kids from trampling the overwhelmed younger kids.

+ The kidsuites are numerous and well priced.

Minuses

− No question: this has to be the loudest, most garish hotel in the world.

— The nonstop stimulation may make it hard to persuade your kids to nap in the afternoon or even go to sleep at night.

— Dining options consist of fast food and buffets, which appeal to kids and are fairly priced but don't offer much variety or nutrition.

Sheraton Vistana   407/238–5000
www.starwood.com

The Sheraton Vistana has been a perpetual favorite with our readers since we first began doing resort surveys. One mom wrote, mirroring many other letters, "We found the resort to be very pretty, very quiet, and very clean. And it took us only 15 minutes to drive to Disney World."

Unusually well decorated and maintained, these villas supply almost anything a family could require, and the location is nearly equidistant between the major Orlando theme parks. One-bedroom villas begin at $149 in the off-season and $279 in the on-season; two-bedroom villas begin at $195 off-season and $339 on-season.

Proximity to Disney World:	Good, via a 15-minute drive
Proximity to Universal:	Good, via a 15-minute drive
Proximity to SeaWorld:	Good, via a 15-minute drive

Pluses

+ Children's programs at the kids' club and in-room babysitting allow parents to have some quiet time.

+ A central location between International Drive and I–4 makes it easy to get to all the theme parks and to family-friendly restaurants and minor attractions along International Drive.

+ The villas are larger and more comfortable than those in most other all-suites hotels.

Minuses

— On-property food options are limited, although there's a casual deli-style restaurant and pool bar. Since most families take advantage of the villa kitchenettes and there are plenty of family-friendly restaurants in the area, the lack of on-site dining options is rarely a problem.

— The resort is wrapping up a major expansion-renovation project, which should be completed by 2010. Even so, when booking a room, ask for a recently renovated room that's not near any ongoing construction.

Budget Off-Site Hotels

Comfort Suites at Maingate East   407/397–7848
www.choicehotels.com

This hotel is cheaper than most of area suite-style hotels, largely because of its location off Route 192. Also called the Irlo Bronson Memorial Highway, Route 192 isn't quite as spiffy as International Drive and, in fact, this particular hotel at present looks out over a creaky little amusement park called Old Town. But the hotel is clean and comfortable, the staff is pleasant, and the price is definitely right. Maingate East is a mere 2 miles from Disney property, and if you're looking for a location that's both affordable and close enough to be able to return to your hotel for a midday break, the Comfort Suites Maingate East is a good option. Prices range from $99–$169 during the off-season and $129–$169 during the on-season.

Proximity to Disney World: Excellent, via a 5-minute
                                  drive
Proximity to Universal: Fair, via a 20-minute drive
Proximity to SeaWorld: Fair, via a 20-minute drive

Pluses

+ Starting at $99 for the smallest suite, it's hard to beat the price.

+ Suites have either partial dividers or separate rooms, plus microwaves, refrigerators, coffeemakers, and sleeper sofas.

+ A deluxe continental breakfast is included.

+ This is as close as you'll get to Disney property at this price point; and the Maingate East entrance means you can skip I–4 traffic altogether.

Minuses

— The one-bedroom suites are comfortable for families of four or fewer. While the Web site says the suites can accommodate a family of six, you'll be cramped.

— Route 192 may be the least scenic part of Orlando.

Holiday Inn SunSpree Lake Buena Vista
www.kidsuites.com   407/239–4500

Although not quite as wild and woolly as its sister, the Nickelodeon Holiday Inn, the SunSpree has lots of ways to keep kids entertained, as well as a smaller price tag and a location that's actually closer to Disney. Kidsuites, rooms with one king bed and two bunk beds in a cheerfully decorated cubicle, begin as low as $99 and standard rooms begin at $78. In-room microwaves and refrigerators allow families to fix snacks and simple meals, and an on-site grocery store makes it easy to get supplies.

A mom from North Carolina expressed her appreciation: "We were at the Holiday Inn SunSpree in the summer when they offer a kiddie program called Camp Holiday. They had games and movies to entertain children in a nice child-care center. Parents can drop off their children, rent a pager so they can be contacted in case of an emergency, and then go out to dinner. It's a marvelous benefit."

Proximity to Disney World:	Good, via a 10-minute drive
Proximity to Universal:	Fair, via a 20-minute drive
Proximity to SeaWorld:	Good, via a 15-minute drive

Pluses

+ Kids will feel special here: there's a separate kid registration desk, an arcade, a sports deck, a playroom, and two pools.

+ Kids eat free at the buffet restaurant.

+ Free shuttle service to Disney.

+ Unusually good prices considering the proximity to Disney.

+ On-site child care in the on-season.

+ A good choice for families who don't need suites with full kitchens, but who would still like some of the amenities, such as a fridge and microwave, that a suite would offer.

Minuses

— The resort is fairly old and some rooms are in need of a little sprucing up. Request a recently refurbished room when you book.

— Like most of the kid-oriented hotels in Orlando, this place is always loud. The noise volume in the main hallway is enough to make your eyes cross.

— As you might anticipate from the lower price, the kid-suites here aren't large and don't have separate bedrooms for parents and kids. What you do get is one big room and a room-within-a-room, really a cubicle, that has bunk beds for kids.

La Quinta International Drive North
www.lq.com   **407/351–4100**

There are plenty of La Quintas in Orlando but this location, an easy drive from all three of the area's major theme parks, is especially appealing to vacationing families. Rooms begin as low as $70 in the off-season, with a junior suite starting at $90. During peak times prices climb to the $100–$130 range. Still a deal.

Proximity to Disney:	Fair, via a 20-minute drive
Proximity to Universal:	Good, via a 10-minute drive
Proximity to SeaWorld:	Good, via a 10-minute drive

Pluses

+ It's an easy drive to SeaWorld and Universal, and a bit farther to Disney. The hotel runs complimentary shuttles to the area theme parks.

+ There are plenty of family-friendly chain and budget restaurants along I-Drive.

+ Complimentary breakfast is included, and there are laundry facilities on-site.

Minuses

— The commute to Disney can be problematic if you're traveling at peak traffic times.

— The I-Drive location, while bringing you close to services, means you'll also have to deal with traffic and noise.

CHAPTER

3

Once You
Get There

Bare Necessities: Strollers, Babies, and First Aid

Whether you're pregnant, traveling with a baby, or nursing a sore ankle, Disney World is prepared to accommodate your needs.

Strollers

Strollers are available for rent at each theme park for $21 (single) and $30 (double). (If you book for multiple days, the price per day drops.)

At these rates, if you need a stroller every day it's obviously most cost-effective to bring one from home. But if you have an older child who will only need a stroller at Epcot, a rental isn't a bad option.

> @ If you're renting a stroller for more than one day, you don't have to get in line every morning. On your first park visit, tell them you want, for example, a four-day stroller rental, and they'll give you coupons for four days. After that you

can skip the rental line and go directly to the stroller pick-up booth.

- All kids 3 and under need a stroller, for napping as well as riding and resting.

- For kids 4 to 6, the general rule is this: Strollers are a must at Epcot, nice in the Magic Kingdom, and less needed at the Animal Kingdom or Hollywood, where the walkable area of the parks is smaller and you spend a lot of time sitting in shows.

Money-Saving Tip

If you plan to park-hop in a single day, you don't have to pay for a stroller twice: Keep your receipt and show it for a new stroller when you arrive at the next park.

- On busy days the Magic Kingdom opens an additional stroller-rental stand outside the main gate, before you enter the bag check area. This location is never as crowded as the rental stand inside the park.

Helpful Hint

Just because your stroller isn't where you left it doesn't mean it's been taken—it may simply have been moved aside. Families often stop in midstride when they see an appealing attraction and abandon their stroller in the middle of the sidewalk. There are Disney cast members whose sole duty it is to collect and rearrange these strollers, lining them up outside rides and packing them as close together as possible. Keep looking—you'll likely find your stroller a few yards away from where you left it.

- Tie something like a bandanna or a balloon to your stroller to mark it; otherwise, when you emerge from a ride it may be impossible to find your stroller in a sea of look-alikes. Also, people sometimes just grab the nearest stroller without checking the name tag, but most people stop short of taking a personal belonging.

- Still can't find your stroller? In the Animal Kingdom and Hollywood, you'll have to go back to the entrance for a replacement. In the Magic Kingdom, check in at Tinker Bell's Treasures in Fantasyland. At Epcot you can get a new stroller at the World Traveler shop between France and the United Kingdom. As long as you've kept your receipt there's no additional charge for a new stroller.

- If at 8 AM your 5-year-old swears she doesn't need a stroller but at noon she collapses in a heap halfway around Epcot's World Showcase, head for the World Traveler shop. The World Traveler is also the place to rent a stroller if you're coming from the Yacht and Beach Clubs, BoardWalk, or the Swan and Dolphin hotels, and using the "back-door" entrance.

- Families staying at one of the more sprawling resorts, such as Pop Century, Caribbean Beach, Coronado Springs, Port Orleans, Fort Wilderness, or the All-Star resorts, should bring a stroller from home for any child under 4. You'll need it just to get from your room to the food court or shuttle bus stop.

Baby Care

Each park has a Baby Care Center where rockers, bottle warmers, high chairs, and changing tables are available; diapers, formula, and jars of baby food are also for sale.

In the Magic Kingdom, Baby Care is beside the Crystal Palace Restaurant. In Epcot it's on the bridge that connects Future World to the World Showcase. At Hollywood it's in the Guest Services (a.k.a. Guest Relations) building; and in the Animal Kingdom it's behind the Creature Comforts gift shop.

Disposable diapers are available in the larger shops, but they're kept behind the counter, so you'll have to ask for them. Changing tables are provided in most women's restrooms and some men's as well. If fathers have trouble locating a changing table in a men's room, they can always make a stop in Baby Care.

Nursing Moms

Disney World is so casual and family-oriented that you shouldn't feel self-conscious about using a towel or blanket and discreetly nursing anywhere that's comfortable. If you're too modest for these methods, or your baby is easily distracted, try the rockers in the Baby Care Center.

Helpful Hint
Seek medical advice the moment you suspect there may be a problem. Waiting it out only makes the solution more painful and more expensive.

First Aid

First-aid clinics are beside the Baby Care Center in each park. Although the clinics mostly treat patients with minor problems such as sunburn, motion sickness, and boo-boos, they're equipped for major emergencies and, when necessary, can provide ambulance service to an area hospital.

If you do suffer a medical emergency, take comfort in the fact that hundreds of families that I've interviewed have given

Insider's Secret

If anyone in your family is prone to a recurring medical condition—your son frequently gets ear infections, for example—bring a prescription from your doctor at home in case you need medication while in Orlando.

ringing endorsements to Disney cast members in times of crisis. I've gotten dozens of e-mails and letters from people who have broken their arms, fainted from heat, gone into premature labor, come down with the chicken pox, and everything else you can imagine—and each person has lauded the Disney cast members for their quick medical response and emotional support. One mother of two from Maryland wrote, "We visited Walt Disney World with our son, who has cystic fibrosis, and found everyone there to be extremely helpful and aware of what our needs might be. In fact, they often anticipated our needs before we did."

General First-Aid Tips

@ If someone begins to feel ill or suffers an injury while in the parks, head for the nearest first-aid clinic. If the nurses there can't fix the problem, they'll find someone who can.

@ All on-site hotels and many off-site hotels have physicians on call 24 hours a day. Contact either the Guest Services (a.k.a. Guest Relations) desk at your own hotel or Centra Care Walk-In Medical Care at 407/238–2000 which, as the name implies, accepts walk-in patients and has in-house pharmacies. There are two locations near Disney World. For directions and more information, call 407/934–2273. Most area hotels provide courtesy transport to medical clinics and pharmacies for guests in need.

@ If you need a pharmacy, try the Walgreens (407/253–6288) on Kirkman Road or the CVS (407/390–9185) on U.S. 192. Both are open 24 hours a day.

@ Of course, no matter where you're staying, in a true emergency call 911.

@ ECVs ($45 with an additional $20 deposit) and wheelchairs ($10 a day or $8 a day for multiday use) are available at all theme parks, so if you're traveling with an older family member, a woman in the late stages of pregnancy, or anyone who might be laid low by the heat, don't hesitate to rent a little mechanical assistance—especially at Epcot, which has the largest walking areas of any Disney park.

More Things You Don't Want to Think About

A Rainy Day

Unless there's a full-out hurricane headed inland, the parks operate as usual. If there's an electrical storm, outdoor rides and shows are suspended until the weather clears, and water parks may close down for the day.

But if you just run into one of those afternoon cloudbursts so common to Florida, soldier on. Rain slickers are available throughout the parks for $7, and they're much more practical than umbrellas because your hands are free to hang on to your kids. The only problem is that on a rainy day half the people in the park are wearing the slickers and thus everyone looks alike. It makes it easier to lose your kids in the crowd, so stay especially alert.

Here are some tips to make sure that a rainy day doesn't turn into a total washout.

- Disney's Hollywood Studios is a good choice when the weather is iffy because most of the rides and shows are indoors. The Animal Kingdom has mostly outdoor attractions, but if it's just misty and not pouring, it can also be a good choice because the animals are more active when a little rain cools off the air. The Magic Kingdom, where many rides are outside, and Epcot, which requires a lot of walking, are a bit tougher to navigate.

- There's always plenty to do at Downtown Disney: shopping, movies, Cirque du Soleil, and DisneyQuest. But be forewarned—DisneyQuest is especially swamped when the weather turns bad.

- Remember, a rainy morning doesn't necessarily mean a rainy day. Weather conditions can change rapidly in Orlando, and if it clears up later in the day the parks will be less crowded than usual. If you see a storm approaching, duck into a show or indoor attraction and give it some time. You may walk out to find sunny skies.

"My advice is to pray for rain," wrote a father of two from Pennsylvania. "We were standing in a long line for Dumbo, and it began to shower. Everyone left, but we just went into a nearby shop and it stopped raining after just a couple of minutes. When we emerged, Fantasyland was practically empty, and we got on Dumbo with no wait at all."

Lost Kids

Obviously, your best bet is not to get separated in the first place. Savvy families set up prearranged meeting places.

If you do get separated and your kids are too young to understand the idea of a meeting place, act fast. Disney employees are well briefed about what to do if they encounter a lost child, so the odds are good that if your preschooler has been wandering around on his own for more than a couple of min-

Insider's Secret

Where and when are kids most apt to get lost? During character signings, in play areas, and just after parades. Everyone designates Cinderella Castle or Spaceship Earth as a meeting spot, which is one of the reasons these places are always mobbed. Plan to catch up with your crowd in a more out-of-the-way locale.

utes, he's been intercepted by a Disney cast member. The cast member has been trained to walk around the area with the child for about 10 minutes and, if they don't find you, they will take the child to the Baby Care Center in that park. So if you've been wandering around looking for longer than 10 minutes, flag down the nearest person you see wearing a Disney name tag, and ask them to call Baby Care and see if the child has been reported found. You can also make things easier if you wear colorful clothing and explain to any child old enough to remember that "Mom is wearing a bright blue shirt today." This increases the chances the cast member will be able to spot you in the crowd.

The one glitch in the system is that lost kids are often so interested in what's going on around them that they aren't crying, and they don't look lost, and, thus, no Disney employee intercepts them. Explain to your kids that if they get separated from you to approach the nearest person wearing a Disney

Insider's Secret

If you stop by Guest Services in the morning, they can give you a tag where you can put your cell phone number on the inside of the child's clothing.

name tag. That person can call in the child's name to Baby Care and, assuming you've also called in to report the child as missing, the attendant can tell you where your child is.

In real emergencies—when the child is very young or disabled, or when you're afraid she's been nabbed—bulletins are put out among employees. So if you lose a child, don't spend a half hour frantically searching on your own. Contact the nearest Disney employee and let the system take it from there.

Parking

When it comes to a day at Disney, by far the most common problem is forgetting where you parked. Be sure to write down your row number as you leave your car in the morning. Pluto 36 seems easy to remember at first, but you may not be able to retrieve that information 14 brain-numbing hours later.

Closed Attractions

Because Disney World is open 365 days a year, there's no downtime for repainting and repairing rides. Because of this two or three attractions throughout Disney World may be closed for refurbishment on any given day. (They try hard to keep major attractions up and going for summer and holidays, so refurbishment is more likely to be an issue in the off-season.) You can check to see which attractions are scheduled to be closed for maintenance during the time you'll be in Orlando by visiting www.disneyworld.com. That way, if the Rock 'n' Roller Coaster is shut down for the week, at least you'll know before you hit the gates.

There's still a slight chance that a ride will be malfunctioning and thus temporarily closed when you visit, but this is relatively rare, and the rides usually come back on line quickly. The one exception to this is Test Track, which is closed for servicing more than any other Disney attraction.

Unexpected Problems

No matter how carefully you plan your vacation, the unforeseen can always occur. Your best bet when trouble brews is to go straight to the nearest Disney cast member and report your problem. There's a reason you're paying these high prices, and one of the biggest is that Disney has created a very responsive team of cast members whose highest priority is to help you have a great experience. Our mail is absolutely full of stories about Disney cast members who have gone above and beyond the call of duty. For example:

"My father lost his cell phone in the Animal Kingdom, and a cast member called every single attraction we had ridden that day until they found the phone. I can't say enough about the helpfulness of Disney employees!"

"Our family missed the last bus leaving the Fantasia Gardens miniature golf course, and we had no idea how we were going to get back to Fort Wilderness. Panic was setting in when an out-of-service bus passed by. My dad flagged him down, and, to our surprise, the driver told us to get aboard, and he would take us there himself. He even calmed my little sister down by singing to her through the loudspeaker. It was the end of his shift, and he could have easily driven by, but that's not the Disney way."

"We had a Princess dinner at Epcot scheduled for our first night, and my daughter's princess dress was packed in our luggage, which hadn't yet been delivered through Magical Express. We called the bell captain at our hotel, who was able to track the bag and get it to our hotel. He had it waiting for us when we got to the bell desk and let my daughter change in the luggage holding room! Then, since by that time we were running late, he even arranged for a special car to take us to Epcot so we wouldn't have to wait on the bus. It was a shining example of Disney customer service."

"One day our 4-year-old was crying hysterically—I think it was because his sister drank the last of the pineapple juice. A street sweeper on Main Street asked us what was wrong, and then said 'Follow me' and led us into Casey's where he got my son a Sprite. I was blown away. Such a kind gesture, especially considering how many crying kids that man probably sees in a day."

Got the picture? If a problem develops, let the Disney cast members try to sort it out. And even if things are going smoothly, stop and chat with them. Many of our readers report that cast member interactions are some of the highlights of their Disney stay.

Saving Money

Saving money at Disney World is somewhat of an oxymoron, but there are ways to contain the damage.

- Be aware that once you cross the Florida state line, there's an inverse relationship between time and money. You have to be willing to spend one in order to save the other. It's worth taking a few minutes to really analyze if cost-cutting measures are worth it; given the high cost of tickets, it doesn't make sense to spend hours trying to save a few bucks.

- How should you spend your arrival day at Disney World? It's tempting to rush straight to the parks, but that's rarely the best use of your money. Since it will probably be at least afternoon before you arrive and settle into your hotel, you'll be using a full day of your expensive ticket for only a few hours in the park. Instead, relax around your resort pool or spend the evening at Downtown Disney, which offers lots of Disney-theme fun but doesn't require a ticket. Then you can start your first full day rested and raring to go.

@ Staying hydrated is essential—and expensive—so bring your own bottles, and keep refilling them at fountains. Also, on-site hotels offer a deal where you can buy a souvenir beverage mug the first day of your trip and get free refills at the resort for the remainder of your stay. Because soft drinks and coffee are so costly, families who plan to eat a lot of meals at their hotel can save as much as $20 per person with the souvenir mugs.

@ If you're not on the dining plan, try to eat at least some of your meals outside the parks. If you get a suite, it's easy to keep breakfast food and snacks in your room. Many off-site Orlando hotels offer free breakfast buffets to their guests, and there are numerous fast-food and family-friendly chain restaurants along the I–4 exits that flank Walt Disney World.

@ Dining in Epcot's World Showcase can be very special, but book those restaurants for lunch, when prices are considerably lower than at dinner. And remember that portions are huge, even for kiddie meals. Consider splitting a meal with a family member. Or toss a few Ziploc bags in your tote and save some of those chips or grapes for a later snack.

@ The dinner shows are expensive, costing a family of four about $150; even a character breakfast can set you back $60 or more. If the budget is tight, skip those extras and concentrate on ways to meet the characters inside the parks.

@ Except for maybe an autograph book and a T-shirt, hold off on souvenir purchases until the last day. By then the kids will really know what they want and you won't waste money on impulse buys.

@ Buy memory cards or film, blank videotapes, diapers, and sunscreen at home before you leave. These things are all for sale in the parks, but you'll pay dearly for the convenience.

@ If you move from park to park in the course of a day, save your parking receipt so you'll only have to pay the fee once. Also, remember that parking is free for on-site guests.

@ Buy your tickets when you make your hotel reservations, so you'll have them before Disney decides it's time for another price increase.

Meeting the Disney Characters

Meeting the characters is a major objective for some families and a nice diversion for all. If your children are young, prepare them for the fact that the characters are big and, therefore, often overwhelming in person. I once visited Disney World with a toddler whose happy babble of "my Mickey, my Mickey" turned into a wary "no Mickey, no Mickey" the minute she entered the Magic Kingdom gates and saw that everyone's favorite mouse was much, much larger than he appears on TV.

That reaction isn't unusual. Many kids panic when they first see the characters, and pushing them forward only makes matters worse. The characters are trained to be sensitive and sensible (in some cases more so than the parents) and will always wait for the child to approach them. It's a good idea to schedule a character breakfast near the end of the trip; by then the kids have had plenty of time to observe the characters around the park, and even cautious youngsters have usually warmed up.

On the other hand, some kids fall in love with the characters from the start. A father from Ohio said, "We were really surprised at how fast our 3½-year-old daughter became a character groupie. Even when in her stroller she could spot them

Insider's Secret

If your child is nervous about meeting the characters, start with the so-called face characters, like Aladdin or Cinderella, who don't wear masks and who can talk. They're far less intimidating to young children.

from a mile away, and she loved getting autographs. This took a lot of time but was worth it just to see the excitement on her face."

Many children, even older ones, enjoy getting character autographs, and an autograph book can become a cherished souvenir. Before lining up, prepare the kids for the fact that the characters don't talk. (With, that is, the exception of characters without masks.) As many as 30 young people in Mickey suits (mostly women, because the suits are pretty small) might be dispersed around Disney World on a busy day, and they can't all be gifted with that familiar squeaky voice. So the characters communicate through body language.

Helpful Hint

The characters are usually available in greeting locations for about 20 minutes before they're whisked away to another spot. There's always a character escort close at hand, and if the line to meet a certain character is long, check with the escort before you line up. He or she can tell you approximately how much longer the character will be there and save you from waiting patiently only to have the heartbreaking experience of having the character leave just as your child makes it to the front of the line.

Also be aware that because of the construction of their costumes, the characters can't always see what's happening beneath them too clearly. Donald and Daisy, for example, have a hard time looking over their bills, and small children standing at their feet might be ignored. If this appears to be happening, lift your child to the character's eye level.

Times and places for meeting the characters are listed on theme park maps, tip boards, and entertainment schedules.

CHAPTER

4

Touring
Tips and
Plans

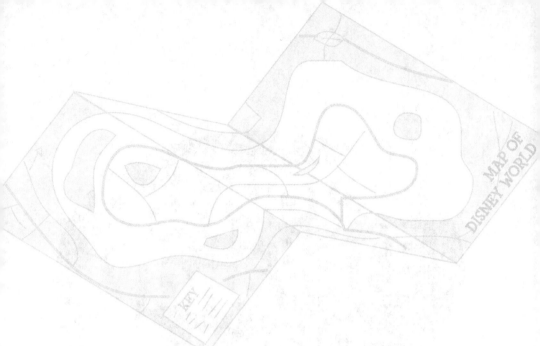

General Disney World Touring Tips

The size of Walt Disney World is often a shock to first-time visitors, many of whom arrive with vague notions that they can walk from Epcot to the Magic Kingdom or even that they are separate sections of the same theme park. There can also be confusion over the names: Some people use "Walt Disney World" and "Magic Kingdom" synonymously, whereas in reality the Magic Kingdom is a relatively small part of the much larger Disney World complex. There's more to this place than Cinderella Castle and Space Mountain. Thus it's vital that you have at least a basic understanding of the Disney World layout and transportation system before you leave home.

The tips in this chapter encourage you to visit more than one park a day—to follow a morning hitting the waterslides at Blizzard Beach, for example, with an afternoon taking in the shows at Hollywood. The best way to avoid overstimulation and burnout is to work a variety of experiences—some active, some passive, some educational, some silly—into each day. (Note that this strategy requires you to have a Park Hopper ticket.)

When it comes to touring, families tend to fall into three groups. The first group sleeps in, has a full-service meal at their hotel, and lollygags over to the parks around 11 AM. They wander around aimlessly, finding the lines for major rides to be so long that their only choices are either to wait 90 minutes for Splash Mountain or to spend the whole afternoon riding minor attractions. By the time they begin to get in a groove (i.e., they figure out time-saving systems like Fastpass), it's 5 PM, and they're exhausted. They retreat to their hotel room frustrated at how little they've seen, irritated by how much they've spent, and carping at each other. This is a vacation?

The second group is what I call Disney World Commandos. These hyper-organized types have elaborate tour plans and march determinedly from ride to ride, checking off their "to do" list as they go. Amanda wants to ride Dumbo twice in a row? No way! It'll throw them off schedule. Jeffrey wants to hang out at Innoventions? Sorry, it's not on the list. If anything unforeseen happens—Space Mountain opens late or there's a glitch in the bus system—the whole group goes into a psychological meltdown. This is a vacation?

Disney-savvy families find the sweet spot between the two extremes. They have an overall plan but make sure to leave empty spaces in the day to allow for spontaneity. They get an early start each morning, but factor in plenty of downtime to rest, particularly in the afternoon. Most important, they're familiar enough with each park and its attractions that they arrive with a clear idea of what they want to see, but they don't feel compelled to do it all. One father of four from Washington State wrote, "People need some kind of plan before they go. Disney World is so big and so overwhelming that the first time we went down we spent hours just aimlessly drifting around."

The following tips should help you make the most of your time without pushing anyone, parents or kids, past their endurance level.

@ For families with kids, it's especially important to avoid the exhaustion that comes with just trying to get there. If you're staying off-site, it can easily take two hours from the time you leave your hotel until you board your first ride, which is enough to shatter the equanimity of even the most well-behaved kid. Your children have been waiting for this vacation a long time, and now they've been flying and driving for a long time. You owe it to them to get into the parks quickly.

Insider's Secret

Come early! If you follow only one tip in the whole book, make it this one. Although in recent years the mornings have become more crowded than they used to be, you'll still find far shorter waits for big-deal rides than you do in the afternoon.

@ Every Disney World guidebook on the market tells people to come early, so it's no shock that in the 20 years since I've written this book's first edition, the mornings have become more crowded. However, the good news for you is that most people visiting Disney World still arrive between 10 and 11 AM, many of them proudly announcing that this is their vacation and they'll sleep in if they want. (These same people seem to take a strange inverse pride in bragging about how long they stood in line and how little they saw.) Arriving early is like exercising regularly: everyone knows you should do it, but most people don't. So an early start is still the best way to ride major attractions with little or no wait time.

@ On the evening you arrive, check with your hotel to see what time the park you'll be visiting the next day opens.

(All on-site and most off-site hotels display this information prominently.) If you learn, for example, that the Magic Kingdom is scheduled to open at 9 AM, be at the gate by 8:30. At least part of the park is usually open early and you can be at the end of Main Street awaiting the rope drop while the other 50,000 poor saps are still crawling along I–4.

@ If you're indeed allowed to enter the first section of the park early, use your time wisely. Take care of any business—get maps and entertainment schedules, rent strollers, take a potty break—before the main park opens. If you haven't had breakfast, there's always a kiosk where you can grab juice

Insider's Secret
What if everyone comes early? They won't.

and muffins. The characters are usually on hand to greet kids, which is a fun way to start the day. But be sure to be at the ropes about 10 minutes before the stated opening times.

@ Because people were practically stampeding after the rope drop, Disney is now controlling how fast you can enter

Time-Saving Tip
To maximize your time in the parks, either eat breakfast at your hotel or buy fast food while you're waiting for the rope drop. There's always at least one sit-down place to get breakfast in each park, but you don't want to waste the relatively uncrowded morning hours in a restaurant.

the main body of the park. Once the whole park opens, proceed quickly but calmly (they'll nab you if you run) to the first ride you'd like to board. Sometimes the Fastpass system doesn't start working until 20 or 30 minutes after the park opens, so it's definitely better to ride your top-priority attraction first and get your Fastpass second.

@ Eat at "off" times. Some families eat lightly at breakfast, have an early lunch around 11 AM and supper at 5 PM.

Helpful Hint
Plan to see the most popular attractions either early in the day, late at night, or during a time when a big event siphons off other potential riders (such as the afternoon parade in the Magic Kingdom).

Others eat a huge breakfast and then a late lunch around 3 PM and have a final meal back at their hotels after the parks close. If you tour late and you're really bushed, all on-site hotels and many off-site hotels have in-room pizza delivery service.

@ Kids usually want to revisit their favorite attractions and parents who overschedule to the point where there's no time for this risk a mutiny. One way to handle this is to save the entire last day of your trip as a "greatest hits" day and go back to all your favorites one more time, even if this means maximum park-hopping. If you feel like lugging the camcorder around only once, make this the day.

@ Use the touring plan to cut down on arguments and debates. It's a hapless parent indeed who sits down at breakfast and asks, "What do you want to do today?" Three different kids will have three different answers.

@ When making plans, keep the size of the parks in mind. Hollywood is small and can be easily crisscrossed to take in various shows. Likewise, the Animal Kingdom can be toured in five or six hours. The Magic Kingdom has more attractions and more crowd density, slowing you down; although some cutting back and forth is possible, you'll probably want to tour one land fairly thoroughly before heading to another. Epcot is so enormous that you're almost forced to visit attractions in geographic sequence or you'll spend all your time and energy in transit.

@ If your kids have the stamina for it, try park-hopping. Families with a multiday pass might figure: We'll spend Monday at the Magic Kingdom, Tuesday at Hollywood, Wednesday at Blizzard Beach, Thursday at Epcot, and Friday at the Animal Kingdom. Sounds logical, but a day at the Magic Kingdom is too much riding, 14 hours at Epcot is too much walking, the Animal Kingdom simply doesn't require that much time, a whole day at Hollywood is too many shows, and anyone who stays at Blizzard Beach from dawn to dusk will wind up waterlogged. Mix it up a bit.

@ If you're trying to predict how crowded a ride or show will be, four factors come into effect:

The newness of the attraction. In general, the newer it is, the hotter it is, especially if it's an attraction that's gotten a lot of media attention like Toy Story Mania.

The quality of the attraction. Space Mountain, Fantasmic!, and other Disney classics will still be mobbed years from now.

Speed of loading. Continuous-loading attractions such as Pirates of the Caribbean, Spaceship Earth, and It's a Small World can move thousands of people through in an hour. The lines at start-and-stop rides such as Dumbo, TriceraTop Spin, and the Mad Tea Party move much more slowly.

Capacity. Shows like Muppet*Vision 3D, Universe of Energy, and Mickey's PhilharMagic have theaters that can accommodate large crowds at once. Lines form and disappear quickly as hundreds of people enter the theater for a show. For this reason, theater-style attractions are good choices in the afternoon, when the park is at its most crowded and you need a rest.

@ Take some time to familiarize yourself with the sprawling WDW transportation system. If you're staying on-site you'll be given a transportation map at check-in, and Guest Services (a.k.a. Guest Relations) can help you decide the best route to take to out-of-the-way locations.

@ For families with young children, seeing the characters is a major part of what makes Disney World special, so don't overplan to the point where you don't have time to hang with Mickey and the gang. Your theme park map indicates when and where they'll appear, but the one place you probably won't see them is just walking down the street. At Disney, the characters are the equivalent of rock stars and security around them is tight. If you want that photo, autograph, or hug, you'll need to either line up or schedule a character breakfast.

@ In the off-season, the Magic Kingdom, Hollywood, and the Animal Kingdom sometimes close at 5 or 6 PM, but Epcot always stays open later, even during the least crowded days of the year. So spend your days at one of the parks that closes early, and evenings at Epcot. This buys you more hours in the parks for your money and besides, many of the best places for dinner are at Epcot.

@ If there's a wide gap in the ages of your kids, check out the maps and develop some strategies in advance. There are plenty of places throughout all four parks where Disney has put kiddie attractions next to rides that appeal to older kids. For example, the Beauty and the Beast show at Hollywood Studios is just down the block from the Tower of Terror and Rock 'n' Roller Coaster. One parent can take the younger kids to the show while the other parent takes the older kids to the thrill rides. Likewise, at the Animal Kingdom, the Dinosaur ride scares the willies out of youngsters, but the nearby Boneyard is a great place for them to play while their older siblings are on the ride. Be aware of which attractions are so intense that you'll need to split up and which—such as Mickey's PhilharMagic, Soarin', and Kilimanjaro Safaris, to name a few—are designed for all ages to experience together.

@ If you'll be at Disney World for more than four days, consider planning a "day off" in the middle of your vacation. A day in the middle of the trip devoted to sleeping in, hanging around the hotel pool, shopping at Downtown Disney, and maybe taking in a character breakfast at an on-site hotel can make all the difference. Not only will you save a day on your multiday ticket, but you'll also start the next morning refreshed and energized.

@ You need a strategy for closing time. Except for the Animal Kingdom, the major parks all have nighttime extravaganzas that result in huge logjams as nearly every guest in the park convenes for the show and then mobs the exits en masse when it's over. See the "Tips for Leaving" sections in each park for specific information on how to best exit each park.

Money-Saving Tips

It isn't easy to save money at Disney, but the following tips will help.

@ Consider the Disney Dining food plan. By turning your vacation into more of an all-inclusive, it helps you better gauge the cost of your trip in advance, a planning tool that some families prefer to showing up and "winging it."

@ Choose wisely when it comes to your hotel. A more expensive hotel with lots of family-friendly perks might end up being more cost-effective than a hotel with a lower nightly rate but no extras.

@ Tickets are expensive, so only use them on days when you can maximize your hours in the park. This might mean not visiting a park on the first or last days of your vacation when your travel schedule cuts into your available time; instead use these days for a character breakfast at a Disney hotel, a visit to Downtown Disney, miniature golf, or just to relax at the hotel pool.

@ Be aware of how little things add up. Bring strollers, sunscreen, water bottles, video supplies, diapers, etc., from home. Make lunch your big meal of the day. Let two family members share a drink or a meal. And bring resealable plastic bags so that you can save leftover chips and fruit for a later snack.

Touring Tips for Visitors Staying On-Site

@ By far the greatest advantage of staying on-site is the shortened commute to the theme parks, making for an easy return to your hotel for a mid-afternoon nap or swim. You can reenter the parks in the early evening. Remember the mantra: Come early, stay late, and take a break in the middle of the day.

@ Take advantage of the Extra Magic Hour program. You're given a brochure at check-in telling you which park is featured on which day of your visit. If you want to use this information in your pre-trip planning, visit www.disney world.com to verify which park will have extended hours on which day.

Touring Tips for Visitors Staying Off-Site

@ Time your commute. If you can make it from your hotel to the theme park gates within 30 minutes, it may still be worth your while to return to your hotel for a midday break. If your hotel is farther out and your commute is longer, it's doubtful you'll want to make the drive four times a day.

@ If it isn't feasible to return to your hotel, find afternoon resting places within the parks. (See the sections headed "Afternoon Resting Places.") Sometimes kids aren't so much tired as full of pent-up energy. If that's the case, take them to the play areas in each park (Tom Sawyer Island and Toontown in the Magic Kingdom; the play fountains in Epcot; the Honey, I Shrunk the Kids Adventure Zone at Hollywood; and the Boneyard at the Animal Kingdom) and let them run around for a bit.

@ The restaurants in the Magic Kingdom resorts are rarely crowded at lunch, and dining there is much more relaxed and leisurely than eating lunch in the parks. An early dinner can also effectively break up a summer day, when you'll be staying at the park until late. If you do take the monorail to a Magic Kingdom resort, be sure to line up for the train marked RESORT MONORAIL and not the express back to the TTC.

@ Off-site visitors tend to tour all day, so get strollers for preschoolers. Few 4-year-olds can walk through a 14-hour day.

@ If you have the Park Hopper option on your ticket, spend the morning in a park where you'll be active (like the Animal Kingdom or Magic Kingdom) and in the afternoon transfer to a park (such as Epcot or Hollywood) that has more shows and thus more places to sit and rest.

Tips to Save Your Sanity

Use Your Time Wisely

This boils down to one thing: Avoid the lines. Big-deal attractions draw long lines early and stay crowded all day.

Head for the most crowded, slow-loading attractions first. In the Magic Kingdom that's Splash Mountain, Space Mountain, and Big Thunder Mountain—although some Fantasyland attractions, such as Dumbo, Peter Pan, and the Many Adventures of Winnie the Pooh, can also draw long lines. In Epcot it's Soarin', Test Track, and Mission: SPACE. At Hollywood it's Toy

Story Mania, Rock 'n' Roller Coaster, and the Tower of Terror. At Animal Kingdom it's Expedition Everest, Kilimanjaro Safaris, and Dinosaur.

Ride as many of the big-deal rides as you can in the morning, when waits are shorter. In general, except for those noted, save theater-style attractions for the afternoon. And if you can't get to all the big-deal rides during the first couple of hours the park is open, try again during the parades, or during the last hour before closing.

Be Willing to Split Up

By this point in the planning process, it's probably beginning to dawn on you that every single member of the family expects something different from this vacation.

Discuss which attractions you'll enjoy as a family; some rides, shows, restaurants, and parades will be a blast for everyone. But there are also bound to be some attractions that won't have such universal appeal and this is especially true if there's a significant gap in the ages of your children.

If an attraction holds appeal for only one or two family members, there's no need to drag the whole crew along. Preteens and teenagers, in fact, often like to split off from the family for an hour or two and simply shop, hang out in arcades, or ride a favorite over and over. Security in Disney parks is tight, so this is an option worth considering. Just make sure to have a clearly designated meeting time and place. About splitting up, one mother of three from Ohio wrote, "Playhouse Disney is a wonderful attraction for young children, but my preteen son wasn't that thrilled with the idea of standing in line for an hour to see the Little Einsteins. We let him shop and walk around on his own for an hour while we took the younger kids to Playhouse Disney. Normally, I would worry about letting him be on his own but at Walt Disney World we felt pretty safe about it. And he was in a much better mood after a break from his little sisters."

Must-See List for WDW

AT THE MAGIC KINGDOM
Big Thunder Mountain

Buzz Lightyear's Space Ranger Spin

Dumbo

Evening parade and fireworks

Mickey's PhilharMagic

Space Mountain

Splash Mountain

AT EPCOT
The American Adventure (in the America pavilion)

Honey, I Shrunk the Audience

IllumiNations

Innoventions

Mission: SPACE

Soarin'

Spaceship Earth

Test Track

Turtle Talk With Crush

World Showcase Entertainment

AT HOLLYWOOD
Beauty and the Beast—Live on Stage!

Fantasmic!

The Great Movie Ride

Lights, Motors, Action!—Extreme Stunt Show

The Magic of Disney Animation

Muppet*Vision 3-D

Must-See List for WDW

Playhouse Disney

Rock 'n' Roller Coaster

Star Tours

Toy Story Mania

Twilight Zone Tower of Terror

Voyage of the Little Mermaid

AT THE ANIMAL KINGDOM

Dinosaur

Expedition Everest

Festival of the Lion King

Gorilla Falls Exploration Trail

It's Tough to be a Bug!

Kali River Rapids

Kilimanjaro Safaris

Maharajah Jungle Trek

Master Fastpass

Disney World's Fastpass system is designed to reduce the time you spend waiting in line. Attractions offering Fastpass are listed in each theme-park chapter.

Here's how it works: Let's say you enter the Animal Kingdom at 10 AM and find that a long line has already formed for Kilimanjaro Safaris. Rather than standing in line for an hour, go to the Fastpass kiosk and insert your theme-park ticket. You'll get the theme-park ticket back, along with a small paper Fastpass that looks like a movie admission stub. The Fastpass (along with a digital clock at the kiosk) will tell you when to return. There's usually an hour-long window of opportunity, which in this case might be between 11:30 AM and 12:30 PM.

Helpful Hint

Only a limited number of Fastpasses are available for each attraction. At the most popular rides on crowded days, Fastpasses can run out by mid-afternoon. So if you want to guarantee you'll get a Fastpass for Splash Mountain or Test Track, visit the kiosk as soon as possible after you enter the park.

Go on to tour the rest of the Animal Kingdom and return to Kilimanjaro Safaris sometime within that one-hour period. Show your Fastpass to the attendant and you'll be allowed to enter a much shorter line and proceed directly to the boarding

Helpful Hint

Be aware that the Fastpass kiosks are located outside of the attraction in question which means that getting a Fastpass from, say, Soarin', and then returning to use it two hours later can involve a lot of walking, especially in a park as huge and sprawling as Epcot. You might want to send one parent to get the Fastpasses for the whole family while the other supervises the kids in a play area or takes them on a less crowded attraction. And if you get caught in a show or restaurant and miss your Fastpass time, not to worry. Guests who show up at 4:15 with a 2:30–3:30 Fastpass will still be allowed into the line.

Insider's Secret

If your older kids want to go on a big-deal attraction such as Expedition Everest or Space Mountain over and over you can use the theme park tickets of younger siblings to obtain multiple Fastpasses. "Our twin 4-year-olds just wanted to hang around the play areas and meet the characters," said one father of four. "So we used their tickets to get Fastpasses for our older two children, who were determined to ride the coasters as many times as possible."

Also, as an Ohio mom said, "Be careful when you're getting your Fastpass to make sure you retrieve your park ticket. We left our multiday tickets in a Fastpass machine in Epcot and didn't realize it for hours. Disney eventually got it straightened out, but it took awhile and it was very stressful."

"We copied the backs and fronts of our tickets when we got them," added a mom from Canada. "And this turned out to be invaluable when we realized on day three that we had somehow managed to lose one of our seven-day passes! The lady at Guest Services was very kind and because we had the numbers written down she was able to reissue us a new ticket in minutes. She said we probably left one of the tickets in a Fastpass machine and that it happened all the time."

area. The waits with Fastpass average 10 to 15 minutes, a vast improvement over the 90-minute waits that big attractions can post on crowded days.

To let as many guests as possible take advantage of the Fastpass system, there are certain limitations to the program. Get the Fastpass for the attraction you most want to see as soon as you can. You can get another (a) once you've used the first

Helpful Hint

Four family members will need four Fastpasses, but that doesn't mean you all have to line up at the kiosk. Let one family member be in charge of holding on to all the tickets and all the Fastpasses. That way you won't find that Tyler has somehow managed to lose his Fastpass just as you're set to board Test Track.

one, (b) after the time indicated at the bottom of your first Fastpass ticket, or (c) after the time on your first Fastpass ticket has expired.

When You Don't Need Fastpass

As great as Fastpasses are, you don't always need one. Don't use the Fastpass system if (a) the wait time in the general-admittance line is 20 minutes or less, (b) the attraction in question is a theater-style show that admits hundreds of people at once, or

Insider's Secret

Fastpass is so popular that Disney is always looking for ways to expand the system, and you never know when they'll be offering some new perk. Check the information flyers you get with your park maps for any new information about the Fastpass program. Disney has already experimented with giving out bonus Fastpasses, wherein a second Fastpass for a different attraction is automatically distributed when you get your first Fastpass of the day. There's also talk that Disney hotel guests may be able to order Fastpasses before they even get to the park through an in-room ordering system.

(c) you plan to later ride an even more popular attraction. Essentially, you want to use your Fastpass privilege where it's most effective, for big-deal rides that get the most crowds.

Tips for Big Families

Disney offers plenty of help to groups, such as family reunions. Specialists can help you arrange rooms, tickets, and dining for the whole party, and they handle details such as individual payment. The following tips may also make things a little less hectic.

@ If you're all on the dining plan, there are certain special experiences designed for dining plan groups of eight or more, including an IllumiNations reception at Epcot, a safari-theme meal at the Animal Kingdom, and a character breakfast at the Magic Kingdom. Your options will be explained to you when you add the dining plan to your package.

Helpful Hint
A gratuity of 18% is added for parties of eight or more—even at buffet restaurants.

@ Consider renting a villa or condo. Many have kitchens so you can save on eating out. On-site resorts with villa-style lodging include Old Key West, Saratoga Springs, BoardWalk Villas, the Beach Club Villas, and the Villas at Wilderness Lodge. There are also plenty of off-site condos and villas for rent; check out the Off-site Hotels section in Chapter 2 for ideas.

@ If you'd like a little less togetherness, book as many rooms as you need at a resort, but ask for adjoining rooms.

@ Transportation can be an issue, especially if there's a wide variation in the ages, stamina, and risk tolerance of the family members. Older kids will probably want to stay at the park all day, while the toddlers and grandparents might be burned out and ready to rest by noon. Either way, stay on-site so you can use the Disney transportation system at your leisure, or, if you're driving, bring more than one vehicle to the parks so that family members have the option to leave early.

@ Bring your cell phones to the theme parks. Large groups tend to scatter and you don't want to spend half your time trying to get the group reassembled.

@ Have everyone wear the same color T-shirt or hat each day. A tour operator passed along this tip, which makes it easier to spot "your people" in a sea of faces.

Money-Saving Tip

If the adults plan to head out for a night, an in-room sitter is generally less expensive than drop-off child care when three or more children are involved.

Tips for Guests with Disabilities

@ Special boarding passes allow people with disabilities, including Down Syndrome and autism, to enter their own queues, which are often shorter than the general lines. Attendants are on hand to help. You can pick up a pass at any Guest Services window.

@ Request a copy of the official *Guidebook for Guests with Disabilities* when you buy your ticket. It's free and it has essential and detailed information on how to approach each attraction. You can also get it at any Disney hotel and Guest Services window, but having it in advance will help you know what to expect.

@ You can rent wheelchairs ($10 per day or $8 per day for multiday use) and ECVs ($45 plus an additional refundable $20 deposit) at any stroller rental booth.

@ Guests with hearing difficulties can pick up a handheld captioning device at Guest Services. This device works on many attractions.

@ People with disabilities give the Disney resorts high marks for convenience at reasonable prices. The All-Star resorts, for example, have several wheelchair-accessible rooms that begin as low as $109 a night. Most of the on-site resorts offer rooms with specially equipped bathrooms and extra-large doors, and if you request it, you can have a complimentary wheelchair waiting for you upon check-in. Plus, life jackets are available at all the pools and water parks.

@ The monorail, buses, boats, and other forms of transportation are all wheelchair accessible.

@ You can refrigerate insulin and other medications at first-aid stations, all on-site hotels, and most off-site hotels.

@ Guests with visual disabilities should be aware that guide dogs are welcome at all parks and many area hotels. You can also rent a tape recorder and cassette describing the attractions at each park and a Braille guidebook with a refundable deposit. Just visit Guest Services.

@ Guests with hearing disabilities can rent listening devices that amplify attraction music and words through Guest

Services with a refundable deposit. TTYs are available throughout Disney World and guests can also contact Disney Reservations via TTY at 407/939–7670.

@ For more detailed information on hotel options for people with disabilities, call Central Reservations at 407/934–7639 (407/W–DISNEY) and ask for the Special Reservations Department.

Finally, not a tip, but a word of reassurance. If you're traveling with someone who has a chronic health problem or disability, rest assured that the Disney World cast members will help you in any way they can. Because Disney World is frequently visited by children sponsored by the Make-A-Wish Foundation and other programs like it, the Disney staff is accustomed to dealing with a wide range of situations, even cases in which visitors are seriously ill. The key is to make sure that Disney employees both at your hotel and within the parks are aware of your presence and that you may need assistance. With a few preliminary phone calls, you'll find that Disney World is one of the best possible travel destinations for such families.

A dad of three, including a special-needs 8-year-old, wrote, "We heard how Disney cast members go out of their way to accommodate special children. We found this to be absolutely true. For any ride that William could go on, we got front-of-line privileges. We also were escorted to special viewing areas for shows and parades."

A mom from Connecticut wrote, "We informed our hotel (the Contemporary), in advance, of our daughter's health problems and when we checked in, we were delighted to learn that our family had been invited to ride in the first car of the afternoon parade at the Magic Kingdom. The cast member told us that there is no way to guarantee such an invitation, but that if they know a special-needs child is visiting, they try to offer some treats. Riding in the convertible and waving to the crowd was the highlight of our daughter's week."

Helpful Hint
The most important tip of all if you're pregnant: check out restroom locations in advance.

Tips for Pregnant Guests

I've personally toured Disney World twice while pregnant and not only lived to tell the tale but honestly enjoyed both trips. However, a few precautions are in order.

- Make regular meal stops. Instead of buying a turkey leg from a vendor, get out of the sun and off your feet at a sit-down restaurant.

- If you aren't accustomed to walking as much as 7 miles a day, begin getting in shape a couple of months before the trip by taking 30- to 40-minute walks at home.

- Dehydration is a real danger. Keep water in your tote bag and sip frequently. You can refill your bottle at water fountains throughout the parks.

- Consider staying on-site so that you can return to your room in the afternoon to rest.

- Mothers-to-be are welcome to rest in the rocking chairs inside Baby Services.

- Standing stock-still can be more tiring than walking when you're pregnant, so let your husband stand in line for rides. You and the kids can join him as he's about to enter the final turn of the line.

Tips for Grandparents

@ Orlando can be the ultimate multigenerational destination for grandparents traveling with their grandchildren, but if possible avoid summers, since the Florida heat and humidity can be very taxing on older adults, and make sure you build in adequate rest stops. Also, any tips on how to reduce the time you spend waiting in line, such as using Fastpass, are especially helpful to older guests.

@ There's no shame in wheelchair or ECV rental (see Tips for Guests with Disabilities, above), even if the older members of the party are mobile. The average amount you walk in a Disney day is 7 miles, and that's a lot for anyone.

@ Grandparents rarely have their grandkids full time and thus might be more likely than parents to "cave," that is, let them skip naps, eat sugary treats, and buy way too many souvenirs. So the "overwhelm" factor that comes into play at a high-stimulation place like Disney World is even more likely to happen with grandparents. Even the best behaved kids can have a meltdown if they're given too much leeway, so set ground rules in advance and try not to let their eating and sleeping routines go totally out the window.

Birthdays and Special Occasions

Celebrating a birthday? Anniversary? Graduation? Is it your first visit? Drop by Guest Services in each park and pick up a free pin announcing your status. Cast members keep an eye out for special visitors and will make a special effort to acknowledge them, especially a child wearing a birthday pin. One mother re-

Insider's Secret

If you're a single parent, consider vacationing with one of your siblings or another single parent. "My daughter is 11 and my son is 4," wrote one mother from Texas. "They like totally different things, and it would have been impossible to give them both the Disney experience they wanted if we'd gone to Orlando by ourselves. So we went with my sister and nephew, rented a nice condo, and had a great time. I did the wild rides with my daughter and meanwhile my sister, who is so prone to motion sickness that she once threw up in an elevator, took the boys around to meet all the characters."

"It's never a good idea to let the kids outnumber the adults," adds another single mother from New Jersey. "My friend Jenny, who doesn't have kids but who loves being an unofficial aunt, has gone down to Disney with us twice. Otherwise, I don't think I'd have the guts to try it."

ported that when the characters in the afternoon parade saw her daughter's birthday pin, they made a special point to come over and high-five her or shake her hand.

If you're celebrating a special occasion, the general rule is "Ask and you shall (probably) receive." If you're staying at a Disney resort, inform Guest Services or the concierge in advance if you'd like flowers or a gift delivered on a special day. Rooms can also be decked out with confetti, balloons, and banners while you're in the park so that the celebrant returns to find things fit for a party. If you want to celebrate with a special meal, make reservations at your restaurant of choice weeks in advance and let the manager know your preferences. You can arrange for a special cake that's themed to the occasion and the

Insider's Secret

During 2009—and possibly beyond since Disney often keeps promotions for longer than announced—Disney will be running a special promotion called "Celebration Vacation." It's an effort to align with a new trend in travel: families hitting the road to commemorate a special event such as a birthday or anniversary. Although it's possible to plan (and pay for) a whole range of special services to celebrate your big day, the main perk of "Celebration Vacation" is free admission to a Disney theme park on your birthday.

To take advantage of the deal you need to register your birthday in advance at www.disneyparks.com. Visitors with multiday passes or who are otherwise already ticketed for their birthdays will get either a one-day one-park pass for use anytime within the next year, Fastpasses for four rides for up to six people, or a gift card with a dollar amount equal to the free ticket usable for food and merchandise.

likes of the birthday boy or girl. (And if you want to have a full birthday party on-site, there are locations for that as well.)

One mother wrote that her son celebrated his birthday at a character breakfast featuring Pooh and friends. The cake was delivered to the table by Tigger, the child's favorite character, who then led the birthday guests in an impromptu parade around the restaurant. Another young birthday girl was serenaded by the doo-wop group preshow at Beauty and the Beast. Or consider the young man who proposed to his girlfriend at the Coral Reef in the Living Seas pavilion at Epcot. The couple was having dinner next to the mammoth glass aquarium when, at the key moment, one of the divers swam by the table carrying a sign that read, "Will you marry me?" When the girl turned to look at her boyfriend, he was on one knee with the ring—and the whole restaurant stood up and cheered when she said yes.

What do these stories have in common? They were arranged in advance. So if you'd like to add some treats and surprises to a special occasion, contact the management at the hotel or restaurant. With their help, you should have no trouble finding a way to make the day memorable.

How to Customize a Touring Plan

Get Some General Information

Request maps and transportation information at the time you make your hotel reservations. Disney's Web site, www. disneyworld.com, is also a good source of preliminary information, including theme-park hours during the time that you'll be visiting.

Ask Yourself Some Basic Questions

Consider how long you'll want to stay at each park. If your kids are under 8, you'll probably want to spend more time in the Magic Kingdom. Older kids? Plan to divide your time fairly equally among the major parks, and save some time for the water parks and Downtown Disney.

The time of year you'll be visiting is a major factor, too; although you may be able to tour Hollywood thoroughly in a single day in October, it will take you twice as long to see the same number of attractions in July. In summer the combination of the crowds, the heat, and extended park hours means you'll need to build in more downtime.

Plan at least one evening each in the Magic Kingdom, Hollywood, and Epcot so that you can see all the closing shows.

Set Your Priorities

Next, poll your family on what attractions they most want to see and build these priorities into the plan. I'd let each family member choose three must-sees per park. For example, at Hollywood, 10-year-old Jeremy wants to ride Star Tours, the Tower of Terror, and Rock 'n' Roller Coaster. His 6-year-old sister, Elyce, chooses Muppet*Vision 3-D, Beauty and the Beast, and Voyage of the Little Mermaid. Mom thinks the '50s Prime Time Café sounds like a hoot and wants to ride The Great Movie Ride and Star Tours. Dad is all over the Tower of Terror/Rock 'n' Roller Coaster thing and thinks the Lights, Motors, Action! stunt show sounds interesting.

Okay, because of some overlap you have nine items on this family's personal must-see list. They should make sure that they experience these attractions even if they don't do anything else. With any luck, they'll have some extra time and may be able to work in a few other things as well, but the key is to make sure you honor everyone's top three choices.

Cut Some Deals

Building each family member's must-sees into the touring plan has many advantages. You're seeing the best of the best, you've broken out of that "gotta do it all" compulsion, and the kids feel that they're giving input and are full partners in the vacation planning.

There's another huge advantage: A customized touring plan minimizes whining and fights. Your 12-year-old is more apt to bear a character breakfast with good grace if she knows that you'll be spending the afternoon at Blizzard Beach, one of her top choices. Kids understand fair. They might fidget a bit in Chefs de France, but if you've already covered Soarin' and Mission: SPACE, you're perfectly justified in saying, "This is Mom's first choice in Epcot, so be quiet and eat your croquette de boeuf."

Break Up the Days

Divide each day of your visit into three components: morning, afternoon, and evening. It isn't necessary to plan where you'll be every hour on the hour—that's way too confining—but you need some sense of how you'll break up the day.

Pencil in things that have to be done at a certain time. You have a character breakfast for Wednesday morning, for example, or you must be in the Magic Kingdom on Friday night because that's the only time the evening parade is scheduled during your visit.

The final product may look something like this:

Monday
Morning: Magic Kingdom
Afternoon: Rest by hotel pool
Evening: Epcot

Tuesday
Morning and afternoon: Animal Kingdom
Evening: Hollywood

Wednesday (rest day)
Morning: Character breakfast
Afternoon: Downtown Disney then early to bed

Thursday
Morning and afternoon: Blizzard Beach
Evening: Epcot

Friday
Morning: Hollywood
Afternoon: Rest by pool
Evening: Magic Kingdom

Note: This plan assumes you have the Park Hopper option on your tickets.

Favorite Attractions for Preschoolers

IN THE MAGIC KINGDOM
Aladdin's Magic Carpet
Country Bear Jamboree
Dumbo
It's a Small World
Jungle Cruise
Mad Tea Party
The Many Adventures of Winnie the Pooh
Mickey's PhilharMagic
Monsters, Inc.
The parades
Peter Pan's Flight
Pooh's Playful Spot
Toontown

IN THE ANIMAL KINGDOM
The Boneyard
Festival of the Lion King
It's Tough to be a Bug!
Kilimanjaro Safaris
TriceraTop Spin
Finding Nemo

AT EPCOT
Soarin'
Family Fun Kidcot Stops
Innoventions
Journey into Imagination
Turtle Talk with Crush

AT HOLLYWOOD
Beauty and the Beast
Honey, I Shrunk the Kids Movie Set Adventure
Muppet*Vision 3-D
Playhouse Disney
Toy Story Mania
Voyage of the Little Mermaid

Favorite Attractions for Kids 5-8

IN THE MAGIC KINGDOM
Aladdin's Magic Carpet
Buzz Lightyear's Space Ranger Spin
Country Bear Jamboree
Dumbo
It's a Small World
Jungle Cruise
Mad Tea Party
The Many Adventures of Winnie the Pooh
Mickey's PhilharMagic
The parades
Peter Pan's Flight
Pirates of the Caribbean
Toontown
Monsters, Inc.

IN THE ANIMAL KINGDOM
The Boneyard
Festival of the Lion King
It's Tough to be a Bug!
Kali River Rapids
Kilimanjaro Safaris
TriceraTop Spin
Expedition Everest (if they're daredevils)
Finding Nemo

AT EPCOT
Honey, I Shrunk the Audience
Innoventions
Journey into Imagination
The Seas with Nemo and Friends
Soarin'
Turtle Talk With Crush

AT HOLLYWOOD
Beauty and the Beast
Honey, I Shrunk the Kids Movie Set Adventure
Muppet*Vision 3-D
Playhouse Disney
Toy Story Mania
Voyage of the Little Mermaid

Whatever you do, save plenty of time to meet the characters. It's a major thrill for kids this age.

Favorite Attractions for Kids 9-12

IN THE MAGIC KINGDOM
Big Thunder Mountain Railroad
Buzz Lightyear's Space Ranger Spin
Haunted Mansion
Mickey's PhilharMagic
Pirates of the Caribbean
Space Mountain
Splash Mountain
Monsters, Inc.

IN THE ANIMAL KINGDOM
Dinosaur
Expedition Everest
The exploration trails, including Gorilla Falls and
Maharajah Jungle Trek
Festival of the Lion King
It's Tough to be a Bug!
Kali River Rapids
Kilimanjaro Safaris
Primeval Whirl
Finding Nemo

AT EPCOT
Honey, I Shrunk the Audience
IllumiNations
Live entertainment around the World Showcase
Mission: SPACE
The Seas with Nemo and Friends
Turtle Talk With Crush
Soarin'
Spaceship Earth
Test Track

AT HOLLYWOOD
Beauty and the Beast
Fantasmic!
The Great Movie Ride
Lights, Motors, Action! Extreme Stunt Show
Muppet*Vision 3-D
Rock 'n' Roller Coaster
Star Tours
Toy Story Mania
Twilight Zone Tower of Terror
Voyage of the Little Mermaid

IN THE REST OF DISNEY WORLD
Blizzard Beach
Cirque du Soleil
DisneyQuest
Typhoon Lagoon
Water Sprite boats

Favorite Attractions for Teens

IN THE MAGIC KINGDOM
Big Thunder Mountain Railroad
Buzz Lightyear's Space Ranger Spin
Haunted Mansion
Mickey's PhilharMagic
Pirates of the Caribbean
Space Mountain
Splash Mountain

IN THE ANIMAL KINGDOM
Dinosaur
Expedition Everest
The exploration trails
It's Tough to be a Bug!
Kali River Rapids
Kilimanjaro Safaris

AT EPCOT
Honey, I Shrunk the Audience
IllumiNations
Live entertainment around the World Showcase
Mission: SPACE
Soarin'
Test Track

AT HOLLYWOOD
Toy Story Mania
Fantasmic!
The Great Movie Ride
Lights, Motors, Action! Extreme Stunt Show
Rock 'n' Roller Coaster
Star Tours
Twilight Zone Tower of Terror

IN THE REST OF DISNEY WORLD
Blizzard Beach
Cirque du Soleil
DisneyQuest
Downtown Disney
Surfing Lessons at Typhoon Lagoon
Typhoon Lagoon
Water Sprite boats

CHAPTER

5

The Magic
Kingdom

The Magic Kingdom

Ariel's Grotto

FANTASYLAND

Fort Sam Clemens

Rivers of America

12

Pinnochio's Village Haus

13

14

19

LIBERTY SQUARE

8

15

16

20

WDW Railroad Frontierland Depot

9

10

Columbia Harbour House

11

Liberty Tree Tavern

Cinderella's Royal Table

17

7

FRONTIERLAND

6

18

Pecos Bill Café

ATM

Sunshine Tree Terrace

Agrabah Bazaar

Central Plaza

El Pirata y El Perico Restaurante

4

5

Aloha Isle

Tip Board

3

Plaza Pavilion

2

Plaza Restaurant

1

Crystal Palace

First Aid & Baby Care

MAIN STREET U.S.A.

ADVENTURELAND

Emporium

Parade Route

Tony's Town Square Restaurant

Town Square

City Hall

Exposition Hall/ Camera Center

WDW Railroad

ATM

Lockers

KEY

Newsstand

Stroller Shop

✕	Restaurants
⚥	Restrooms
—+—	Rail Line
≈≈≈	Monorail
•••	Parade Route

Guest Relations

Monorail Station

Entrance Turnstiles

Seven Seas Lagoon

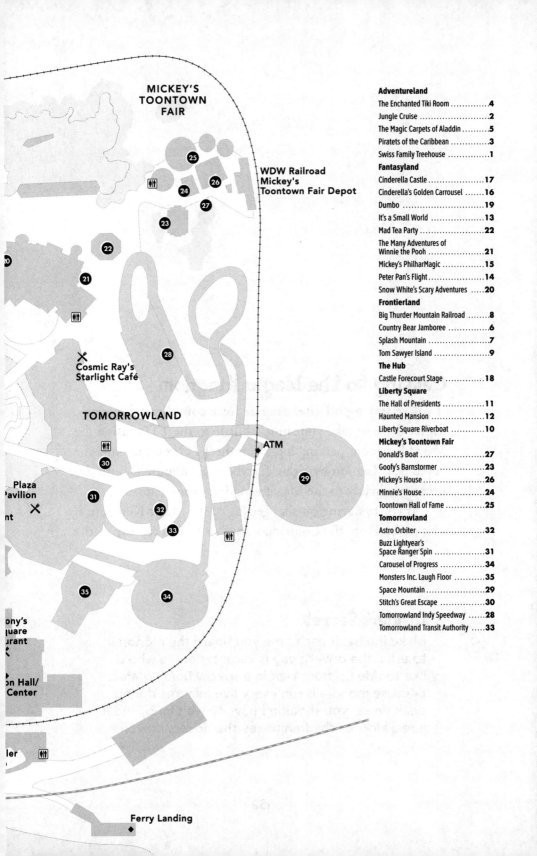

MICKEY'S TOONTOWN FAIR

WDW Railroad
Mickey's
Toontown Fair Depot

Cosmic Ray's
Starlight Café

TOMORROWLAND

ATM

Plaza
Pavilion

ony's
quare
urant

on Hall/
Center

ler

Ferry Landing

Getting to the Magic Kingdom

If you're staying off-site, prepare for a complicated journey. Either drive or take your hotel shuttle to the TTC inside the Magic Kingdom parking lot. From the TTC you can cross the Seven Seas Lagoon by either ferryboat or monorail. Both deliver you directly to the Magic Kingdom front gates.

If you're staying on-site, getting to the Magic Kingdom is a lot easier. From the Contemporary Resort, you can bypass the

Insider's Secret

Make it a habit each time you board the monorail to ask if the driver's cab is vacant; people who'd like to ride up front wait in a special holding area. Because monorails run every five minutes during peak times, you shouldn't have to wait long, and it's a real kick for children to see the drivers at work.

TTC and take the monorail to the Magic Kingdom or walk to the park. From the Grand Floridian, you can either take the monorail or the ferry. From Fort Wilderness Campground or Wilderness Lodge, take the ferry. Polynesian guests have all the options: the monorail, a water taxi, or the ferry.

Guests at Disney hotels that aren't Magic Kingdom resorts will take shuttle buses that deliver them directly to the Magic Kingdom gates, bypassing the TTC. Sometimes families who stay on-site but have a car prefer to drive to the parks, which can save time at every park except the Magic Kingdom. If you're headed for the Magic Kingdom, take Disney transportation even if you have your own car just so you can avoid the TTC.

Helpful Hint

Driving? The Magic Kingdom parking lot is the most confusing of the four parks. Even if you come early enough to park near the gate, still take the tram just to make sure you wind up at the right place.

Through the Turnstiles

If you're staying off-site, each of your park tickets will be a different color and have a different scene or character on the front. When you get your tickets, assign each one to a different family member and have everyone write their name on the back of their ticket. If you're staying on-site with a package, your plastic room key will also be your theme-park ticket. Either way, copy and carry with you the identifying numbers on your tickets in case they're lost—a problem that has become more pressing in the last few years because using the Fastpass system requires people to take out their tickets several times during the day, increasing the risk of dropping one. Plus, in the heat of the moment it's all too easy to forget to retrieve one or more of your theme-park tickets from the Fastpass machine.

You can designate one person (i.e., Mom) to hold on to all the tickets, but when you get to the turnstiles, everyone will need to hold their own ticket. Disney's security system, called Ticket Tag, requires each ticket holder to place their second finger into an electronic reader as they slide their ticket through a machine at the turnstiles. Disney makes a quick electronic measurement of your finger, allowing the system to link your park ticket to you and you alone.

Getting Around the Magic Kingdom

The Disney World Railroad leaves from Main Street with stops near Splash Mountain in Frontierland and Toontown. A lap around the park takes 20 minutes; trains depart from Main Street every 4 minutes during busy times and every 10 minutes during slower times. Even so, this isn't your fastest way to get around the park. In the morning, when crowds are heaviest, you may have to wait for a second or even third train; by that time, you could have walked.

Helpful Hint

Be prepared to make frequent rest stops while touring the Magic Kingdom. You won't walk as much as you do in Epcot, but you're likely to spend more time standing in line. Standing still is ultimately harder on the feet—and the nerves— than walking.

Walking, in fact, is the fastest means of transport in the Magic Kingdom. The train, vintage cars, and horse-drawn carriages are cute, but think of them as rides, not as a serious means of getting around the park.

Tips for Your First Hour in the Magic Kingdom

@ Be through the gates 30 minutes earlier than the stated opening time. Get strollers and pick up a map and entertainment schedule as you enter. The entertainment schedule is crucial because it gives you showtimes and character meeting times for that day.

Helpful Hint

On days that are anticipated to draw large crowds, guests are allowed to travel the length of Main Street before the park officially opens. On less crowded days, people are usually held in the town square just in front of the railroad. Either way, several characters will be on hand to give the kids something to do while you're waiting for the ropes to drop.

@ On Extra Magic Hour mornings, Fantasyland and Tomorrowland open first. Older kids should head straight for Space Mountain and Buzz Lightyear while younger kids should start with Dumbo, Peter Pan's Flight, and The Many Adventures of Winnie the Pooh.

@ On regular mornings all sections of the park open at once. If your kids are up for it, head for Splash Mountain when the ropes drop, then on to Big Thunder Mountain Rail-

Quick Guide to Magic

Attraction	Location	Height Requirement
Astro Orbiter	Tomorrowland	None
Big Thunder Mountain Railroad	Frontierland	40 inches
Buzz Lightyear's Space Ranger Spin	Tomorrowland	None
Carousel of Progress	Tomorrowland	None
Cinderella's Golden Carrousel	Fantasyland	None
Country Bear Jamboree	Frontierland	None
Dumbo	Fantasyland	None
The Enchanted Tiki Room	Adventureland	None
Goofy's Barnstormer	Toontown	35 inches
The Hall of Presidents	Liberty Square	None
Haunted Mansion	Liberty Square	None
It's a Small World	Fantasyland	None
Jungle Cruise	Adventureland	None
Liberty Square Riverboat	Liberty Square	None
Mad Tea Party	Fantasyland	None
The Magic Carpets of Aladdin	Adventureland	None

Scare Factor

0 = Unlikely to scare any child of any age.

! = Has dark or loud elements; might rattle some toddlers.

!! = A couple of gotcha! moments; should be fine for school-age kids.

!!! = You need to be pretty big and pretty brave to handle this ride.

Kingdom Attractions

Speed of Line	Duration of Ride/Show	Scare Factor	Age Range
Slow	2 min.	!	5 and up
Moderate	3 min.	!!	5 and up
Fast	6 min.	0	3 and up
Fast	22 min.	0	10 and up
Slow	2 min.	0	All
Moderate	15 min.	0	All
Slow	1 min.	0	All
Fast	20 min.	0	All
Moderate	1 min.	!!	5 and up
Fast	20 min.	0	10 and up
Slow	9 min.	!!	7 and up
Fast	11 min.	0	All
Slow	10 min.	0	All
Fast	15 min.	0	All
Slow	2 min.	0	4 and up
Slow	1 min.	0	All

(continued)

Quick Guide to Magic

Attraction	Location	Height Requirement
The Many Adventures of Winnie the Pooh	Fantasyland	None
Mickey's PhilharMagic	Fantasyland	None
Monsters, Inc. Laugh Floor	Tomorrowland	None
Peter Pan's Flight	Fantasyland	None
Pirates of the Caribbean	Adventureland	None
Snow White's Scary Adventures	Fantasyland	None
Space Mountain	Tomorrowland	44 inches
Splash Mountain	Frontierland	40 inches
Stitch's Great Escape	Tomorrowland	40 inches
Swiss Family Robinson Treehouse	Adventureland	None
Tomorrowland Indy Speedway	Tomorrowland	None
Tomorrowland Transit Authority	Tomorrowland	None
Tom Sawyer Island	Frontierland	None

Scare Factor

0 = Unlikely to scare any child of any age.
! = Has dark or loud elements; might rattle some toddlers.
!! = A couple of gotcha! moments; should be fine for school-age kids.
!!! = You need to be pretty big and pretty brave to handle this ride.

Kingdom Attractions

Speed of Line	Duration of Ride/Show	Scare Factor	Age Range
Moderate	5 min.	0	All
Moderate	20 min.	0	All
Moderate	22 min.	0	All
Moderate	3 min.	0	All
Fast	8 min.	!!	6 and up
Slow	3 min.	!!	5 and up
Moderate	3 min.	!!!	7 and up
Moderate	10 min.	!!	5 and up
Moderate	15 min.	!!!	7 and up
Slow	n/a	0	4 and up
Slow	5 min.	0	2 and up
Fast	10 min.	0	All
Slow	n/a	0	4 and up

road. Both may have long lines even by 9:15—if you arrive to find more than a 20-minute wait, get a Fastpass.

@ If there's a gap in the ages of your children and the 9-year-old is ready for a coaster but the 5-year-old isn't, consider splitting up during this crucial first hour of the day when you can ride popular attractions with relatively short waits. Mom can take one child, Dad the other, and you can meet back up in an hour.

@ Want to ride lots of big-deal rides? Get your first Fastpass early in the day, but only after you take advantage of the usually uncrowded first hour to ride your first-choice attraction.

Attractions in the Magic Kingdom Offering Fastpasses

Big Thunder Mountain Railroad

Buzz Lightyear's Space Ranger Spin

Jungle Cruise

The Many Adventures of Winnie the Pooh

Mickey's PhilharMagic

Peter Pan's Flight

Space Mountain

Splash Mountain

Stitch's Great Escape

Main Street

Main Street is where the stage is set. With its pristine sidewalks, Victorian shops, flower stalls, and antique cars, strolling down

The Magic Kingdom Don't-Miss List

IF YOUR KIDS ARE 8 OR OLDER

Any Fantasyland rides that catch their fancy

Big Thunder Mountain Railroad

Buzz Lightyear's Space Ranger Spin

Haunted Mansion

Mickey's PhilharMagic

The parades

Pirates of the Caribbean

Space Mountain

Splash Mountain

IF YOUR KIDS ARE UNDER 8

Buzz Lightyear's Space Ranger Spin

Country Bear Jamboree

Dumbo

It's a Small World

Mad Tea Party

The Magic Carpets of Aladdin

The Many Adventures of Winnie the Pooh

Mickey's PhilharMagic

The parades

Peter Pan's Flight

Pirates of the Caribbean

Splash Mountain and Big Thunder Mountain, if they're
bold enough and if they pass the height requirement.

Toontown

Main Street is like walking through an idealized circa-1890 American town. It also provides a transition from the unglamorous parking lots and buses to the charms of the park, and people visibly relax as they move closer toward Cinderella Castle. Usually by the time they arrive, they're thoroughly Disney-fied.

Main Street Touring Tips

@ Although you might spend a few minutes mingling with the characters as you enter, don't take too much time checking out the shops and minor attractions of Main Street. One mom who made the mistake of shopping too early said, "We bought souvenirs on the way into the park, and I spent the whole day dragging things around. I looked like a Disney bag lady!" Instead, focus on getting to the major rides.

@ A blackboard posted near the end of Main Street provides information about the approximate wait times of the major attractions, plus showtimes and character meeting places. Consult it whenever you're unsure about what to do next.

@ As you come down Main Street, you may be waylaid by a Disney photographer wanting to snap a family shot with the castle in the background. Let him. He'll then hand you a PhotoPass, which looks like a credit card. You can have more professional shots added to it throughout the week, even photos that are taken on rides. Once you get home, use the number on the card to access all the pictures at www.disneyphotopass.com. This allows you to peruse your photos at leisure—a vast improvement over the old system where everyone lined up to view their pictures before leaving the parks at day's end, usually missing a fair amount of evening fun in the process. If you see anything

Helpful Hint

"Take a picture of your PhotoPass ID with your iPhone or home camera," a dad from Michigan advises. "That way, if you lose the card, you can still find your pictures online."

you like, prints are $12.95 for a 5-by-7, with additional copies for $9.95. You can also consolidate all of your pictures into a PhotoCD.

@ You might want to return to Main Street around noon for lunch or some early shopping when the stores are relatively uncrowded. But if you're not planning to see the parade, be off Main Street by 2:30 PM. After that, it's a mob scene.

@ If you're touring the Magic Kingdom late and your party splits up, choose a spot on Main Street as your meeting place. Disney cast members clear people out of other sections of the park promptly at closing time, but Main Street stays open at least an hour after the rides shut down. It's the best place to reassemble the family before heading home.

Insider's Secret

After shopping, either stow your purchases in the lockers beneath the Railroad Station or, if you're a guest at a Disney resort, have them returned directly there for free.

Fantasyland

Fantasyland, directly behind Cinderella Castle, is home to many of the Magic Kingdom's classic kiddie rides. It's also the most congested section of the park.

Fantasyland Touring Tips

- Visit Fantasyland either before 11 AM, after 7 PM, or during the parades.

- Wait times for Dumbo, Peter Pan's Flight, and The Many Adventures of Winnie the Pooh are always longer than for other Fantasyland rides. Visit these first or use Fastpass.

- Don't eat or shop in Fantasyland. Similar foods and souvenirs are available elsewhere in less-crowded areas of the Magic Kingdom.

- Park your strollers in one spot and walk from ride to ride. Fantasyland is geographically small, so this is easier than constantly unloading and reloading the kids, only to push them a few steps.

Helpful Hint

Stay alert. Because the kiddie rides tempt them to wander off, this is the most likely spot in all of Disney World to lose your children.

Fantasyland Attractions

Mickey's PhilharMagic

A 3-D show projected onto a mammoth screen, Mickey's PhilharMagic, which rates high with all age groups, is one of the best attractions in Walt Disney World.

The story begins when maestro Mickey is called away from the stage and Donald steps in as conductor. He promptly loses

The Scare Factor

Although the theater is dark and some of the special effects are startling—Donald leaps right out of the screen at you more than once—the presence of beloved Disney characters usually calms the kids down. Unless you have a baby or toddler who is afraid of loud noises, children of any age will love the show.

control of the orchestra and is whisked away on a madcap journey. A slew of other Disney characters get into the act—you see Donald falling in love with Ariel, dancing with Simba, and sailing through the skies with Aladdin. The show is funny, the animation is breathtaking, and the music is stirring; in short, it's a great introduction to the 3-D experience for kids. "It was our 4-year-old's favorite attraction at the Magic Kingdom," concurs one dad from Ohio. "We were surprised at how much she enjoyed all the shows (even more than the rides), but this was the best."

Insider's Secret

Mickey's PhilharMagic offers Fastpass, but you'll only need it during the on-season. The theater seats many people at once, so during the off-season, you'll probably be able to get in with a minimal wait. Save your Fastpass for rides that always have lines, like Peter Pan and Pooh.

It's a Small World

During this 11-minute boat ride, dolls representing children of all ages greet you with a song so infectious that you'll still be humming it at bedtime. (Which may or may not be a good thing.) The line moves steadily, even during the most crowded parts of the afternoon. Babies, toddlers, and preschoolers seem to be especially enchanted.

Helpful Hint

Although beloved by preschoolers, It's a Small World can be torture for older siblings. One 10-year-old wrote that Disney should offer an "I Survived It's a Small World" T-shirt similar to those they sell outside of Splash Mountain or the *Twilight Zone* Tower of Terror. In other words, if older kids opt to skip the ride, don't press the point.

Peter Pan's Flight

Tinker Bell flutters overhead as you board miniature pirate ships and sail above Nana's doghouse, the night streets of London, the Indian camp, and Captain Hook's cove. Of all the Fantasyland attractions, this one is most true to the movie that inspired it and the level of detail is so captivating that even older kids tend to enjoy the ride. It only lasts three minutes, though, so if the wait's longer than 30 minutes, use Fastpass or come back during the parade.

The Many Adventures of Winnie the Pooh

This upbeat attraction follows Pooh and friends through a "blustery" day, so be prepared for your honey pot–shaped car to swirl and sway along the way. Designed especially for younger kids, the ride is gentle and fine for any age. Pooh's Thotful Spot, at the exit, has great souvenirs for Pooh fans.

Insider's Secret

Many Disney purists mourned the passing of Mr. Toad's Wild Ride, an original Fantasyland attraction that was torn down to make way for Pooh. In a nod to the dear departed amphibian, there's a painting inside the ride that shows Mr. Toad passing along a deed to Owl.

Pooh's Playful Spot

This small play area just across from The Many Adventures of Winnie the Pooh has spurting fountains of water, crawl-through logs and honey pots, a slide, and a tree house for climbing. Everything is pint-size and geared toward the toddler set (and there are benches for parents to rest while the kids play). The Playful Spot is a great place for the youngest members of the family to romp around while older siblings ride some of the more intense attractions in Fantasyland.

Helpful Hint

Upon entering Fantasyland, immediately get a Fastpass for either The Many Adventures of Winnie the Pooh or Peter Pan's Flight. Both attractions draw longer-than-average lines.

Cinderella's Golden Carrousel

Seventy-two white horses prance while a pipe organ toots out "Chim Chim Cheree" and other classic Disney songs. The carousel is especially gorgeous at night.

Snow White's Scary Adventures

The main focus of this ride is on the part of the movie when Snow White flees the evil witch. You ride mining cars through

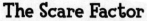

The Scare Factor

It's hard to decide exactly whom this ride was designed for. It's boring for older kids and too scary for preschoolers. The music, the witch, and the mood of the ride are foreboding enough to give toddlers the willies. Next to Stitch's Great Escape, I have received more negative mail about this attraction than any other in the Magic Kingdom, with most parents telling tales of preschoolers so shaken up that they leave the ride in tears. "My 2-year-old didn't seem to realize what was going on," wrote one mother, "but my 4-year-old was crying within 20 seconds."

the dark, and the witch, with her toothless grin and gleaming red apple, appears several times quite suddenly.

Dumbo

There's something very special about Dumbo. Although the lines move slowly—you could stand in line an hour for the 90-second ride—most kids seem willing to wait for a chance to ride in one of Disney's most enduring icons: a flying elephant. If you visit first thing in the morning, you can cut the wait time

The Scare Factor

You control the height of your flight via a joystick, so the ride is appropriate for any age. All the elephants do rise for a couple of high-flying laps at the end, but by then kids are generally used to the sensation.

way down. And if all you want is the Dumbo shot, there's an earthbound elephant parked beside the ride, just for photo ops.

Mad Tea Party

Spinning pastel cups, propelled by their riders, swirl around the Soused Mouse, who periodically pops out of his teapot. Because you largely control how fast your teacup spins, this ride can be enjoyed by all ages. Just don't go right after lunch.

Dream Along with Mickey

The characters come out in full force for the Castle Forecourt stage show, running several times daily in front of the castle. While the premise of these 20-minute shows changes every year or so, they're always full of songs, dancing, and fun. Consult your map for show times, and if you want the best view, try to arrive 15 minutes in advance. Everyone stands for the show and it can be tiring, especially on a hot day, so don't worry if you arrive late and have to watch from the sidelines. These shows are entertaining, but it's not worth missing other Magic Kingdom attractions to see them.

Time-Saving Tip

Rider volume ebbs and flows at the Mad Tea Party. If the line looks daunting, grab a drink or make a bathroom stop. By the time you return, the crowd may have dispersed.

Insider's Secret

Princess alert! The Bibbidi Bobbidi Boutique, fash-
ioned on the popular Downtown Disney location, is
appropriately situated inside Cinderella Castle. A
variety of packages ranging $50–$55 let young
princesses receive fairy-tale makeovers: new hair-
styles, shimmering makeup, glittery nails. If their
parents have completely lost their minds, for $205
the girls can even be outfitted in a complete
princess costume and have the event captured on
film. (In a gesture toward gender equality, boys can
get the $10 "cool dude" package, which translates
to hairstyling with colored gel and sparkles. That
said, you don't see a lot of little boys hanging
around the BBB, and those who are there look trau-
matized.) Children must be at least 3 years old and,
for the Magic Kingdom salon, theme-park admission is required. Reservations, which can be made
180 days in advance, are a must. Call 407/939-3463
(407/WDW–STYLE).

Mickey's Toontown Fair

Mickey's Toontown Fair (most often referred to as just "Toontown") makes you feel as if you're immersed in a giant cartoon.
The land is really just one giant play area designed to appeal to
the 2- to 8-year-old set.

Begin by walking through Minnie's pastel house where the
oven bakes a cake before your eyes. Mickey's house is right
down the block, and Donald's Boat is a great play area with
squirting fountains.

Toontown is the best place in the park to meet the characters. After you tour Mickey's house, signs lead you to a back-

yard tent where the Main Mouse is holding court. You enter in small groups and have time for pictures, autographs, and hugs. In Toontown Hall of Fame, three lines lead to three rooms where you can meet more characters for pictures and autographs. Signs that say PRINCESSES, VILLAINS, or THE HUNDRED ACRE WOOD tell you who's inside. After you've visited one group, you can rejoin the line and visit another. "If you have little girls, take the time to visit the Princesses in Mickey's Toontown," advised one mom. "We saw Cinderella, Belle, and Aurora without having to pay for a princess breakfast. The room is beautiful—they really lay the princess atmosphere on thick!—and there was plenty of time for autographs and photos."

Toontown Touring Tips

- Toontown can become unbearably crowded in mid-afternoon. By early evening, the crowds thin out.

- The Donald's Boat water-play area is a great place to cool off. Many parents let their children wear bathing suits under their clothes, then have them strip down to the suits when they want to get wet. They'll get semidry pretty quickly in the hot weather, at which point you can dress them again. Babies can play in waterproof diapers. There's a changing table in the Toontown restrooms.

- The best time to visit Mickey and other Toontown characters is Sunday morning, when the crowds are light.

- When you're lining up to meet the characters in the Toontown Hall of Fame, be aware that any queue featuring "face characters," such the princesses or Tinker Bell and her fairy friends, will move slowly. The reason is that face characters, unlike Mickey and his gang, can talk and interact with the children. This can slow the line to a crawl, but once at the front, your kids are in for a real treat.

@ On most days Toontown opens at 10 AM. Be at the ropes for 9:45 and proceed directly to the Hall of Fame.

Toontown Attractions

Goofy's Barnstormer

The centerpiece of Toontown is this zippy little roller coaster, which takes you on a wild trip through Wise Acre Farm with the Goofman himself as the pilot. The ride only lasts 60 seconds, but it's more intense than it looks.

The Scare Factor

Goofy's Barnstormer is a good test to see how kids will handle the bigger coasters like Splash Mountain. The drops are steep, and there are thrills, but the ride is so short that you barely have time to get out a scream before it's over. Watch it go around once or twice before riding. "Goofy's Barnstormer is much faster than you think it would be, considering it's in Toontown," wrote a mom from New York. "My 6-year-old was terrified." The height requirement is 35 inches.

Tomorrowland

Tomorrowland has a 1930s sci-fi look of "the future that never was." We're talking metal, chrome, robots, and neon.

Tomorrowland Touring Tips

@ Ride Space Mountain early—by 9:15 it has substantial lines. If there's a 30-minute wait, get a Fastpass.

@ The arcade across from Space Mountain is a good place for the less adventurous members of your party to wait while the coaster warriors tackle Space Mountain.

@ Looking for fast food during peak dining hours? Tomorrowland stands are rarely as busy as those in other lands. Cosmic Ray's Starlight Café, the largest such place in the Magic Kingdom, moves you in and out fast.

Tomorrowland Attractions

Space Mountain
This three-minute roller-coaster ride through inky blackness is one of the few scream-rippers in the Magic Kingdom. The cars move at a mere 32 mph, a tame pace compared to other monster coasters, but since the entire ride takes place in the dark, it's almost impossible to anticipate the turns and dips.

The Scare Factor
This is the most intense ride in the Magic Kingdom, with a 44-inch height requirement. Most kids in the 3 to 8 age range find Space Mountain too scary, but the 9 to 11 age group gives it a solid thumbs-up. It's the highest-rated attraction in the park among teens.

Bad news for thrill seekers: at this writing, Space Mountain is slated to be closed for refurbishment until April 2010. Visiting after April? These things can take longer than predicted, so check the Disneyworld.com site to make sure the ride has re-opened before you make any promises to the kids.

Buzz Lightyear's Space Ranger Spin

This attraction is an "interactive fantasy in which riders help Buzz save the world's supply of batteries." Huh? The ride transports you into the heart of a video game where you pass through various scenes, spinning your cars and shooting at targets. Your car tallies your score and you learn whether you're a Space Ace or a lowly Trainee. Buzz is addictive, but the lines do move swiftly and Fastpass is available. "Buzz Lightyear is great for all ages," wrote a mother from Texas. "Our family members ranged from 2 to 83, and this was one ride everybody got into. Of course, we all got a little too competitive . . ."

Insider's Secret

Attention Space Ace wannabes: The tougher the target, the higher the points. Don't waste time taking cheap shots. There are 100,000-point targets on the palm of the orange robot's left hand in the Robot Attack scene and another on the bottom Z of the spaceship in Zurg's Secret Weapon. Also, if you hit a target multiple times, it gives you more points.

Astro Orbiter

A circular thrill ride similar to Dumbo, Astro Orbiter is a bit too much for preschoolers and a bit too little for teens. If you ride at night, the astro-ambience is more convincing.

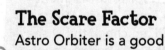

The Scare Factor

Astro Orbiter is a good choice for children ages 5 to 10 who might not be quite up to Space Mountain. But it's not for anyone prone to motion sickness.

Tomorrowland Indy Speedway

Tiny sports cars circle a nifty-looking racetrack and although the ride itself isn't anything unusual, kids under

11 rate it highly, perhaps because young drivers can steer the cars themselves. (Kids 52 inches and taller can drive solo; others must be at least 32 inches tall and accompanied by an adult.)

Helpful Hint
Persuade your child not to rush through the Speedway; loading and reloading the cars takes time—better to drive slowly than sit for five minutes in the pit waiting to be unloaded.

Tomorrowland Transit Authority
This little tram circles Tomorrowland and provides fun views, including a glimpse inside Space Mountain and the Buzz Lightyear attraction. The trip lasts 10 minutes, and the ride is never crowded so the attendant usually lets you stay on for more than one cycle. The rocking of the train has lulled many a cranky toddler into a nap; cast members report that the ride is often full of parents holding sleeping youngsters.

Carousel of Progress
This is a fairly long show (22 minutes) and a high-capacity attraction, so it's good for the crowded times of the afternoon. Kids might be bored by this salute to modern inventions, especially once they've seen the more high-tech presentations of Epcot. That said, it has a nostalgic appeal; Carousel of Progress was one of Walt's contributions to the 1964 World's Fair. Note: This is often closed during the off-season.

Stitch's Great Escape
Stitch's Great Escape tells the story of what Stitch was like before he came to Earth in the hit movie *Lilo & Stitch*. Stitch is captured by the Galactic Federation and taken to a prisoner

processing facility. Since Stitch's reputation as a troublemaker precedes him, visitors to the attraction are recruited to provide additional security. But you can't keep a good alien down, and Stitch eludes security, causing mayhem everywhere he goes. The show features sophisticated audio-animatronics, including the remarkable, three-dimensional Stitch figure. It's also loud, dark, and far more forbidding than the advertisements indicate.

The Scare Factor

We receive a lot of mail about Stitch's Great Escape—most of it negative. While the height requirement to see Stitch is only 40 inches, the prevailing complaint is that the darkness and volume of the ride are simply too scary for many preschoolers. It seems Disney missed the boat here in much the same way they did years ago with Snow White's Scary Adventures. They named an attraction after a familiar movie character beloved by young children and then created an experience so intense that it scares the daylights out of the age group it attracts. While Disney is constantly tinkering with the Stitch attraction (e.g., raising the light level during the most intense scenes), it remains, as one 7-year-old put it, "scary scary, not fun scary."

A mom from Delaware echoed the sentiment. "The worst thing about shows like Stitch (and It's Tough to be a Bug! in the Animal Kingdom) is that they take beloved Disney characters and make children afraid of them. My son wanted to ride Stitch, but now he's telling everyone at home that he would never go on it again." Unless you have brave preschoolers and you love Stitch, you should have your young ones skip this attraction.

Stitch's Party Blast

This new mini-attraction, between Space Mountain and the Carousel of Progress, uses the same technology as the popular Turtle Talk With Crush at Epcot. Stitch interacts with the audience via a big screen on the stage. It's sillier, more fun, and far less frightening than Stitch's Great Escape, so it's a better option for young kids.

Monsters, Inc. Laugh Floor

This show lets you laugh, joke, sing, and interact right along with your one-eyed "monster of ceremonies" Mike Wazowski and other characters from *Monsters, Inc.* While the show technology is highbrow, the humor is lowbrow. Children as young as 5 should be able to enjoy the silly jokes and slapstick, and even if they miss a joke here or there, they'll still have fun. Oh, and even if the spotlight doesn't fall on you, you can still get in on the action—while you're waiting in the preshow area, you can text message jokes for possible use in the show.

Monsters, Inc. was created in response to the way-popular Turtle Talk with Crush in the Living Seas at Epcot. Kids love shows in which characters on-screen interact with people sitting in the audience. It's high-tech with heart.

Adventureland

Thematically the most bizarre of all the lands—sort of a Bourbon Street meets Trinidad by way of Congo—Adventureland definitely conveys an exotic mood.

Adventureland, Frontierland, and Liberty Square Touring Tips

- If you have two days to spend touring the Magic Kingdom, begin your second day in Frontierland, at Splash Mountain. Move on to Big Thunder Mountain, then the

Haunted Mansion in Liberty Square. All three attractions are relatively easy to board before 10 AM.

@ These lands stay crowded between noon and 4 PM, when the crowds lined up to watch the afternoon parade finally disperse. If you miss Splash Mountain, Big Thunder Mountain Railroad, or the Haunted Mansion early in the morning, wait until early evening to visit them.

@ Should you find yourself stuck in these lands in the afternoon, you'll find a bit of breathing space on Tom Sawyer Island or in The Enchanted Tiki Room or the Hall of Presidents. Surprisingly, Pirates of the Caribbean can be a smart choice even when the park is crowded. At least you wait inside, and this is one of the fastest-loading attractions in Disney World.

Time-Saving Tip

If you hustle to Frontierland only to find that Splash is posting a 30-minute wait, get a Fastpass and ride Big Thunder Mountain Railroad first.

Adventureland Attractions

Jungle Cruise

You'll meet up with headhunters, hyenas, water-spewing elephants, and other varieties of frankly fake wildlife on this 10-minute boat ride. It's dated-looking in comparison to the attractions in the Animal Kingdom but it's still fun, thanks largely to the amusing patter of the tour guides, who somehow manage to tell jokes and puns so corny that you're groaning and laughing in the same breath.

The cruise isn't at all scary and is fine for any age. You can use Fastpass, but I'd recommend saving your Fastpass appointments for more important attractions and riding Jungle Cruise later in the day.

The Magic Carpets of Aladdin

This colorful, appealing attraction is a circular aerial ride similar to Dumbo. The twist is that you can make your carpet tilt, rise, or drop on command—evasive maneuvers that are necessary if you wish to avoid the spitting camels that guard the ride.

The Scare Factor
Because the carpets pitch around a bit, the Aladdin ride is slightly more intense than Dumbo, but most kids love it.

The Enchanted Tiki Room

These singing and talking birds represent Disney's first attempt at the audio-animatronics that are now such an integral part of theme-park magic. The addition of Iago from *Aladdin* and Zazu from *The Lion King* as co-owners is good news for kids,

The Scare Factor
The revamped show is louder than the original version. When the Tiki gods are angered, the theater darkens and lightning and thunder begin. The noise level frightens some toddlers.

and although this is hardly the most exciting show in the Magic Kingdom, the theater is a good place to get off your feet and out of the heat. Be sure to stick around for Iago's stream of insults as you exit the theater; it's the funniest part of the show.

Pirates of the Caribbean

This attraction inspires great loyalty and, since the success of the movie series by the same name, the Pirates are hotter than ever, especially Captain Jack Sparrow. If you've been on the ride before, you'll notice an updated twist to the story line as Sparrow races to a cache of plundered treasure. It's a kick to see the

The Scare Factor

The queue winds through a dark, drafty dungeon, so many kids are nervous before they even board. After that, the scariest elements of the ride occur in the first three minutes—there are skeletons, cannons, periods of shadowy darkness, and a sudden manifestation of Davy Jones in the mist. By the time you get to the mangy-looking and politically incorrect buccaneers themselves, however, the mood is up-tempo, as evidenced by the cheerful theme song. This ride is fine for most kids over 6, unless they're afraid of the dark.

new figures interacting with some of the older animatronic buccaneers. All the audio-animatronics figures are remarkably lifelike, right down to the hair on their legs, and the theme song is positively addictive. Even though the story is dark, violent, and brutal, in the hands of Disney it all somehow manages to come off as a lighthearted, happy adventure.

Insider's Secret

If you can't get enough of Captain Jack Sparrow and crew, stop by the Pirate League in Adventureland. In this interactive experience, kids receive a pirate identity, meet a Pirate Master, and gain access to a treasure room.

Swiss Family Robinson Treehouse

There's a real split of opinion here—some visitors revel in the details and love climbing through this replica of the ultimate tree house, while others rate it as dull. Kids who have seen the movie tend to like it a lot more.

Insider's Secret

There's been a persistent rumor that the Treehouse is due for a major revamp to tie the theme into a more contemporary movie and make it more interesting to the younger set. Stay tuned.

Frontierland

Kids love the rough-and-tumble Wild West feel of Frontierland, which is home to several of the Magic Kingdom's most popular attractions.

Frontierland Attractions

Big Thunder Mountain Railroad

A roller coaster designed as a runaway mine train, Big Thunder Mountain is one of the most popular rides in the park with all age groups. The glory of the ride is in the setting. You zoom through a deserted mining town and although the details are best observed by day, the lighting effects make this an especially atmospheric ride after dark. Be warned that the ride is very bouncy and jerky, but the effects are more apt to make you laugh than to make you scream.

The Scare Factor

When it comes to coasters, Big Thunder Mountain is more in the rattle-back-and-forth style than the lose-your-stomach-as-you-plunge style. Most children over 7 should be able to handle the dips and twists and many preschoolers adore the ride as well. The height requirement is 40 inches. If you're debating which of the three mountains—Space, Splash, or Big Thunder—is most suitable for a child who has never ridden a coaster, Big Thunder is your best bet.

Splash Mountain

Based on *Song of the South* and inhabited by Br'er Rabbit, Br'er Fox, and Br'er Bear, Splash Mountain takes riders on a winding, watery journey through swamps and bayous.

Because it's the first thing you see as you approach, most of the attention is given to that 40-mph drop over a five-story waterfall, but there's a great story to the ride as well. You get into a log boat and follow Br'er Rabbit's adventures throughout the attraction, and each time he gets into trouble, you get into

The Scare Factor

The intensity of that last drop, which gives you the feeling that you're coming right out of your seat, along with the 40-inch height requirement, eliminates some preschoolers. Watch a few cars make the final drop before you decide. Our mail indicates that most kids over 5 love the ride.

Hidden Mickey

When you and the kids are keeping an eye out for Mickey Mouse, you may not realize that you're walking right past him. No, we're not talking about the life-size Mickeys, we're talking about those silhouettes and abstract images that are cleverly tucked throughout Walt Disney World.

These "Hidden Mickeys" began as an inside joke among the Imagineers and artists who design theme-park attractions. Spotting a Hidden Mickey is a real treat. In the final scene of Splash Mountain, as you pass the Zip-a-Dee-Lady paddleboat, look for a pink cloud floating high in the sky. It's a silhouette of Mickey lying on his back.

trouble, too. In other words, each dangerous moment is followed by an escape through a water drop, and the ultimate danger culminates in the ultimate water drop. The interior scenes

Helpful Hint

Just because your toddler can't ride Splash Mountain doesn't mean she can't get a thrill. There's a certain place you can stand to watch the log boats on their final drop. The shrieks combined with the sprays of water will delight any child. A father of three from Florida agreed. "Our 2-year-old's favorite ride was Splash Mountain. She couldn't ride it, of course, but she stayed outside with Dad while Mom and her brothers rode, and she loved watching the boats splash down. Water shoots up after the boats, and she squealed every time."

are delightful and "Zip-a-Dee-Doo-Dah," perhaps the most hummable of all Disney theme songs, fills the air.

Splash Mountain can get very crowded; ride early in the morning or in the last hour before closing. You can get soaked, really soaked, especially if you're in the front-row seats of the log, and especially if you're sitting on the right. This can be great fun at noon in June, less of a kick at 9 AM in January. Some people bring ponchos or big black garbage bags for protection and then discard them after the ride.

Country Bear Jamboree

Younger kids usually enjoy the furry, funny, audio-animatronics critters featured in this 15-minute show. From the coy Trixie, who enters via a ceiling swing, to the wincingly off-key Big Al, each face is distinctive and lovable.

Time-Saving Tip

A clock outside the *Country Bear Jamboree* tells you how long you have until the next show. Don't enter the waiting area until the countdown is 10 minutes or less.

The Jamboree seats large numbers of guests for each show, and it's a good choice for the afternoon, when you'll welcome the chance to sit and rest. Kids 10 and up often think the bears are hokey, so parents can take younger kids to the Jamboree while their older siblings visit Splash Mountain and Big Thunder Mountain Railroad.

Tom Sawyer Island

A getaway playground full of caves, bridges, forts, and windmills, Tom Sawyer Island is the perfect destination for kids full of pent-up energy who just need to run wild for a while.

You'll want to accompany them through the Mystery Cave and Injun Joe's Cave, however; both can be dark, confusing, and a little scary. Across the bouncy suspension bridge is Fort Sam Clemens, the perfect spot to play cowboy.

The big drawback is that the island is accessible only by raft, which often means you have to wait to get there and back. If your kids are under 5, don't bother making the trip. The terrain is too wild and widespread for preschoolers to play without careful supervision; young kids can better blow off steam in the padded playgrounds of Toontown. Likewise, there's little on the island for teenagers and adults to do. But for kids 5 to 12, a trip to Tom Sawyer Island is the ideal afternoon break. "Tom Sawyer Island was my 6-year-old's favorite place in the Magic Kingdom," wrote a mom from Texas. "It's so detailed with a lot for a boy his age to do. We definitely thought it was worth the wait to catch the raft."

Liberty Square

As you walk between Frontierland and Fantasyland, you find yourself transported back in time to colonial America, strolling the cobblestone streets of Liberty Square.

Liberty Square Attractions

Haunted Mansion
More apt to amuse than to frighten, the recently revamped mansion is full of clever special effects—there's a fascinating

Hidden Mickey

Look at the arrangement of dishes on the table in the Haunted Mansion banquet scene. Do any of the place settings look like you-know-who?

ballroom scene where spirits waltz, and, at one point, a ghost hitchhikes along in your doom buggy. The cast members have great costumes (including the bat-in-a-hat that ladies wear), and they add to the fun with their mortician-like behavior and such instructions as, "Drag your wretched bodies to the dead center of the room." The mansion is full of clever insider jokes. For example, the tombstones outside feature the names of Imagineers who designed the ride and Madame Leota's face on her recently added tombstone; keep watching it for a while and you may be surprised. And be sure to take a glance at the pet cemetery when you leave.

The mansion draws long lines in the afternoons, especially just before and after the parade. Try to see it mid-morning, or—if you have the courage—after dark.

The Scare Factor

A significant number of kids 7 to 11 list the Haunted Mansion as one of their favorite attractions. While some kids in this age group are frightened by the opening story, the setting, and the darkness, once they get going, they're usually okay. The attraction is richly atmospheric, but the spooks are mostly for laughs. In contrast, many toddlers are intimidated by the ambience. One mother said that her daughter, age 3, referred to "that ugly house with the bad people" for weeks after their Disney visit.

Liberty Square Riverboat

The second tier of this paddle-wheel riverboat offers nice views of the Rivers of America, but the 15-minute cruise is a bit of a snooze for kids. It would be fine if they could really nap, but there are few seats on the boat, so most riders stand. Board only if you have time to kill and the boat is at the dock.

The Hall of Presidents

The residents of the Hall of Presidents are so lifelike that it's a bit eerie (and Disney cast members report that this is a very "interesting" attraction to clean at night). The show opens with a film about the Constitution (otherwise known as "nap time" for the preschool set) and then moves on to the real highlight, the presidential roll call. Each chief executive responds to his name with a nod of the head or similar movement, while in the background the other presidents fidget and whisper.

The hall seats 700, with new shows every 20 minutes, and thus is a good choice during the most crowded parts of the afternoon. Ask one of the attendants at the lobby doors how long it is before the next show and amble in about five minutes early.

Insider's Secret
Disney has added kid-friendly entertainment in every park in the form of seemingly spontaneous sidewalk shows. For example, in the Magic Kingdom, kids can become a pirate at Captain Jack Sparrow's Pirate Tutorial in Adventureland. These small, simple shows are the ultimate interactive experience. Check your entertainment schedule for locations and showtimes.

Food Choices in the Magic Kingdom

Let's face it, the Magic Kingdom is not the fine-dining park of Walt Disney World. Even so, some options are better than others.

If you want to have a sit-down meal and see the characters, consider Cinderella's Royal Table, which is inside the castle. The princess breakfasts and lunches are especially popular with young girls (generally ages 10 and under) who want to meet Cinderella, Snow White, Belle, and some of the other princesses. (In the evening only the Fairy Godmother is present.) Reservations are always snapped up months in advance, so be sure to reserve early, preferably 180 days ahead of time, by calling 407/939–3463 (407/WDW–DINE). Little girls like to wear their princess regalia when they dine in the castle, so pull out those tiaras and magic wands before you go. One mother reported that she brought her daughter's princess gear with her and let her change in a nearby bathroom just before her character meal. "I noticed a lot of families doing the same," she said. "It makes sense because afterwards you can change your child back into play clothes for the rest of the day."

Other character options include the Crystal Palace, where Winnie the Pooh and his friends circulate among diners for breakfast, lunch, and dinner. There's a wide debate on the quality of the Crystal Palace experience; while one mom considered

Helpful Hint

We thought the following note from a conscientious mom of two hit the nail on the head. "The one thing we learned about the Magic Kingdom princess breakfast is not to promise this treat unless you already have advance reservations. It took us six days of getting up at 6:30 AM to start trying to get through the phone line at 7 before we got lucky enough to get seats. I was already trying to figure out how to tell my then-5-year-old daughter there wasn't room for us at the castle."

it, "perfect for our family since we love the Pooh characters, and the food selection was really nice," another mom described the food as "inedible, even by theme park standards." Buffets are served, so you can get your food quickly, and there's plenty of variety.

At Liberty Tavern, expect an all-you-can-eat dinner with down-home cooking like turkey, pork chops, mashed potatoes, and macaroni and cheese. The Plaza Restaurant on Main Street, thematically the plainest of all Magic Kingdom restaurants, offers a variety of salads and sandwiches, along with elaborate ice cream–based desserts. Tony's Town Square, also on Main Street, offers generous servings of Italian food and a charming Lady and the Tramp theme.

In terms of fast food, your choices abound, but Cosmic Ray's Starlight Café in Tomorrowland is the largest fast-food spot in the park and the lines move fast. For snacks try the fruit cobblers at Sleepy Hollow in Liberty Square or the pineapple whips at Aloha Isle in Adventureland.

Insider's Secret

Closed out of the princess character meals at Cinderella Castle? Try the lesser-known princess meals in the Norway Pavilion of Epcot.

Insider's Secret

If you've visited the Magic Kingdom before and want to try something a little different, consider the Family Magic Tour. This adventure is designed for kids 4 to 10 and their families. You follow clues throughout the park and end by solving the mystery and finding a character. See Chapter 10 for details.

Afternoon Resting Places

- @ Country Bear Jamboree

- @ The Disney World Railroad (you can rest while you ride)

- @ The Enchanted Tiki Room

- @ Hall of Presidents

- @ Mickey's PhilharMagic

- @ Monsters, Inc.

- @ Pooh's Playful Spot or the Toontown play area (for kids to get out of the stroller and blow off steam while parents rest on benches)

- @ The small park across from Sleepy Hollow in Liberty Square

Best Vantage Points for Watching the Parade

The Magic Kingdom has two basic parades: the afternoon parade (usually 3 PM), which runs daily, and the evening parade, which runs nightly in the on-season and periodically during the off-season.

The 3 PM parade emerges from the gate just to the left of Splash Mountain, winds its way through Frontierland, and finishes by coming down Main Street. The evening parade follows the same route in reverse, starting from the gate to the right of City Hall on Main Street and ending in Frontierland. Specialty parades—such as those held during the Halloween and Christmas parties—follow the same route as the 3 PM parade.

If time is of the essence, take a second to note which direction the parade will be coming from. (And if you have any doubt, ask a nearby cast member.) Being near the beginning of the route not only saves you 20 minutes of waiting for the fun to reach you but also ensures that you won't be trapped in the mob that swarms the streets the minute the parade is over.

Stake your curb space about 30 minutes before the parade is due to start. If you're willing to show up an hour early, you might snag a seat on the second floor of the railway station. Being high in the air spoils your chance of interacting with the characters, but for some families the bird's-eye view more than makes up for it.

Tips for Your Last Hour in the Magic Kingdom

- @ Some rides—most notably Big Thunder Mountain Railroad, Cinderella's Golden Carrousel, Astro Orbiter, Dumbo, and Splash Mountain—are particularly beautiful at night.

- @ If you're visiting on an evening when the parade is scheduled, make sure you're stationed as close as possible to the beginning of Main Street. This way you can turn in your strollers and make a final potty run before the parade begins and make a quick exit after the fireworks end. Otherwise you risk being stuck in the exiting crowds, which can be really difficult to navigate, especially if you're trying to carry small children or push a stroller.

- @ Not watching the evening parade? It pulls almost everyone in the park to one place at one time, so about an hour before the parade starts you'll notice a definite shift in the crowd. This is a great time to squeeze onto a couple of rides that had long lines earlier in the day. Then take the train from Frontierland or Toontown back to the Main Street station. That way you can exit the Magic Kingdom without having to work your way through the crowds lining Main Street. Just be sure to board the train

Insider's Secret

The best place to watch the Magic Kingdom fireworks isn't in the Magic Kingdom at all. It's the California Grill, high atop the Contemporary Resort. The California Grill is a beautiful upscale restaurant, with some of the best cuisine in all of Orlando. Despite the restaurant's reputation, it isn't formal or stuffy. Kids are welcome.

To see the fireworks, reserve a time about 30 minutes before the parade is due to start. (This needs to be done before you leave home. First call 407/824–4321 to determine the evenings and times the parade is scheduled, and then reserve a table by calling 407/WDW–DINE.) Since so many guests have been showing up at the restaurant just to see the fireworks, the restaurant has been forced to implement the policy that only diners are allowed to view the show. (Can't get a perfectly timed reservation? If you dine at California Grill earlier that evening, ask if you can return at fireworks time. Some families have reported that if they kept their dining receipt they were allowed back at fireworks time for the viewing. A large outdoor walkway area keeps the restaurant from getting too packed.)

Once the fireworks begin, the restaurant dims its lights and pipes in the theme music from the fireworks show. You have a fabulous view of the pyrotechnic display and a bona fide magical moment.

And while the vantage point isn't quite as perfect, you can also see the fireworks from Narcoossee's and Citricos, two restaurants in the Grand Floridian.

Insider's Secret

The evening fireworks are preceded by a nifty little extra called Tinker Bell's Flight. Look toward the castle and you'll see a young gymnast dressed like Tink descend via wire from the top of the castle.

at least 20 minutes before the parade is due to start. The train stops running during the parade and if you fail to catch the last one, you'll be stuck deep in the park behind the departing crowds.

@ Wishes, the fireworks display in the Magic Kingdom, is absolutely beautiful, and the pyrotechnics are perfectly synchronized to the musical score. Wishes is presented nightly at closing time, even on nights when the parade is not scheduled to run, and it's clearly visible from any location.

Insider's Secret

The Magic Kingdom has interactive parades throughout the day. The current manifestation is called "Move It, Shake It, Celebrate It," and most of the action takes place in front of Cinderella Castle. At one point in this parade—which is really more of a street party since the floats stop and characters jump off to mingle with the crowd—you're invited to conga, sing, and dance. It's great fun but keep an eye on your kids. It's easy to lose track of them in the celebration.

@ The rides stop running at the park's official closing time but Main Street stays open for up to an hour longer. If the crowd looks bad going down Main Street, you can be sure it looks even worse at the bus stop or monorail station. Pause, have a snack, and wait for the crowds to thin before you exit the park.

Tips for Leaving the Magic Kingdom

@ Upon exiting, visitors staying off-site should pause and survey their options. If a ferry is in dock at your far left, that's your fastest route back to the TTC. Otherwise, queue for the express monorail back to the TTC.

@ Guests of the Contemporary Resort should either take the monorail or, if stamina permits, the footpath. Guests of Wilderness Lodge and Fort Wilderness should take the water-taxi launch. Guests of the Polynesian or Grand Floridian resorts should glance down at the launch dock. If a water taxi is in sight, take it back to your hotel. Otherwise, head for the resort monorail. Guests of other Disney hotels should return to the shuttle bus station.

CHAPTER

6

Epcot

Epcot

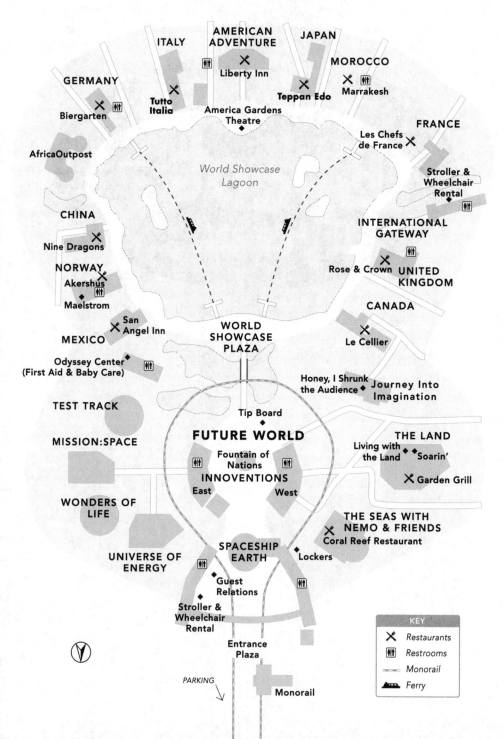

WORLD SHOWCASE

AMERICAN ADVENTURE

ITALY

JAPAN

MOROCCO

✕ Liberty Inn

✕ Teppan Edo

✕ Marrakesh

GERMANY

✕ Tutto Italia

✕ Biergarten

America Gardens Theatre

FRANCE

Les Chefs de France ✕

AfricaOutpost

Stroller & Wheelchair Rental

World Showcase Lagoon

INTERNATIONAL GATEWAY

CHINA

✕ Nine Dragons

Rose & Crown ✕

UNITED KINGDOM

NORWAY

Akershus

✕ Maelstrom

CANADA

✕ San Angel Inn

WORLD SHOWCASE PLAZA

Le Cellier ✕

MEXICO

Odyssey Center
(First Aid & Baby Care)

Honey, I Shrunk the Audience ◆ **Journey Into Imagination**

TEST TRACK

Tip Board ◆

FUTURE WORLD

THE LAND

Living with the Land ◆ ◆ Soarin'

MISSION:SPACE

Fountain of Nations

INNOVENTIONS

East   West

✕ Garden Grill

WONDERS OF LIFE

THE SEAS WITH NEMO & FRIENDS

✕ Coral Reef Restaurant

UNIVERSE OF ENERGY

SPACESHIP EARTH

◆ Lockers

◆ Guest Relations

Stroller & Wheelchair Rental

Entrance Plaza

PARKING

Monorail

KEY

✕	*Restaurants*
🚻	*Restrooms*
	Monorail
⛴	*Ferry*

Getting to Epcot

Many off-site hotels and all on-site hotels offer shuttle buses to Epcot, and it is also easy to reach by car. If you arrive early in the morning, you can park close to the entrance gate and forgo the tram. If you arrive a bit later, however, the trams do run quickly and efficiently. Just be sure to write down the number of the row where you parked your car.

If you're staying at the Contemporary or Grand Floridian resorts, your fastest route is to take the monorail to the TTC and then transfer to the Epcot monorail. If you're staying at the Polynesian, it's probably fastest to walk to the TTC and take the Epcot monorail from there.

The Yacht and Beach Clubs, and the BoardWalk, Swan, and Dolphin resorts are connected by bridge to a special "back-door" entrance into Epcot's World Showcase. You can get there either by water taxi or by walking.

Getting Around Epcot

Epcot is an acronym for Experimental Prototype Community of Tomorrow—although some Disney insiders insist that Epcot really stands for "Every Person Comes Out Tired."

Epcot is indeed sprawling—more than twice the size of the Magic Kingdom. It's composed of two circular sections, Future World and the World Showcase, which form a basic figure-eight shape. The only in-park mode of transportation is the two FriendShips that cross the World Showcase Lagoon; most of the time, you'll walk.

Tips for Your First Hour at Epcot

@ If you're an on-site guest and visiting Epcot on an Extra Magic Hour morning, only a few attractions will be open, but those will have a significantly reduced wait time.

@ On regular mornings, you're usually allowed into the entrance plaza around Spaceship Earth before the rest of the park officially opens. You'll have time to get a map and entertainment schedule, and rent a stroller before the ropes drop.

@ If you're staying at the Yacht and Beach Club, BoardWalk, Swan, or Dolphin and thus entering through Epcot's back-door entrance, walk through the United Kingdom and Canada until you get to the rope. It's a bit of a hike to start the day, but the payoff is that you're in a good position to beat the main crowd to Soarin' once the ropes drop.

@ Once you're allowed into the main body of the park, ride Soarin' first. This attraction, popular with literally all age groups, can draw such long lines that Fastpasses frequently run out by midday. If you think you might want to ride again later in the day, go ahead and get a Fastpass. Next, assuming your kids are up for it, cross Future World and head for Mission: SPACE and Test Track. If you didn't get a Fastpass at Soarin', get one for Test Track and ride Mission: SPACE first. If you did use your Fastpass option back at Soarin', ride Test Track first and then Mission: SPACE. Confused? The main issue is that these three rides are the ones most apt to get crowded later in the day so you want to ride them relatively early and use your Fastpass option judiciously.

@ Next, visit The Seas with Nemo & Friends and after you disembark, head for Turtle Talk with Crush.

Attractions at Epcot That Offer Fastpass

Honey, I Shrunk the Audience (seasonally)

Living with the Land (seasonally)

Maelstrom (seasonally)

Mission: SPACE

Soarin'

Test Track

Epcot Touring Tips

@ Take Epcot in small doses if you're traveling with young kids; four hours at a time is enough.

@ In the off-season, Epcot hours are often staggered. Future World is generally open from 9 AM to 7 PM (although Soarin', Test Track, and Mission: SPACE generally remain operative until Epcot closes) and the World Showcase is open from 11 AM to 9 PM.

@ Tour Future World in the morning and then drift toward the World Showcase in the afternoon. You can escape to the films and indoor exhibits during the hottest and busiest times of the day.

@ On entering a World Showcase pavilion that has a show or film—France, Canada, America, or China—ask the attendant how long until the show begins. If your wait is 10 minutes or less, go on inside. If the wait is longer, browse the shops or take a bathroom break and return 10 minutes before showtime. Epcot theaters are so large that even people in the back of the line can get in.

@ Innoventions provides a nice break from the enforced passivity of the rides. But ride first and save the exhibits for the afternoon.

@ Check out your entertainment schedule and save time for some of the shows that take place in the pavilions of the World Showcase. Shows like Off-Kilter or the Chinese acrobats have major kid-appeal.

@ If you miss Soarin', Mission: SPACE, or Test Track in the morning, return in the evening. Although they're packed throughout the afternoon, it's often easier to slip onto these popular rides while everyone else is eating dinner in the World Showcase or watching IllumiNations.

@ If you're touring off-season and plan to spend mornings in the other parks and evenings at Epcot, make your dinner reservation times early, like around 5 PM. That leaves you several hours to tour after dinner.

@ Another alternative: If the kids have had a good afternoon nap and can keep going until 11 PM, arrange your reservations for 8:30. The restaurants keep serving as the park closes down, so eating late buys you maximum hours in the park—assuming your kids can handle the schedule,

Time-Saving Tip

Your morning is best spent moving among continuous-loading attractions such as Mission: SPACE, Test Track, The Seas with Nemo & Friends, and especially Soarin'. Save theater-style attractions for the afternoon.

that is, and assuming that you'll be seeing IllumiNations on another night.

@ If you're not staying for IllumiNations, begin moving toward the exit gates while the show is in progress.

Future World

Future World comprises nine large pavilions, each containing at least one major attraction, and is very much like a permanent

The Epcot Don't-Miss List

The American Adventure (in the America pavilion)

Honey, I Shrunk the Audience

IllumiNations

Innoventions

Mission: SPACE (if the kids are old enough and pass the 44-inch height requirement)

Soarin' (if the kids pass the 40-inch height requirement)

Spaceship Earth

Test Track (if the kids pass the 40-inch height requirement)

Turtle Talk With Crush

World Showcase entertainment

World's Fair, mixing educational opportunities with pure entertainment. Most visitors are drawn first to the rides with their spectacular special effects, but don't miss Innoventions and the chance to play with the smaller interactive exhibits. These hands-on exhibits encourage young visitors to learn while doing and help kids avoid what one mother termed "audio-animatronics overload."

Future World Attractions

Spaceship Earth

Whatever their age, few travelers can remain blasé at the sight of Spaceship Earth, the most-photographed and readily recognizable symbol of Epcot. Even preschoolers rate it highly, probably because of the excitement of actually entering the "big ball."

Hidden Mickey

We all know Mickey is a star, and he actually has his own constellation in Spaceship Earth. Look for him in the starry sky at the beginning of the ride, just after you load.

The ride inside, which coils toward the top of the 17-story geosphere, traces developments in communication from cave drawings to computers. You climb past scenes of Egyptian temples, a performance of Oedipus Rex, and the invention of the Gutenberg press. Thanks to a revamp in 2008, the show has been spiffed up a bit. Judi Dench is the new narrator, there's a new musical score, four new scenes, jazzed-up costuming, and better special effects. A simple interactive game near the end lets you answer some questions and then see your own "future"—complete with your own face.

Take a few minutes to check out the postshow as you exit the ride. Sponsored by Siemens, the mega electronics and engineering company, most of the exhibits are technology-based and geared toward older kids, but children of any age will enjoy watching their image flash on the screen and their hometown light up on a global map that indicates the hometowns of past guests.

The Seas with Nemo & Friends/Turtle Talk with Crush

The Seas saltwater aquarium is so enormous that Spaceship Earth could float inside it, and the Finding Nemo ride within is a hit with preschoolers. You board "clamobiles" (similar in shape to the Haunted Mansion doom buggies) and travel through a coral reef looking for Nemo. On the way, you meet Dory, Bruce, and other stars from the film. At the end of the ride, you disembark at Sea Base, with its interactive exhibits. Don't miss the lighthearted and funny Turtle Talk with Crush,

Insider's Secret

If you really want to experience the Living Seas, a program called DiveQuest ($150) lets visitors 10 and over scuba dive in the aquarium, while the Epcot Seas Aqua Tour ($115) lets guests 8 and up snorkel. Whether you go under the sea or stay on top, these three-hour programs give you bragging rights and a cool T-shirt. Call 407/WDW–TOUR if you're interested.

in which the laid-back animated turtle interacts with the kids in the audience through real-time animation technology. Encourage your child to sit up front on the floor and ask Crush questions. We get tons of positive mail about this show. "Adorable," wrote a mom from Canada. "Our children considered it one of the highlights of the day."

Quick Guide to

Attraction	Location	Height Requirement
The American Adventure	World Showcase	None
Circle of Life	Future World	None
Gran Fiesta Tour	World Showcase	None
Honey, I Shrunk the Audience	Future World	None
Impressions de France	World Showcase	None
Innoventions	Future World	None
Journey Into Imagination	Future World	None
Living with the Land	Future World	None
Maelstrom	World Showcase	None
Mission: SPACE	Future World	44 inches
O Canada!	World Showcase	None
Reflections of China	World Showcase	None
The Seas with Nemo and Friends	Future World	None
Soarin'	Future World	40 inches
Spaceship Earth	Future World	None
Test Track	Future World	40 inches
Universe of Energy	Future World	None

Scare Factor

0 = Unlikely to scare any child of any age.

! = Has dark or loud elements; might rattle some toddlers.

!! = A couple of gotcha! moments; should be fine for school-age kids.

!!! = You need to be pretty big and pretty brave to handle this ride.

Epcot Attractions

Speed of Line	Duration of Ride/Show	Scare Factor	Age Range
Fast	30 min.	0	All
Fast	20 min.	0	All
Fast	9 min.	0	All
Fast	25 min.	!!	5 and up
Fast	20 min.	0	10 and up
n/a	n/a	0	3 and up
Fast	13 min.	!	3 and up
Fast	10 min.	0	All
Moderate	15 min.	!!	4 and up
Slow	15 min.	!!!	7 and up
Fast	20 min.	0	10 and up
Fast	20 min.	0	10 and up
Moderate	8 min.	0	All
Moderate	15 min.	!	5 and up
Moderate	15 min.	0	All
Slow	25 min.	!!!	7 and up
Slow	30 min.	!!	3 and up

Helpful Hint

Turtle Talk with Crush is starting to generate a lot of buzz. If you have preschoolers, try to get here before 11:30 AM. Afternoon shows are very crowded.

The Land

This cheerful pavilion, devoted to the subjects of food production and the environment, is home to three attractions, a rotating restaurant, and one of Epcot's most elaborate fast-food courts. Because there are so many places to eat here, the Land is crowded from 11 AM to 2 PM, when everyone heads in for lunch.

@ *Living with the Land.* You travel by boat past scenes of farming environments, ending with a peek at fish farming, drip irrigation, and other innovative agricultural technologies. It's a fairly adult presentation, but it moves swiftly, so kids shouldn't be too bored. Fastpasses are seasonally available but rarely necessary. If you have older kids who might benefit from doing a school project on the subject of futuristic farming, consider the $15 "Behind the Seeds" greenhouse tour. The sign-up booth is tucked away near the entrance to the Garden Grill restaurant.

@ *Circle of Life.* This 20-minute film stars Simba, Pumbaa, and Timon from *The Lion King,* and the beloved characters do a terrific job of pitching the conservation message. Simba explains how humans affect, both positively and negatively, their environment, so the show is both educational and entertaining. And because the Harvest Theater is large, with comfortable seats, Circle of Life is the perfect choice for afternoon.

@ *Soarin'.* Soarin' provides a bird's-eye view on an exhilarating flight above the beautiful state of California. It works like this: you're lifted 40 feet off the ground inside a giant dome. The interior of the dome is actually an enormous screen with images of redwood forests, Napa Valley, Yosemite, and the Golden Gate Bridge. You'll feel like you're hang gliding as you gently climb, bank, and descend your way through the scenery. The details make the ride: you'll feel the wind blowing through your hair and smell orange blossoms and pine trees. One mother of three from New York raved about the experience: "Soarin' was the favorite of everyone in our family, including our 5-year-old. She is normally afraid of heights but insisted on riding it three times, and the last time she actually wanted to sit on the highest row so she could see better!"

@ *Soarin' is madly popular,* and to compensate for the greater-than-anticipated crowd flow, Disney has created a fun preshow to keep you entertained while you wait in line. (They're so fun, in fact, that you might forget to keep moving!) The preshow, which is basically a group game played on five large video screens, lets you virtually fly a bird through a canyon and "launch" paintballs against a digital canvas to reveal hidden images.

Time-Saving Tip

Use Fastpasses for Soarin' whenever you can and remember that on busy days all the Fastpasses may be gone by noon.

Journey Into Imagination

The ride's premise is that Dr. Nigel Channing (Eric Idle), the rather stuffy head of the Imagination Institute, must be broken out of his shell and taught the true meaning of imagination, and the lovable purple creature known as Figment is just the dragon for the job. The ride is pretty simple, especially in contrast to other Future World attractions, but younger kids like it and there's rarely a wait.

After the ride, stop off at the ImageWorks Lab where interactive exhibits allow you to distort your facial image, produce sounds by stepping on pictures of lightning and lions, or morph your face onto a sunflower or koala and e-mail the results back to your friends. It's a fresh, funny, and free way to say, "Wish you were here."

Honey, I Shrunk the Audience

As you enter the theater, remember that closer is not always better, especially when it comes to a 3-D show like Honey, I Shrunk the Audience. For best viewing, sit about two-thirds of the way back.

The Scare Factor

Honey, I Shrunk the Audience is highly rated by kids of all ages. If your child is afraid of snakes or mice, have him take off the 3-D glasses and either pull up his legs into the seat or sit on your lap. That way he won't see the images clearly or feel the sensations.

The presentation, which is based on the movie series, begins as Dr. Wayne Szalinski (played by Rick Moranis) is about to pick up the award for Inventor of the Year. The scene quickly dissolves into mayhem when the audience is accidentally "shrunk," one son's pet snake gets loose, and the other son's pet mouse is reproduced 999 times. Although the 3-D images are dazzling, the effects go far beyond the visual—you actually feel the "mice" running up

Insider's Secret

Heat getting to you? As you exit Honey, I Shrunk the Audience, check out Splashtacular, a fun fountain show that gives kids the chance to get wet.

your legs, and the finale is a real "gotcha." Popular or not, there are rumors that this show might be closed down to make way for an updated attraction. We'll keep you posted.

Test Track

Test Track is the fastest ride in all of Disney World—we're talking 34 separate turns, 50-degree banking, and speeds of 65 mph.

The cars replicate tests at the GM proving grounds, and each vehicle is independently powered and controlled. In other words, this isn't the Tomorrowland Speedway. Thanks to an on-board computer, the cars are constantly adapting to road conditions, vehicle weight, and the location of the other 28 cars on the track.

The Scare Factor

Children must be 40 inches tall to ride Test Track. It's all about speed, with no flips or plunges, so kids 5 and up should be fine.

You begin the ride inside, checking out how your vehicle responds to cold, heat, sharp turns, rough roads, and other stresses. The stress level of the passengers soars when you move to the impact test, break through a barrier, and then zoom outside the building to the track. Here cars reach their top speeds—well, actually, they could go higher than 65 mph, but Imagineers didn't think it would be prudent to break the Florida speed limit—as they go through a mile of curves, hills, and turns. It's one powerful ride.

Test Track can draw some of the longest lines in all of Disney World. Fastpasses are almost always necessary; don't wait too long to get one. A whole day's supply of Fastpasses is often gone by early afternoon. If the Fastpasses are all gone and your kids are old enough to handle the intensity, consider going through the Singles Line. You won't get to ride together, but your wait time will be cut significantly.

Helpful Hint

Mission: SPACE is right beside Test Track and together they share the most crowded real estate in Epcot. Ride these two either in the morning or in the evening, after the crowds have moved into the World Showcase.

Mission: SPACE

Epcot's most technologically advanced thrill ride launches guests into a simulated space adventure, from the excitement of liftoff to the wonder of flight. To develop the story and design, Disney Imagineers worked with 25 space experts from NASA, and the result is completely immersive and interactive.

You're grouped into teams of four and each person is given a crew position—Commander, Navigator, Pilot, or Engineer—and assigned the tasks that go along with their role. Once you board your pod, everything happens fast. If you've opted for the spinning version of the ride, the motion is so rapid that it really feels like flight. The sustained G-forces during the launch are by far the most intense part of the ride. And before you fully recover, you're required to take on your crew role and push a few buttons (made somewhat more difficult by the gravitational pull of the ship's movement) as directed by mission control. (These "tasks" engage the kids, especially if

Time-Saving Tip

"I wasn't sure my kids could handle the G-forces [of Mission: SPACE] so I talked them into going into the green non-spinning line," said one mom. "An added bonus is that the green line is much shorter. We waited 5 minutes on a day when the regular line had a 40-minute wait."

they're a bit nervous about flying, but if you mess up, not to worry. You'll land safely back in Orlando just the same.)

In motion simulators, you can avoid motion sickness by looking away from the screen, but on the spinning version of Mission: SPACE, where your cabin is actually moving, the opposite is true. If you begin to feel queasy, keep your head back against the seat and focus intently on the screen. Shutting your eyes is the worst thing you can do.

The Scare Factor

There was tremendous concern over Mission: SPACE after two people died on the ride in 2006. It was ultimately shown that the victims had preexisting conditions, and the ride was not to blame, but Disney decided to offer a tamer—in other words, non-spinning—version of the ride for younger children and anyone with health concerns. As you approach the attraction, signs direct you toward either the orange team who boards the spinning capsules or the green team, who boards the non-spinning capsules. If you opt not to spin you have the same engaging preshow and postshow, and the same visual effects; the main difference is you don't feel the dramatic G-forces during the liftoff portion of the ride. That said, there's a fair amount of bouncing around in both sets of capsules.

The height requirement is 44 inches for either version. Take Disney's safety recommendations seriously: no pregnant women, children under 7, or anyone with high blood pressure or back, neck, or motion-sickness problems, especially on the spinning version of the ride.

As you exit, there's a small Space Base crawl area for younger kids and a cool competitive group game called Space Race for older kids.

Universe of Energy

This technologically complex presentation can be enjoyed by any age on any level. The preshow features Ellen DeGeneres, Alex Trebek, and Jamie Lee Curtis. Ellen has a dream in which she's a contestant on the game show *Jeopardy!*, and when she's thoroughly skunked by smarty-pants Jamie Lee, she realizes she needs to know a lot more about energy. Luckily for her, neighbor Bill Nye the Science Guy is happy to help.

The Disney twist comes when the 97-seat theater begins to break apart in sections that align themselves in sequence and form a train. A curtain lifts, and you begin to move through a prehistoric scene that carries you back to the era when coal deposits first formed on Earth. All around you are those darn dinosaurs, among the largest audio-animatronics figures Disney has ever created. After your train has once more morphed into a theater, there's a final film segment in which a newly educated Ellen gets her *Jeopardy!* revenge. Note: The Universe of Energy is often closed in the off-season, and there are rumors that it might close permanently.

Time-Saving Tip

When entering the Universe of Energy, ask the attendant how long it is until the next show begins, or check the digital clock. Don't enter sooner than 10 minutes before showtime; this is a 30-minute presentation, and there's no point in wearing out the kids before you begin. The theater can seat many people, so there's rarely a reason to line up and wait.

Despite its proximity to the front gate, Universe of Energy isn't a good choice for the morning; save it for the afternoon when you'll welcome the chance to sit down for 30 minutes.

Innoventions

Innoventions is the arcade of the future, where you can try out new video games before they hit the market, experience virtual reality, and play with beyond-state-of-the-art technology. There are games, quiz shows, and interactive exhibits to pull everyone into the action.

Cast members are on hand to answer questions or help you get the hang of the games and experiments. Exhibits change frequently, keeping things fresh, and many of the stations are kid friendly. Even preschoolers will find plenty to do.

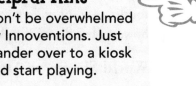

Helpful Hint
Don't be overwhelmed by Innoventions. Just wander over to a kiosk and start playing.

Insider's Secret
On a hot day, stop for a few minutes to check out the Coca-Cola Tasting Station (to the right of the entrance fountains), where you can sample the (sometimes unbelievably icky, at least to American palates) flavors of soft drinks from around the world.

World Showcase

Pretty by day and gorgeous by night, the World Showcase comprises the pavilions of 11 nations: Mexico, Norway, China, Germany, Italy, America, Japan, Morocco, France, the United Kingdom, and Canada. The countries are like links in a chain that stretch around a large lagoon. Really large. Making a full circle is a 1.2-mile trek.

Some of the pavilions have full-scale attractions while others have only shops and restaurants. Wonderful live entertainment is also available; check your entertainment schedule for showtimes.

Each pavilion is staffed by citizens of the country it represents. Disney goes to great pains to recruit, relocate, and if necessary, teach English to the shopkeepers and waiters here, bringing them to Orlando for a year and housing them with representatives from the other World Showcase nations. It's a cultural exchange program on the highest level. These young men and women save the World Showcase from being merely touristy and provide your kids with the chance to rub elbows, however briefly, with folks from other cultures.

World Showcase Attractions

O Canada!
This 20-minute Circle-Vision 360 film has recently been updated and now stars actor Martin Short. The film is gorgeous, stirring, and difficult to view with kids under 6. To enjoy the effect of the circular screen, you must stand during the presentation, and no strollers are allowed in the theater. This means babies and toddlers must be held, and preschoolers, who can't see anything in a room full of standing adults, often clamor to be lifted up as well.

Impressions de France
What a difference a seat makes! Like all the Epcot films, Impressions de France is exceedingly well done, with lush music and a 200-degree wide-screen feel. It's easy to get in, even in the afternoon, and no one minds if babies take a little nap. The 20-minute film shows on the hour and half hour and there is rarely a wait to get in.

Insider's Secret

One of the best ways to get kids involved in the World Showcase experience is by visiting the Kidcot Fun Stops. Children begin a craft project (at present it's a mask but sometimes you can make musical instruments as well) at the first booth they visit and as they move to the next country, they receive another element to add to their project. It's a great icebreaker and gets them interacting with people from other countries.

The American Adventure

This multimedia presentation, combining audio-animatronics figures with film, is popular with all age groups. The technological highlight comes when the Ben Franklin robot walks up the stairs to visit Thomas Jefferson, but the entire 30-minute presentation is packed with elaborate sets that rise from the stage, film montages, and moving music.

It's worth noting that some guests find the patriotism of The American Adventure a little heavy-handed. There seem to be two primary reactions to the show—some people weep through it and some people sleep through it. Most of our readers rate it as one of the best attractions in Epcot.

Reflections of China

Another lovely 360-degree film. But again, it's not an easy attraction to view with young children.

Maelstrom

In this Norwegian boat ride, your Viking ship sails through fjords and storms, over waterfalls, and past a threatening three-headed troll—all within four minutes. You disembark in a North Sea coastal village, where a short film is presented. (If

The Scare Factor

Maelstrom sounds terrifying but the reality is much tamer than the ride description. The much-touted "backward plunge over a waterfall" is so subtle that passengers in the front of the boat are not even aware of the impending doom. The darkness and the troll put off some preschoolers but the ride is generally fine for kids 5 and up.

Hidden Mickey

Check out the mural of Vikings in the line before you board Maelstrom. One of them is wearing mouse ears!

you want to skip the film, no biggie . . . just keep on walking through the theater. Most families do.) The adjacent Kringla Bakeri Og Kafe is one of the best places in the World Showcase for a quick snack or lunch.

Gran Fiesta Tour

This mild little boat ride stars the Three Caballeros. The story line has Donald skipping out on a singing gig and José and Panchito searching throughout Mexico for their friend. The Gran Fiesta Tour is a very simple ride, somewhat reminiscent of It's a Small World on a more limited scale, but younger kids like it.

Food Choices at Epcot

Epcot is *the* food park. It has such an embarrassment of riches that it's hard to choose.

For sit-down dining, one perennial favorite is the San Angel Inn in Mexico, which is a great place to escape on a hot sunny day. A shadowy waterway gurgles by, and the scene is that of an evening marketplace, romantically dark even at high noon. Another popular spot is Chefs de France in—you guessed it—France. Here the feel is of a Parisian sidewalk café with white tablecloths and bustling waiters. Le Cellier is perhaps the most popular Epcot restaurant, due to its tasty steaks and elaborate desserts, and the Tutto Italia Ristorante in Italy serves up delicious classics. Kids enjoy the show-style teppanyaki dining at the Teppan Edo in Japan, and the food—which includes such upscale items as Kobe beef—is outstanding.

Not up for full-service dining? For a quick, casual meal in Future World, head for the Sunshine Seasons food court in the Land, where you can choose from healthy salads, hearty sandwiches, and a variety of well-prepared ethnic dishes at different counters.

In terms of World Showcase fast food, you have plenty of possibilities. The Tangierine Café in Morocco has Mediterranean wraps, hummus, salads, and platters of chicken and lamb. The food is served in a pretty patio area with a perfect view of the pavilion. Don't miss the pastry counter in the back for baklava and other honeyed delights, not to mention Turkish coffee so strong that you may set a land-speed record on your next lap around the World Showcase.

Helpful Hint

If you're worried about how the kids will react to unfamiliar cuisine, not to worry. On kiddie menus, the food is a nod to the country in question—for example, skewered chicken in Morocco or fish-and-chips in the United Kingdom—but the entrées are smaller and less spicy than the adult meals and look enough like chicken nuggets and fish sticks that the kids will eat them.

While the Tangierine Café is right in the middle of the action, the Yakitori House in Japan is tucked away in the back of the pavilion with a soothing view of the manicured gardens and koi ponds. The food—especially the broiled skewers of chicken, shrimp, and beef—is tasty and a bit lighter than many of the counter-service options. Another good choice is Kringla Bakeri Og Kafe in Norway, which has wonderful open-face salmon sandwiches and delicious pastries.

The Yorkshire County Fish and Chips stand in the United Kingdom is always popular. Carry your food into the back garden and sit on a park bench while you listen to the British Invasion sing Beatles classics.

The Boulangerie Patisserie in France emits such phenomenal aromas of coffee and croissants that there's always a line, even though the café is in an out-of-the-way back alley. Drop by for sandwiches, quiche, and a wide selection of decadent pastries, which are so good that they make the Boulangerie a favorite with Disney cast members. *Bon appétit!*

Money-Saving Tip

Not on the dining plan but you'd still like to size up a few of Epcot's posh restaurants? To save both time and money, stick to fast-food places for meals and make reservations at a sit-down restaurant for a truly off-time, like 3 PM or 10 PM and just have dessert. You can soak up the ambience for an investment of 30 minutes and 20 bucks.

Alternatively, as the average Epcot dinner for four costs about $100 without wine or beer, you can slice that bill in half if you visit the sit-down restaurant of your choice at lunch instead of dinner.

Epcot Extras

The Magic Kingdom isn't the only place to see the characters, catch a show, watch fireworks, or buy souvenirs. Epcot provides a whole range of entertainment, but with an international spin.

Characters

The character meetings and shows at Epcot are rarely as crowded as those at the Magic Kingdom. A well-marked character spot to the right of the fountains in Future World is your best bet to meet Mickey and his pals, and, in the World Showcase, the backdrops for individual character appearances can't be beat. You might meet Aladdin in Morocco, for example, or Mary Poppins in the United Kingdom. Check your entertainment schedule for times.

World Showcase Performers

Singers, dancers, jugglers, and artisans from around the globe perform throughout the World Showcase daily. Times are outlined on your entertainment schedule.

Some of these presentations are more child-oriented than others. Children especially enjoy the young acrobats in China and the balancing act in France. Older kids can enter into the raucous action of the King Arthur skit in the United Kingdom or catch the "High-energy progressive Celtic music" of Off-Kilter in Canada. This translates to rock music with bagpipes—a must-see. The British Invasion, a talented '60s-style group that plays in the United Kingdom, is also popular.

The shows are set up so that you can pretty much flow from one to the other as you work your way around the World Showcase. If you're there 10 minutes before showtime you can usually get a decent spot. Be forewarned that for most of the shows you'll either be standing or sitting on the sidewalk; only

Insider's Secret

The princess character meals at Epcot are popular but not as well known as those in the Magic Kingdom. Restaurant Akershus in Norway is the host, and at present the princesses show up at breakfast, lunch, and dinner. They only stay for about an hour though, so book your meal at the time they're slated to appear. Also note that you'll probably see Belle, Snow White, and Sleeping Beauty, but Cinderella only appears in the Magic Kingdom. Reservations are a must; call 407/WDW–DINE up to 180 days before the date you wish to attend. The earlier the better!

The princess meals aren't just for girls. Consider this note from a mother of two in Delaware: "Even though it's somewhat geared toward girls, my 7-year-old son really enjoyed the princess breakfast in the Norway pavilion. The waiter greeted him by calling him 'Prince,' which he loved, and the princesses treated him like royalty throughout the whole meal. He seemed quite smitten with them."

the stage where Off-Kilter appears has actual seats and even that venue is way too small for the crowds the group attracts.

A mother of two from Illinois wrote to us, "Please stress how great the World Showcase performers are. We got wonderful pictures of our children with the Living Statues, and the Chinese acrobats were so good that we went back for another show. You don't hear much about the live entertainment in the World Showcase, but we found it to be the highlight of our day at Epcot."

Kim Possible

Want to save the world—or at least make the World Showcase more appealing to your kids? The Kidcot Fun Stops were created to give preschoolers a reason to explore the World Show-case, but now their older siblings also have an inducement: a high-tech mission as part of the Kim Possible Adventure.

It works like this: in the morning, as you're passing through Future World, you'll see the Kim Possible booths (one inside of Innoventions East, the other on the bridge into the World Showcase Plaza). If you'd like to go on a mission, stop by and pick up a free ticket. You'll be directed to a second booth inside one of the World Showcase countries, and there you'll be given a cell phone and mission information. As you follow the clues into specific sections of the park, your phone will period-ically ring and vibrate, giving you updated information and di-recting you to the next location.

Although the complicated plot lines seem to confuse adults, kids catch on fast and enjoy the chase. The fact that the game leads them through every nook and cranny of an Epcot country is a bonus. It takes about 30 minutes to play, and if they have fun, they can go on another mission in a different country.

IllumiNations

This display of lasers, fireworks, syncopated fountains, and stir-ring music is a real-life fantasia and an unsurpassed Disney World classic. Very popular, very crowded, and the perfect way to end an Epcot day, IllumiNations takes place over the World Showcase lagoon at the 9 PM closing time. If you watch from

Insider's Secret

The show produces a lot of smoke. Before you select your vantage point, note which way the wind is blowing. If you have a pleasant breeze in your face now, you can be sure you'll catch the full brunt of the smoke during the show.

the Mexico or Canada pavilions, you'll be able to beat the crowd to the exits afterward. Guests staying at the Yacht and Beach Clubs, or the BoardWalk, Swan, or Dolphin resorts, and thus leaving via the "back-door" exit, can watch from the bridge between the United Kingdom and France pavilions.

Shopping

You'll see things in Epcot that aren't available anywhere else in Disney World: German wines, Chinese silk robes, Mexican piñatas, Norwegian sweaters, and English teas are all within strolling distance of each other. Once you've made your purchases, either have them sent to Package Pick-Up near the front gate and retrieve them as you exit or, if you're staying on-site, have them delivered to your hotel. Both services are free.

International Food and Wine Festival

Dining your way around the World Showcase is always a treat, but it gets even better during one of the park's premier special events, the annual Epcot Food and Wine Festival. It runs for approximately eight weeks, from late September through November. You can get exact dates and information by calling 407/WDW–FEST.

Open-air booths serving the food, wine, and beer of more than 60 nations are set up around the World Showcase, offering everything from New Zealand lamb chops to Bavarian strudel. The sample-size servings range from $1.50 to $4.50 so you can happily nosh your way around the world, indulging in WDW's biggest buffet. If you want to learn more about what you're eating and drinking, cooking demonstrations and wine tastings are scheduled daily and are usually free.

True foodies and wine enthusiasts should consider one of the special-event dinners. The Party for the Senses, Winemaker Dinners, and Reserve Dinners are very heady events, held in se-

Insider's Secret

If you're intrigued by the Segways zipping around Epcot, guests 16 and up can sign up to learn how to ride and take a lap around the World Showcase—in the morning, before the park opens to the general public. Call 407/WDW–TOUR for details.

cluded glamour points all around Disney property, and they sell out weeks in advance. Call 407/WDW–FEST for a list of participants, dates, prices, and reservations. Details are also posted at www.disneyworld.com.

Afternoon Resting Places

- The American Adventure
- Circle of Life in the Land pavilion
- Honey, I Shrunk the Audience
- Impressions de France
- Universe of Energy

Helpful Hint

Epcot has many shows, so if the kids need to run off a little energy between presentations, check out the play fountains. One set is near Mission: SPACE and the others are just to the right of the bridge leading to the World Showcase. They're a great place to cool off on a hot afternoon, especially if you bring along bathing suits or waterproof diapers.

Tips for Your Last Hour at Epcot

@ If you're staying for IllumiNations, find a spot around the World Showcase lagoon 30 minutes in advance during the off-season, 45 to 60 minutes in advance during the on-season. Have a snack to help pass the time.

@ When staking out the perfect spot to watch Illumi-Nations, remember that much of the show takes place above you. If you sit beneath a tree or awning you'll have trouble seeing the fireworks in their full glory.

@ Not staying for IllumiNations? This is the perfect chance to swing back through Future World and ride Soarin', Mission: SPACE, or Test Track on your way out. Just be sure you're at the exit gates by the time the fireworks end and the onslaught of people begins.

Tips for Leaving Epcot

@ Lights are kept low during closing time to accentuate the effects of IllumiNations. This makes it easy to get separated from your party, so hang on tight to younger kids and make plans to meet at a certain place in case you lose each other in the crowd.

Disney's Hollywood Studios

Disney's Hollywood Studios

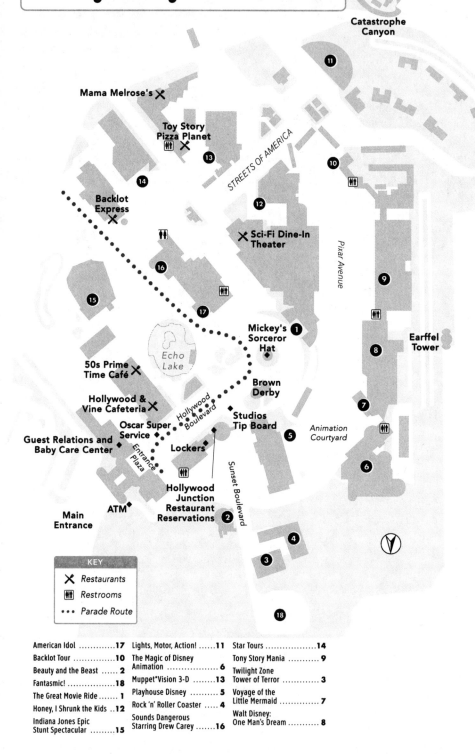

Catastrophe Canyon

11

Mama Melrose's ✕

Toy Story
Pizza Planet ✕

13

14

STREETS OF AMERICA

10

12

Backlot
Express ✕

✕ Sci-Fi Dine-In
Theater

Pixar Avenue

16

9

15

17

Echo
Lake

Mickey's **1**
Sorceror
Hat

Earffel
Tower

8

50s Prime
Time Café ✕

Brown
Derby

Hollywood &
Vine Cafeteria ✕

Hollywood Boulevard

Studios
Tip Board

Animation
Courtyard

7

Oscar Super
Service ◆

5

Guest Relations and
Baby Care Center ◆

Entrance Plaza

Lockers ◆

6

Sunset Boulevard

Hollywood
Junction
Restaurant
Reservations

2

ATM ◆

Main
Entrance

4

3

18

Getting to Disney's Hollywood Studios

Compared with the Magic Kingdom, getting to Disney's Hollywood Studios—formerly Disney-MGM Studios—is a snap. Shuttle buses run approximately every 15–20 minutes from all on-site hotels. Guests staying at the Swan, Dolphin, and Board-Walk resorts or the Yacht and Beach Clubs are a 15-minute water taxi ride from the Hollywood gate.

If you're driving to the parks, note that the Hollywood parking lot is small. If you get there at opening time and park close to the entrance, then you can forgo the parking lot tram and walk to the front gate.

Getting Around Hollywood

Hollywood is a relatively small park with no trains, boats, or buses. In other words, you'll walk.

Tips for Your First Hour at Hollywood

@ Pick up a map and entertainment schedule as you enter. If you need a stroller, rent one at Oscar's Super Service Station. If you haven't yet arranged reservations for meals, stop by the dining information booth on the right near the end of Hollywood Boulevard.

@ If you're at Hollywood on an Extra Magic Hour morning, a blackboard beside the dining information booth will let you know which attractions are operative; the whole park doesn't open early but several major rides will be up and going.

@ New rides are naturally the hottest tickets and Toy Story Mania appeals to all age groups and therefore is very hot indeed. Visit it as early as possible. Fastpasses for the whole day are often gone by mid-morning.

@ After riding Toy Story Mania ask yourself: Are your kids old enough and bold enough for a couple of big-deal rides? If so, turn onto Sunset Boulevard and head straight toward Rock 'n' Roller Coaster and the Twilight Zone Tower of Terror. Waits are usually minimal in the morning but if it's a busy day, get a Fastpass for one attraction, then immediately board the other. If your kids are younger, move on to Playhouse Disney or Voyage of the Little Mermaid.

Hollywood Touring Tips

@ In general, you should save theater-style presentations—Playhouse Disney; Beauty and the Beast; Voyage of the Little Mermaid; Muppet*Vision 3-D; Sounds Dangerous; Indiana Jones; and Lights, Motors, Action!—for the afternoon. Tour continuous-loading attractions such as the Tower of Terror, The Great Movie Ride, Toy Story Mania, Rock 'n' Roller Coaster, and Star Tours early in the day.

@ The one exception to this rule is if your kids are so young that you won't be going on most of the major rides. If so, ride Toy Story Mania first and then catch one of the

Disney's Hollywood Studios Don't-Miss List

Beauty and the Beast—Live on Stage!

The Great Movie Ride

Lights, Motors, Action!—Extreme Stunt Show

Muppet*Vision 3-D

Playhouse Disney—Live on Stage!
(if your kids are under 8)

Star Tours

Rock 'n' Roller Coaster (if your kids are 8 and up)

Toy Story Mania

Twilight Zone Tower of Terror (if your kids are 8 and up)

Voyage of the Little Mermaid

morning shows of Playhouse Disney and Voyage of the Little Mermaid.

@ No matter what the ages of your kids, save the Backlot Tour and Animation Academy for after lunch.

Attractions at Hollywood Offering Fastpasses

Indiana Jones Epic Stunt Spectacular (seasonally)

Lights, Motors, Action!—Extreme Stunt Show

Rock 'n' Roller Coaster

Star Tours

Toy Story Mania

Twilight Zone Tower of Terror

Voyage of the Little Mermaid

Hollywood Attractions

On Sunset Boulevard

Twilight Zone Tower of Terror

The Twilight Zone Tower of Terror combines the spooky ambience of a decaying, cobweb-covered 1930s-style Hollywood hotel with sheer thrills. For the clever preshow, Imagineers spliced together clips from the old Twilight Zone TV series, bringing back the long-deceased Rod Serling as narrator.

Hidden Mickey
During the preshow, take note of the child actress boarding the elevator. She's holding a Mickey Mouse toy.

The story begins on a dark and stormy night in 1939 when five people— a movie star and starlet, a child actress and her nanny, and a bellboy—board a hotel elevator. The hotel is struck by lightning, the elevator drops, and the five passengers are transported into the Twilight Zone. One of the cast members who works at the attraction reports that the most common questions people ask her are "Is this a real hotel?" and "Am I going to die?" (The answer to both is "No.")

After the creepy preshow, you file through a dark basement queue at the end of which you board a freight elevator much like the ill-fated one that disappeared years earlier. Your seat has a lap bar and each "elevator" holds about 25 people.

Your car moves out of its elevator shaft and through a hallway with holographic images before eventually settling into a second elevator shaft. (This is all drawn out with agonizing slowness.) Then the doors of your elevator car open to reveal a panoramic view of the park from nearly 150 feet in the air, then you free-fall.

The Scare Factor

The Tower of Terror has a 40-inch height requirement, which means that many preschoolers are tall enough to ride. Nonetheless, our suggestion is 8 and up, both because of the spooky setup and the drop. The expanded drop sequence means you're bouncing around in the shaft for a good 20 to 30 seconds, which can feel like forever to a terrified child.

When the ride first opened, you only dropped once, but Imagineers have since introduced a random drop pattern, which means that computers controlling the ride select from several possible drop sequences. You may be hauled up and dropped as many as seven times, and the trip up is as exhilarating as the trip down.

Rock 'n' Roller Coaster

The Rock 'n' Roller Coaster is one of the best rides in Disney World. The sound track, featuring Aerosmith, is perfectly synchronized to the movements of the coaster and the volume is cranked to the max.

The premise is simple. You play the part of fans that have shown up at an Aerosmith taping but, unfortu-

Time-Saving Tip

Lines for both Rock 'n' Roller Coaster and Tower of Terror are long in the afternoon. Use Fastpass.

Hidden Mickey

As you walk through the rotunda area before boarding check out the floors; two Hidden Mickeys are in the tiles.

Quick Guide to

Attraction	Location	Height Requirement
American Idol	Hollywood Blvd.	None
Backlot Tour	Pixar Ave.	None
Beauty and the Beast—Live on Stage!	Sunset Blvd.	None
Fantasmic!	Sunset Blvd.	None
The Great Movie Ride	Hollywood Blvd.	None
Honey, I Shrunk the Kids Movie Set	New York St.	None
Indiana Jones Epic Stunt Spectacular	Hollywood Blvd.	None
Lights, Motors, Action! Extreme Stunt Show	New York St.	None
The Magic of Disney Animation	Animation Courtyard	None
Muppet*Vision 3-D	New York St.	None
Playhouse Disney—Live on Stage!	Animation Courtyard	None
Rock 'n' Roller Coaster	Sunset Blvd.	48 inches
Sounds Dangerous Starring Drew Carey	Hollywood Blvd.	None
Star Tours	Hollywood Blvd.	40 inches
Toy Story Mania	Pixar Ave.	None
Twilight Zone Tower of Terror	Sunset Blvd.	40 inches
Voyage of the Little Mermaid	Animation Courtyard	None
Walt Disney: One Man's Dream	Pixar Ave.	None

Scare Factor
0 = Unlikely to scare any child of any age.
! = Has dark or loud elements; might rattle some toddlers.
!! = A couple of gotcha! moments; should be fine for school-age kids.
!!! = You need to be pretty big and pretty brave to handle this ride.

Hollywood Attractions

Speed of Line	Duration of Ride/Show	Scare Factor	Age Range
N/A	35 min.	0	7 and up
Fast	35 min.	!	5 and up
Fast	30 min.	0	All
Fast	25 min.	!!	3 and up
Fast	25 min.	!	5 and up
Slow	n/a	0	2 and up
Fast	30 min.	!	All
Moderate	25 min.	!!	All
Moderate	35 min.	0	All
Fast	20 min.	!	2 and up
Moderate	15 min.	0	All
Moderate	3 min.	!!!	8 and up
Slow	15 min.	!!	7 and up
Moderate	10 min.	!!	5 and up
Moderate	12 min.	0	All
Moderate	10 min.	!!!	8 and up
Slow	20 min.	!!!	6 and up
Moderate	20 min.	0	8 and up

nately, the group is in the process of leaving for a concert. They insist you come along to the show, so you're boarded into 24-passenger stretch limos, which their manager promises are "real fast," and you're off on a rock-and-roll trip through the highways of L.A.

Takeoff is amazing—0 to 60 in 2.8 seconds—and then you're quickly thrown into your first total flip. The maze-like track will make a total of three inversions and at one point you rip through an "O" in the HOLLYWOOD sign. The coaster is smooth and fast and offers uneasy riders one comfort: since the whole ride takes place inside a building, you never go very high, so there's no plunging sensation. Rock 'n' Roller Coaster is more about speed than big drops.

The Scare Factor

Loud, fast, and wild, especially at takeoff, this coaster is for older kids and teens. With a 48-inch height requirement, suffice it to say that Rock 'n' Roller Coaster will be much too much for kids under 8.

Beauty and the Beast—Live on Stage!

The Theater of the Stars is modeled on the Hollywood Bowl, and it's the perfect setting for this appealing 30-minute show. The costuming, choreography, and production are first-rate. The plot is drastically compressed, but since approximately 99.9% of the audience has seen the movie, it's really not a problem. Beauty and the Beast is a good choice for the afternoon. The theater is covered and large enough to seat 1,500, so if you show up 20 minutes before showtime you should easily get a seat.

Insider's Secret

One problem that arises with all Disney's theater-style attractions is especially acute in huge venues like the Hollywood Bowl, where Beauty and the Beast plays. Let's say you arrive 30 minutes before the stated showtime and find yourself a terrific seat. As others file into the theater, cast members encourage you to move over and make room, and this goes on all the way until the split second the show starts. Ironically, those who came earliest often end up politely sliding their way into the far corners of the theaters, while stragglers end up with the best seats. And if you try to avoid this by swooping in at the last minute, you may not get a seat. Try this: instead of staking out aisle seats in side sections (where you'll find yourself being pushed to the walls), arrive early and sit along one of the aisles in the center section. You'll still be asked to keep sliding, but at least you'll end up near the middle of the theater.

Fantasmic!

Fantasmic! may be the best show in any Disney park. It has everything—lasers, fireworks, lighting effects, music, fountains, a 6,900-seat amphitheater, 1.9 million gallons of water, 45 cast members, and a 50-foot fire-breathing dragon. The show plays at closing every night and twice nightly on busy days.

Mickey performs in his role as the Sorcerer's Apprentice, fighting off a horde of

Helpful Hint

At Fantasmic!, sit at least 15 rows from the front to avoid being sprayed with water.

evil Disney characters with a variety of special effects, including the projection of film images onto a screen of water. For a while it looks like the bad guys are winning, and these dark scenes are upsetting for some children. In due time, however, Mickey's imagination conjures up images of happiness, love, and friendship, and the good-guy characters show up in force. Children

Insider's Secret

Fantasmic! is always packed, but one surefire way to guarantee you get in is to purchase a Fantasmic! Dinner Package. It includes a prix-fixe meal at one of three Hollywood restaurants (the Brown Derby, Mama Melrose, or Hollywood & Vine) plus access to a priority-seating area of the Fantasmic! theater. Prices depend on the restaurant you choose and range from $27 to $47 for adults and $10 for kids ages 3 to 9. Prices don't include park admission, tax, gratuity, or drinks (except at Hollywood & Vine, where nonalcoholic drinks are part of the buffet).

Plan to eat early—maybe two or three hours before the show. After dinner, as you pay, you're given a voucher that lets you into the priority-seating area, which is to the far right of the stage. Don't arrive at the last minute though—you aren't guaranteed a specific seat, just a seat within a specific area. Two caveats: Fantasmic! is an outdoor show, and if the weather is truly inclement it can be canceled at the last minute. You still get your dinner, but you're not reimbursed for losing out on the preferred seating for the show. Also, remember that this is a secured reservation that you can't casually blow off: They'll ask for a credit card guarantee when you make your reservation, and if you don't show up (or at least don't cancel within 48 hours), you'll be charged.

The Scare Factor

Every Disney villain you can think of shows up for the cartoon Armageddon and the middle scenes of the show are emotionally wrenching for preschoolers. Mickey rallies to save the day, of course, and most kids adore the show. The noise level is high enough to frighten some babies and toddlers.

of all ages rate the show highly, and it's surprisingly moving, even for adults.

On Hollywood Boulevard

The Great Movie Ride

Beginning in the Chinese Theater at the end of Hollywood Boulevard, The Great Movie Ride is a bona fide classic. Disney's largest ride-through attraction, it loads steadily and fairly swiftly and is best toured either mid-morning or in the last hour before the park closes.

Your tour guide provides an amusing spiel as you glide past soundstage sets from *Casablanca, Alien, The Wizard of Oz,* and other great films. The audio-animatronics figures of Gene

The Scare Factor

You'll encounter the Alien from *Alien,* the Wicked Witch from *The Wizard of Oz,* and any number of no-gooders on your trip. Some of the scenes are startling for preschoolers—the pretend gunfire as well as the confrontations, however campy, can be jarring to some—but the fact that your tram driver disappears and reappears does underscore the fact that it's all "just pretend."

Kelly, Julie Andrews, and Clint Eastwood are among Disney's best. But things suddenly turn ugly as your car stalls and the movie scenes come to life. Depending on which car you've boarded, you're about to be overrun by either a Mafia-style gangster or a Western desperado. Your tram will be taken hostage, but don't fret too much. In a later scene, drawn from *Indiana Jones and the Temple of Doom*, justice prevails. Was there ever any doubt there would be a happy ending?

Afternoon Parade

A theme parade—the latest manifestation is a tribute to Disney-Pixar films called "Block Party Bash"—runs every afternoon, and the exact time and route are outlined on your map. Stake out curb space 30 minutes in advance during the on-season. Because the parade route is so short, the crowds can be 8 to 10 people deep, and no vantage point is significantly less crowded than another. It's worth it though; the athleticism of the performers will amaze you.

On Echo Lake

Star Tours

Motion-simulation technology and a jostling cabin combine to produce the real feel of flight in Star Tours. With the hapless Captain Rex at the helm, you're off for what's supposed to be a routine mission to the Moon of Endor. "Don't worry if this is your first flight," Rex comforts visitors, "it's my first one, too." One wrong turn later, and you're ripping through space at

The Scare Factor

Most kids love Star Tours and find it's like being inside a very exciting, very authentic video game. There's a 40-inch height requirement. One warning: Star Tours can cause motion sickness.

Insider's Secret

Younglings will jump at the chance to participate in the Jedi Training Academy, held several times a day on a stage outside of Star Tours. A Jedi knight leads them through some basic light saber moves and suddenly (who could have seen this coming?) Darth Vader and his Storm Troopers show up looking for trouble. Each young Jedi-in-training gets a chance to show off his or her fighting skills in defense of the Force. Check your schedule for showtimes.

hyper speed, headed toward combat with the dreaded Death Star.

George Lucas served as creative consultant, and the ride echoes the charming as well as the terrifying elements of the Star Wars series. The chatter of R2-D2, C3PO, and assorted droids makes even the queues enjoyable. Star Tours is the best of both worlds—visual effects so convincing that you'll clutch your arm rails but actual rumbles so mild that only the youngest children are eliminated as passengers.

Lines move at an agreeable pace, but it's still best to ride in the morning if you can. Fastpass is available.

As you exit, be sure to check out the Jedi Training Academy. Showtimes are marked on your entertainment schedule and there's plenty of audience participation, with some lucky kids brought up on stage. "My 6-year-old son loved this attraction," reported one father from Michigan. "We ended up coming back for another show."

Sounds Dangerous Starring Drew Carey

In Drew Carey's spy spoof, you wear headphones and listen as Drew upends a jar of killer bees, drives a car, has a haircut, and

The Scare Factor

For long periods of Sounds Dangerous you sit in total darkness to accentuate the sound effects, and this unnerves some young kids. At nearly every performance at least one toddler is shrieking, which obviously undercuts the enjoyment of everyone in the theater, not to mention the terrified child. For kids with no fear of the dark, the show is an entertaining introduction to the lost world of radio, where sound told the story.

visits the circus. The effects are remarkably convincing, and the show is a crash course on behind-the-scenes sound production.

The postshow interactive area called "Sound Works" allows you to create video sound tracks and play around with 3-D sound effects in darkened booths. Most of the attractions are geared toward older kids but this is definitely a fun place to kill a few minutes; you can either stop in here after the show, or skip the show and enter through a separate entrance.

Helpful Hint

Sounds Dangerous is a good choice for the afternoon. It's rarely crowded and you can sit for a while.

Indiana Jones Epic Stunt Spectacular

This stunt show is loud, lively, and full of laughs. Audience volunteers are a key part of the action and your odds of being tapped improve if you show up early and are near the front of the line. Professional stunt people re-create daring scenes from the Indiana Jones movies, and this 30-minute show is a great

The Scare Factor

The gunfire and explosions are loud enough to startle some kids, but the fact that the theater is outdoors does dilute the intensity.

chance to see how some of those difficult and dangerous stunts actually wind up on film.

Lines can look daunting, but the 2,200-seat theater is so huge that even people in the back are usually seated. That said, if you're visiting on a truly crowded day, you could always use Fastpass or wait until the less-crowded evening shows.

In Animation Courtyard

Voyage of the Little Mermaid

Using puppets, animation, and live actors to retell the story of Ariel and Prince Eric, Voyage of the Little Mermaid remains one of the most popular shows at Hollywood.

The special effects in this 20-minute show are among the best Disney has to offer. You'll feel as if you're really underwater and the interplay between the animation, puppetry, and live actors is ingenious.

The Scare Factor

Voyage of the Little Mermaid does have some frightening elements. The storm scene is dark and loud, and Ursula the Sea Witch is one big ugly puppet. That said, most kids have seen the movie and know enough to expect a happy ending, so they usually make it through the dark scenes without becoming too upset.

The Magic of Disney Animation

The Magic of Disney Animation opens with a fast and funny show starring Mushu, the pint-size dragon from *Mulan* with the voice of Eddie Murphy, and a live Disney animator. The animator describes how a character evolves in the animation process, and Mushu learns, to his horror, that he originally wasn't destined to be a dragon at all.

After the show, it's on to the interactive exhibits. These are designed to be fun for all ages, and you can stay as long as you like. "You're a Character," a quiz that tells you which Disney character is most like you, will save you years of money, otherwise spent on therapy. (Don't like your character? Try the test again!) Or you can insert your own voice into clips of animated classics, digitally color a cartoon, or—the most exciting part for youngsters—meet the stars of Disney's latest film. While stars from the older flicks circulate through all the parks, Hollywood is usually the only one where you can meet the newest stars.

The best part of the attraction for older kids is the Animation Academy, where you can learn to draw a Disney character. Your drawing becomes a great free souvenir that you can take home. Many kids like to have the character they drew autograph the picture the next time they see him or her in the park. Or you can buy a frame for your masterpiece as you exit the attraction. If you get hooked and want to draw more than one character, you can reenter the Animation Academy later without going back through the entire attraction. Just duck in through the Animation Gallery shop. "Learning to draw Pooh was an unexpected highlight for our family," wrote one mom. "I think we may have discovered an unknown talent in our 8-year-old son!"

Playhouse Disney—Live on Stage!

Younger kids love this stage show where they sing, dance, and play along with costumed cast members from such Disney Channel shows as "Mickey Mouse Clubhouse," "Little Einsteins," and "Handy Manny." (Characters are updated periodically to make sure they're from currently popular Playhouse Disney programs.) The performance space holds large crowds, with the children (largely preschoolers) grouped on the floor where they can participate in the show, i.e., they can stand, jump, sing, and shriek within the confines of your claimed spot on the carpeted floor. Show emcees and performers are skilled at drawing even the youngest and the shyest of children into the action.

Although the show is simple, it's a big hit with toddlers and preschoolers and substantial lines begin forming about 30 minutes before showtime. Visit whenever your kids are at their happiest and most rested.

Oh, and there's more excitement as you exit. Characters are often on hand for meet and greets in the Animation Courtyard, and this is the only place you'll see Playhouse Disney stars. Consult your entertainment schedule for times, try to line up early, and keep a sharp eye on your kids. All character meeting sessions have the potential to get wild but the Playhouse Disney ones—perhaps because most of the fans are preschoolers—is more like Madhouse Disney.

On Pixar Avenue

Walt Disney: One Man's Dream

This is more of an exhibit than an attraction, but it does remind you that almost everything in Disney World sprang from the extraordinary vision of a single man. There are plenty of artifacts and memorabilia, as well as a film about Walt Disney's life.

Backlot Tour

The Backlot Tour begins with a stop at the special-effects water tank, where audience volunteers help film a naval battle scene. Then you stroll through the props department before boarding a tram that stops in Catastrophe Canyon where you're caught in an earthquake and flash flood. (If you're sitting on the left side, prepare to get wet.) After the rumbles subside, you ride behind the canyon to see how the disasters were created. Note that the Backlot Tour is frequently closed in the off-season, and there are rumors that it might close for good.

Toy Story Mania

Ever fancied being one of the toys in *Toy Story*? Well, going on this ride may be the closest you ever get, and there's no doubt you'll feel—ahem—animated. Toy Story Mania combines a ride through a cartoon toy box with the challenge of playing carnival midway games. You put on 3-D glasses and suddenly you've been shrunk into a toy spinning around with Woody, Hamm, Rex, and other familiar characters. Just when you're starting to get the hang of being in a cartoon, you come across the first interactive games. Using spring-action shooters, you'll launch rings at aliens, shoot darts at balloons, and hurl eggs at barnyard targets. Best of all, the ride gauges your skill level during the practice round and then adjusts the difficulty for each rider in order to create a level playing field. So a 5-year-old can compete mano a mano with her 12-year-old brother.

Toy Story Mania is similar in concept to Buzz Lightyear's Space Ranger Spin in the Magic Kingdom, but the technology

Time-Saving Tip
Toy Story Mania is hot, hot, hot, so go early and use Fastpass. "We arrived at 10:30 AM to find that all the Fastpasses for the day had already been distributed," says one mother from Philadelphia. "We ended up standing in line for 90 minutes."

is considerably more advanced. As you play, you see the "virtual objects" you've launched from your shooters either hit or miss targets. And at times it even seems as if objects are whirling past you as they pop out of the 3-D scenes. Like any attraction with scoring, Toy Story Mania is addictive, with riders coming back time after time to try and beat their own scores. "The best ride in Hollywood," enthused one mother of three, "and maybe in all of Disney World. The kids loved it and it took me and my husband back to our childhoods."

On Streets of America

Honey, I Shrunk the Kids
This playground is based on the popular film of the same name. "Miniaturized" guests scramble through a world of giant LEGOs, 9-foot Cheerios, and spiderwebs three stories high. It's the perfect place for kids to blow off steam and very popular with the under-10 set. The only complaint is that it needs to be about four times larger!

Insider's Secret
Stay alert inside Honey, I Shrunk the Kids. When a child enters a tunnel or climbs to the top of a slide, it's often difficult to judge exactly where she'll emerge. For that reason, the attraction could be called "Honey, I Lost the Kids."

Muppet*Vision 3-D
The Muppets combine slapstick and high wit, so everyone from preschoolers to adults will find something to make them laugh. Kids love the 3-D glasses and the eye-popping special effects. And the preshow is nearly as clever as the 20-minute main

Helpful Hint
The 3-D effects are more convincing if you sit near the center toward the back of the theater.

The Scare Factor
Although Muppet*Vision 3-D tested highly among kids ages 2 to 5, some parents reported that children under 2 were unnerved by the sheer volume of the finale.

show. This is a good choice for early afternoon when you've ridden several rides and would like to just sit and laugh for a while.

Lights, Motors, Action!—Extreme Stunt Show
Based on the popular Moteurs . . . Action! Stunt Show Spectacular at Disneyland Paris, this show features special cars, motorcycles, and Jet Skis built to blow up, split in half, and perform other high-octane stunts. When the show starts you've been

Helpful Hint
Lights, Motors, Action! shows in a large arena, but you should still try to be there 20 minutes in advance. Showtimes will be listed on your entertainment schedule and the tip board on Hollywood Boulevard.

The Scare Factor
The volley of engines is very loud and may startle babies and toddlers.

transported to a movie set where the director is filming chase scenes and other daring feats with a cast and crew of 50. The show is fast, furious . . . and a great addition to the Backlot area, which has gotten a general sprucing up in the last two years.

"The Lights, Motors, Action! stunt show was incredible," wrote one mother of two from Massachusetts. "We saw it twice. It's an especially good show for boys since some of the other shows at Hollywood are a little girly."

American Idol

Fans of the TV show will love Hollywood's newest attraction. A sign as you enter the park directs would-be superstars on where to audition, and the most promising performers are given a quick vocal lesson, a mini-makeover, and a slot to perform during one of the day's scheduled shows. Theme-park guests—with the help of critiques by professional judges who humorously fill the shoes of Randy, Paula, and Simon—choose a winner from each show, and these singers move on to the last show of the day. Whoever wins this Finale Show gets front-of-the-line access to audition for the real Idol judges for the 2010 season.

Even if you're too tone-deaf to audition, watching the shows and voting is a lot of fun, and the studio is an amazing mock-up of the Idol set. Showtimes are listed in your entertain-

Insider's Secret

Any *High School Musical* fans in the crowd? Then check out the "pep rally" held several times a day in front of The Great Movie Ride. The show is a simple, lip-synched affair, but this doesn't seem to matter to the squealing young girls who show up in droves. "The show gives kids the chance to go out and interact with the performers, learning part of the dance," said one father. "For my daughter, this was a priceless experience." Note: Themes for the street shows change quickly at Disney, so don't make any promises until you verify that HSM is still in town.

ment guide, and, needless to say, the Finale Show is the hardest to get into. Show up early to get a seat. For the sake of the understandably nervous amateur singers, kids need to be old enough to enjoy watching the "filming" of a mock TV show and sit in reasonable silence during a 35-minute presentation.

Meeting the Characters at Hollywood

Hollywood is a great place to meet the characters. Consult your map or the tip board, which is midway down Hollywood Boulevard, for the times and places they'll appear and check out these locations.

- A variety of characters greets you at park opening and return to the entrances around 3 PM.

- The Pixar characters can be seen across from Toy Story Mania.

- The stars of Cars can be found in their own little garage to the right of the entrance into Lights, Motors, Action! Extreme Stunt Show.

- The newest Disney stars are inside the Animation Studio.

- Playhouse Disney stars are in the Animation Courtyard.

Food Choices at Hollywood

The Hollywood Brown Derby is one of the best restaurants inside a Disney theme park—or any theme park, for that matter. Although it has gourmet cuisine and a beautifully urbane setting, it's still casual and friendly enough to take the kids. The menu changes seasonally and is frequently updated, but one thing that's always available is the signature Cobb Salad.

Helpful Hint

It's always a good idea to make reservations for sit-down restaurants, but if you arrive at Hollywood without a reservation, drop by the dining information booth on Hollywood Boulevard and see what's left. If you're willing to eat at an off time like 4 PM, you may still get in.

Other Hollywood restaurants offer big doses of fun for kids. The '50s Prime Time Café plunks you down in the middle of a television sitcom and serves comfort food like meat loaf, milk shakes, and mac and cheese. TVs play nonstop, you're seated in replicas of baby-boomer kitchens, and the waitress pretends to be your mom. Before the meal is over, everyone gets into the act, and "Mom" is likely to inspect your hands for cleanliness before she'll feed you or she may force the kids to finish their green beans using the dreaded airplane technique.

Equally campy is the Sci-Fi Dine-In Theater Restaurant, where you eat in cars as if you were at a drive-in movie. Your waiters are carhops, the film clips are unbelievably cheesy, and the waiters add to the fun by presenting your bill as a speeding ticket. (Kids are often "driving" so they're usually presented with the bill. If they can't pay they may have to wax the car.) Drinks even come with glow-in-the-dark ice cubes. The one drawback to the Sci-Fi is that the monster clips which are shown on the drive-in screen are so graphic and so huge that they alarm some children, and the creepiness is accentuated by the fact that the restaurant is extremely dark.

Due to its out-of-the-way location near Muppet*Vision 3-D, Mama Melrose's is definitely the least crowded and the fastest of the sit-down places. The pizzas and salads are very good; the veal saltimbocca and penne *alla vodka* are excellent.

Helpful Hint

Villains in Vogue is the perfect place to shop for Halloween costumes because all the bad guys (and girls) are represented. Rather go as a princess? Check out In Character near Voyage of the Little Mermaid. If there's a Wookiee in the party, head to Tatooine Traders, just outside of Star Tours, to find costumes of your favorite *Star Wars* characters.

If you just want a quick nosh, the Backlot Express lives up to its name and serves burgers and salads fast. The ABC Commissary has a fairly unusual menu for a fast-food place, with some Mexican and Chinese dishes mixed in with the sandwiches and salads. If your party can't agree on what to eat, head for the open-air food court called the Sunset Ranch Market on Sunset Boulevard. You can each go in different directions for pizza, hot dogs, turkey legs, ice cream, and fruit, then all meet back at your table.

Tips for Your Last Hour at Hollywood

@ To guarantee yourself a seat for Fantasmic!, you'll need to enter the stadium at least an hour in advance, 90 minutes during the on-season. That's quite a wait, so you may want to eat dinner while you hold your seat. The stadium sells hot dogs and such, but if you want a more elaborate meal, you can buy fast food from anywhere in the park and carry it in.

@ If you're not watching Fantasmic!, the last hour before closing is a great time to hit any attraction you missed early in the day or to revisit favorites. Just be sure to be out of the park before the show wraps up. The big fireworks salvo at the end is your cue to get moving toward the exits.

Tips for Leaving Hollywood

@ Although a terrific show that more than justifies any inconvenience, Fantasmic! draws virtually everyone in the park to one spot at closing. Ergo, exiting afterward is a nightmare. Since navigating the crowd is so difficult, many families abandon their rental stroller before the show and simply carry their kids out.

Insider's Secret
You can save yourself some waiting if you buy the Fantasmic! Dinner Package, which includes a meal at one of Hollywood's sit-down restaurants plus reserved seating (in a specific part of the theater, not in specific seats). The seating area is way over to one side of the stadium, hardly the best view, but at least you know you'll be seated. Present Fantasmic Dinner prices for adults are $33 at Mama Melrose's, $27–$31 at Hollywood and Vine, and $47 at the Hollywood Brown Derby.

@ Try to sit near the back of the Mickey section so you'll not only have the best view but also the best shot at getting out fast and beating the crowds to the buses, trams, or water taxis. But be forewarned—this is prime real estate and fills up early. If you end up near the water or in one of the sections to the extreme right or extreme left of the stadium, you've got no choice but to deal with the crowd. One option is to sit tight and wait for the stadium to at least partially empty then eat or shop your way through the park, allowing most of the people to exit ahead of you.

ⓔ Exiting the park, especially in the midst of the post-Fantasmic! crowd, can be intense, slow, and, at times, claustrophobic. Be patient, and keep track of everyone in your party.

8. The Animal Kingdom

Disney's Animal Kingdom

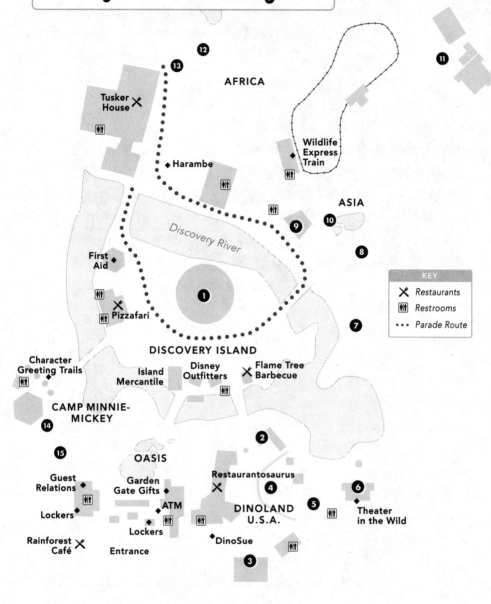

AFRICA

Tusker House ✕

Harambe ◆

Wildlife Express Train

❶❷

❶❸

❶❷

ASIA

❿

Discovery River

❾

First Aid ◆

❽

❶

✕ Pizzafari

❼

DISCOVERY ISLAND

Character Greeting Trails

Island Mercantile

Disney Outfitters

Flame Tree ✕ Barbecue

CAMP MINNIE-MICKEY

❶❹

❶❺

OASIS

Garden Gate Gifts

Restaurantosaurus ✕

❷

Guest Relations ◆

ATM

❹

❻

Lockers ◆

DINOLAND U.S.A.

❺

Theater in the Wild ◆

Rainforest ✕ Café

Lockers

Entrance

DinoSue ◆

❸

KEY

✕	Restaurants
🚻	Restrooms
•••	Parade Route

Getting to the Animal Kingdom

The Animal Kingdom parking lot is relatively small; all on-site hotels run direct shuttles and many off-site hotels do as well. If possible, arrive by bus. If you're coming by car, try to arrive early, before the main parking lot is filled. Otherwise, you'll be directed to an auxiliary lot.

Getting Around the Animal Kingdom

With more than 500 acres, technically the Animal Kingdom is the largest of all the Disney parks, but most of the space is earmarked for animal habitats, such as the huge 100-acre savanna featured in Kilimanjaro Safaris. The walkable part of the park is relatively compact—a good thing since the only real means of getting around is on foot. The layout is basically circular, with the 14-story Tree of Life in the center. This may sound like the Animal Kingdom is easy enough to navigate, but in the middle of the day the area around the main entrance can become so crowded that it's nearly impassable. If you're trying to move around the park, your best bet is to cut through the Asia section, essentially going behind the Tree of Life. It looks like you're going out of your way (and, to some degree, you are), but the traffic flow works more in your favor.

At Disney World it's easy to fall into the trap of thinking "the faster you go, the more you'll see," but at the Animal Kingdom, the opposite is true. Slow your pace a little, because this park is designed for savoring. There are more than 1,700 live animals representing more than 250 species in the Animal Kingdom, and the park is also a botanical marvel, showcasing more than 3,000 species of plants. So, relax and enjoy the incredible natural beauty of the park and the many small-animal habitats tucked along the way.

Tips for Your First Hour in the Animal Kingdom

- On Extra Magic Hour mornings, only a few attractions will be operative during the first hour, but they will be indicated on a sign as you enter.

- The Oasis is the entry area, much like Main Street in the Magic Kingdom, and it often opens 30 minutes before the stated entry time. Characters are usually on hand to keep the kids entertained.

Insider's Secret

When the park opens, attendants are usually standing near the Tree of Life, directing you toward attractions. Because they're on walkie-talkies with the operators of the rides, these cast members can give you approximate wait times and save you from hotfooting it to a ride only to find a 40-minute wait. The tip board in front of the Tree of Life also lists upcoming showtimes and the approximate wait time for major attractions.

@ The animal habitat areas in the Oasis are charming, but don't visit them in the morning. You'll be stampeded by the people behind you hustling to get to the big rides . . . not to mention the fact that you need to hustle to the big rides yourself. It's better to visit the Oasis in the afternoon or evening, on your way out of the park. That way it's not a big deal if you stand there for 20 minutes waiting for the three-toed sloth to move.

@ Head first to Expedition Everest. If the wait is less than 20 minutes, ride.

@ Next, cross through Asia to Africa and ride Kilimanjaro Safaris.

Attractions at the Animal Kingdom Offering Fastpasses

Dinosaur

Expedition Everest

It's Tough to be a Bug!

Kali River Rapids

Kilimanjaro Safaris

Primeval Whirl

Animal Kingdom Touring Tips

@ Because of the relatively small number of attractions, you can tour the Animal Kingdom in about six hours. The park is often mobbed between 10 AM and 3 PM, but it usually begins to clear out by mid-afternoon. If you can't be there first thing in the morning, consider arriving after lunch.

Quick Guide to

Attraction	Location	Height Requirement
The Boneyard	DinoLand	None
Character Greeting Area	Camp Minnie-Mickey	None
Dinosaur	DinoLand	40 inches
Expedition Everest	Asia	44 inches
Festival of the Lion King	Camp Minnie-Mickey	None
Finding Nemo—the Musical	DinoLand	None
Flights of Wonder	Asia	None
Kali River Rapids	Asia	38 inches
Kilimanjaro Safaris	Africa	None
Maharajah Jungle Trek	Asia	None
Pangani Forest Exploration Trail	Africa	None
Pocahontas and Her Forest Friends	Camp Minnie-Mickey	None
Primeval Whirl	DinoLand	48 inches
Rafiki's Planet Watch	Africa	None
Tree of Life—It's Tough to be a Bug!	Discovery Island	None
TriceraTop Spin	DinoLand	None

Scare Factor

0 = Unlikely to scare any child of any age.
! = Has dark or loud elements; might rattle some toddlers.
!! = A couple of gotcha! moments; should be fine for school-age kids.
!!! = You need to be pretty big and pretty brave to handle this ride.

Animal Kingdom Attractions

Speed of Line	Duration of Ride/Show	Scare Factor	Age Range
n/a	n/a	0	All
Moderate	n/a	0	All
Moderate	10 min.	!!!	7 and up
Moderate	10 min.	!!!	8 and up
Moderate	25 min.	0	All
Moderate	30 min.	0	All
Fast	25 min.	0	All
Moderate	7 min.	!	4 and up
Moderate	20 min.	!	6 and up
Fast	n/a	0	All
Moderate	n/a	0	All
Fast	12 min.	0	All
Slow	7 min.	!!	5 and up
Fast	20 min.	0	All
Slow	10 min.	!	All
Slow	4 min.	!	All

Insider's Secret

In your dash to get to the rides and shows, don't forget that the Animal Kingdom is really all about the animals. The Maharajah Jungle Trek and Pangani Forest Exploration Trail are major attractions, as well designed as any zoo, and there are other small enclaves of animal habitats around the Tree of Life.

© Don't feel that you have to see all the live shows, which may be too much sitting for young children. Festival of the Lion King and Finding Nemo are must-sees, but read the descriptions of the others, and choose those that sound the most interesting or age-appropriate.

© Because of their proximity, consider combining a morning visit to the Animal Kingdom and an afternoon visit to Blizzard Beach. The parks are five minutes apart by car and many hotel buses stop at both.

The Animal Kingdom Don't-Miss List

Dinosaur (if your kids are 7 or older)

Expedition Everest (if kids are 8 or older and at least 44 inches tall)

Festival of the Lion King

It's Tough to be a Bug!

Kali River Rapids

Kilimanjaro Safaris

Maharajah Jungle Trek

Pangani Forest Exploration Trail

@ The Animal Kingdom closes early (between 5 and 7 PM depending on the season) and has no closing show.

Animal Kingdom Attractions

The attractions may be few in number, but they're powerful in impact. Most of the rides and shows are designed for the whole family to enjoy together.

On Discovery Island

Mickey's Jammin' Jungle Parade

This cute 15-minute parade, featuring the characters "on safari," runs every afternoon, usually at 4 PM. (Check the tip board to confirm showtime and your map to confirm the parade route.) Expect beautiful animal puppetry, amazing stilt-walkers, and a lot of wacky visual humor. Although crowds don't get as thick as those at the Magic Kingdom parades, it's a good idea to stake your space at least 15 minutes before showtime.

Tree of Life—It's Tough to be a Bug!

This state-of-the-art 3-D film is a real highlight for all ages. First of all, it's shown inside the Tree of Life, which is an absolutely amazing edifice with 325 animals carved seamlessly into its trunk. Perfect for pictures.

The show combines visual, sensory, and tactile effects and the cast of characters, including an accurately named Stinkbug, is so funny that everyone leaves the attraction laughing. The best effect of all is at the very end of the show.

The Scare Factor

It's Tough to be a Bug! is a huge hit with most kids, but there are a couple of scary scenes. At one point, large spider puppets drop from the ceiling and dangle over your head. Later, the theater goes dark, you hear the sounds of swarming wasps, and there's the chance that the back of your seat might give you a small electrical zap, indicating you've been stung. (Not into pain? Simply lean forward in your seat.) Most children seem to find Flik and friends to be great fun, but there's usually at least one child crying in the audience at every performance, and we've gotten letters from quite a few readers who ended up actually having to carry kids out. If your kids are scared of the dark or bugs, skip the show. "My 7-year-old girl is normally a brave thing," wrote a mom from England. "She went on Tower of Terror, Space Mountain, Expedition Everest, etc., with no problem at all. But It's Tough to be a Bug! scared her so badly she was ready to leave. Stress to parents that sometimes shows with a dark, scary atmosphere are more upsetting to children than wild roller coasters."

In Africa

Kilimanjaro Safaris

This is the Animal Kingdom's premiere attraction, a ride that simulates an African photo safari. The animals have a great deal of open space around them and, in fact, appear to be running free—although cleverly incorporated water and plant barriers ensure that the cheetahs don't meet up

Time-Saving Tip

Want to ride twice? Get a Fastpass.

with the ostriches and graphically illustrate the circle of life in front of you.

Your guide helps you tell the impalas from the gazelles and at times your vehicle (called a lorry) comes startlingly close to the wildlife. The story line is that you're helping the reserve's game warden look for poachers who have abducted a baby elephant.

Because the animals do have so much room to roam along the 2-mile route, some safari trips yield more sightings than others do. Safari drivers say that the animals are often active in the morning, but that you have a better chance of seeing cheetahs, rhinos, and warthogs later in the day. And because of the attraction's mammoth and unpredictable animal cast, Kilimanjaro is, in essence, a different adventure every time. You could go on one safari in the morning and return in the afternoon for a whole new show. Consider this report from a grandmother of seven: "Because we live near Orlando we visit Disney World often and never tire of the Animal Kingdom. We have found the best time to see lots of animals on Kilimanjaro Safaris is on a rainy, drizzly day. If you can time your visit for just after a shower, you'll see plenty of animals walking around enjoying the cool fresh air."

Pangani Forest Exploration Trail
Near the exit of Kilimanjaro Safaris is a self-guided walking trail. The highlight is seeing the jungle home of Gino, the silverback gorilla, and his harem. (The dominant male in a gorilla troop is called the silverback because he is ordinarily older than the other males and often has gray hairs mixed in with the black.) Along the trail you also pass everything from mole rats to hippos to birds in an enclosed aviary, but children seem to especially enjoy the warthogs and meerkats in the savanna exhibit. Trail Guides are on hand to answer questions and help point out the animals.

Helpful Hint

Save Rafiki's Planet Watch for early afternoon, when you've toured most of the major attractions.

Rafiki's Planet Watch

If you're interested in learning more about how Disney cares for the animals in the park, this attraction will answer many of your questions.

You board a nifty train called the Wildlife Express for a five-minute ride to Rafiki's Planet Watch. Along the way, you'll see where the animals sleep at night—a cool peek behind the scenes that older

Helpful Hint

The actual conservation station is a 10-minute walk from where the train lets you out so if you have younger kids who need strollers, plan accordingly.

kids appreciate. You disembark at Rafiki's Planet Watch, an utterly out-of-the-way station in the farthest-flung section of the park. There you'll find exhibits on the subjects of conservation and animal endangerment. Kids especially enjoy touring the veterinary labs where newborns and sick animals get a lot of attention and the Affection Station, where they can pat and touch the friendly goats, llamas, and sheep. Rafiki is often on hand to do autographs, pictures, and hugs. Check your entertainment schedule for times he is due to appear.

Helpful Hint

Rafiki's Planet Watch, a bit like Tom Sawyer's Island in the Magic Kingdom, requires time and effort for the round trip. If you're on a tight schedule you can save this one for another visit.

In DinoLand

Dinosaur

You're strapped into "high-speed" motion vehicles and sent back in time to the Cretaceous period to save the gentle, plant-eating iguanodon from extinction.

Helpful Hint

A character greeting area is to the right just before you cross the bridge into DinoLand. A sign tells you which characters you'll find waiting.

It's a noble mission, but it ain't easy. Along the way, Disney throws everything it has at you: asteroids, meteors, incoming pterodactyls, and ticked-off people-eating dinosaurs. The dinosaurs are extremely lifelike and in some cases, extremely close. The jeeps bounce around like mad, so Dinosaur can be a bit rough—but it's also a powerfully fun ride.

The Scare Factor

Dinosaur combines atmospheric scariness with a wild-moving vehicle. The height requirement is 40 inches, which means that plenty of preschoolers qualify to board; nonetheless, based on the realism of the dinosaurs, we say wait until kids are at least 7 to ride, and even then consider whether they're brave enough to handle very big, very loud dinosaurs jumping out at them while the car takes steep drops. "As much as our young son (age 7) loves dinosaurs, this ride proved to be too much for him," wrote a mom of two. "We are planning another trip to Disney this year, and he still reminds us that he is not going on the dinosaur ride again. The size and closeness of the effects just proved to be too much."

Finding Nemo—the Musical (In Theater in the Wild)

Based on the animated film, *Finding Nemo,* this kid-pleasing musical combines performances by puppets, dancers, and acrobats, all choreographed to envelop you in Nemo's big blue world. The puppets, created by the same team who brought *The Lion King* to Broadway, are especially amazing and the special effects are dazzling.

The story will be familiar to anyone who's seen the movie—Nemo and his father, Marlin, go on separate journeys that ultimately teach them how to understand each other. The catchy pop music and the multigenerational humor are designed to appeal to all age groups. Finding Nemo is a great attraction for the whole family.

 Time-Saving Tip
Because of the proximity of the two attractions, Finding Nemo is a good place to take younger kids while older siblings wait in line and ride Expedition Everest. Arrive at the theater 30 minutes ahead of showtime to get good seats.

The Boneyard

A great attraction for kids 7 and under, the Boneyard is a playground designed to simulate an archaeological dig site. Kids can dig for "fossils," excavate "bones," and play on bridges and slides. The playground is visually witty—where else can you find slides made from prehistoric animal skeletons?—and has fun surprises, such as a footprint that roars when you jump on it.

Visit the Boneyard after you've toured the biggies and the kids are ready to romp for a while. The play area can get very hot on a Florida afternoon, however, so remember the sunscreen and water bottles. If it's a really roasting day, head for the woolly mammoth dig site area, which is covered and has large

Helpful Hint

The good news is that kids can lose themselves in the Boneyard and happily play for an hour. The bad news is that parents can lose their kids as well. The Boneyard is sprawling, so keep your eyes on young children at all times, especially when they're playing on the slides. When they enter at the top, it's often hard to tell what chute they're in or where they'll emerge.

fans to cut down on the heat. "My 3-year-old loved the dig site," reported one father. "We hung out there for about an hour while my wife took the older kids on Dinosaur."

A "mini-land" in the middle of DinoLand, Chester and Hester's Dino-Rama is a tribute to the owners of the campy T-shirt and trinket shop near the exit to Dinosaur. Expect traditional midway games and a pair of we-guarantee-you'll-learn-nothing-here rides.

Hidden Mickey

In Boneyard's woolly mammoth dig, there's a Hidden Mickey formed by two hard hats and a fan.

TriceraTop Spin

The first is the kid-friendly TriceraTop Spin, a circular ride similar to Dumbo, except that you fly in dinosaurs, naturally. The beasts tilt back and forth as you climb or descend.

The Scare Factor

If they loved Dumbo, they'll love TriceraTop Spin.

Helpful Hint
The Boneyard and TriceraTop Spin are a good place for parents to take younger kids while their older siblings ride Dinosaur.

Primeval Whirl
The second ride in Chester and Hester's Dino-Rama is Primeval Whirl, a crazy mouse–style coaster with spinning cars, hairpin turns, and numerous dips. Primeval Whirl is a slow-

The Scare Factor
A bit surprisingly, Primeval Whirl has a 48-inch height requirement. The ride is faster than it looks and has many spins. Most kids over 5 (assuming they make the height requirement) love it, but if you have any doubts, watch it make a cycle or two before joining the queue. And this is not a good choice for anyone prone to motion sickness.

boarding, low-capacity ride and can draw major lines. If you're visiting on a busy day, use Fastpass.

In Camp Minnie-Mickey

Character Greeting Area
Camp Minnie-Mickey is the Animal Kingdom equivalent of Toontown. You can find separate greeting areas where you can line up to meet the characters, all adorably decked out in safari gear. The greeting areas are especially busy just after a showing of Festival of the Lion King.

Festival of the Lion King
This is one of the best attractions in the Animal Kingdom.
　　Festival of the Lion King features what you might expect—singers, dancers, the characters—as well as acrobatic

"monkeys" twirling fire batons, and "birds" that dramatically take flight. The costuming is incredible, the music is wonderful, and the finale is guaranteed to give you goose bumps.

The performers interact directly with the audience, and at one point small children from the crowd are invited to join in a simple circular parade. Children sitting near the front are more apt to be tapped.

Festival of the Lion King is very popular. Showtimes are printed on your entertainment schedule; be there at least 30 minutes beforehand if you'd like to sit near the front.

Helpful Hint

For the big shows, factor in not only the time you'll spend in the show but also the time you'll spend in line. "We visited on a crowded summer day when they were suggesting that people be at the theaters 45 minutes before showtime for both Finding Nemo and the Lion King," wrote one mom. "That cut into our eight-hour day so badly that we had to end up just picking one show."

Pocahontas and Her Forest Friends

This sweet little show is a good choice for younger kids but tends to bore older siblings. Pocahontas, Grandmother Willow, and live animals team up to deliver a gentle lesson about protecting our wildlife. Although the animals featured vary, you might see an armadillo, a skunk, snakes, and birds. The theater is small so you can sit quite close to the stage—and the animals.

Showtimes are indicated on your entertainment schedule, and it's rarely necessary to show up more than 10 minutes early. Visit in the afternoon when the rest of the park is crowded and you'll enjoy resting a bit. Showtimes for the animal training sessions are indicated on your entertainment schedule.

In Asia

Kali River Rapids

For this water ride, you board an eight-passenger raft for a descent down a meandering river through rapids, geysers, and waterfalls. Expect to get very wet, possibly soaked, depending on where you're sitting in the raft. (And since the rafts are circular and constantly turning throughout the ride, it's impossible to predict which seats will catch the most spray.) Stow cameras and other water-sensitive valuables in lockers before you board, and bring your trusty poncho.

It's also a good idea to keep your feet up on the center bar. A wet fanny is an inconvenience, but wet shoes and socks can lead to blisters and ruin your whole day. Also consider bringing a change of clothes. One mom said her soaking wet child burst into tears and had to be taken back to the hotel to change. Here are comments from another: "They aren't kidding when they say you'll get wet on Kali River Rapids. We rode first thing in the morning, expecting to get splashed, and we really got soaked. It was so uncomfortable we had to go back to our room to change clothes. Now we know to ride it later in the day, preferably just as we're about to leave the Animal Kingdom."

The Scare Factor

The height requirement is only 38 inches, reflecting the fact that Kali River Rapids is a very mild ride, with only one sizable descent along the way. It's fine for anyone who isn't afraid of getting wet.

Maharajah Jungle Trek

Another lovely walking path, this one goes through habitats of Asia. The Bengal tigers are the undisputed stars of the show, but you'll also encounter Komodo dragons, gibbons, and, most

Insider's Secret

Are some of your kids too young or too short to ride? Let them man Kali's water cannons on the bridge as you approach the ride; there they can take aim against their older siblings as they pass in the rafts below. Revenge is sweet! And to be honest, soaking strangers can be fun, too.

intriguing of all, giant fruit bats. Take time along the path to appreciate the glorious landscaping and the beauty of the architecture. In fact, if you only have time to choose one animal path, the Maharajah Jungle Trek gets the nod over Pangani Forest Exploration

Hidden Mickey

The Maharajah Jungle Trek is Hidden Mickey city. There are several in the drawings on the ruins just as you enter the tiger habitat.

Trail, largely because the tigers lie around more—and thus are more likely to be in viewing range—than the gorillas.

Flights of Wonder

The Caravan Stage is home to this lovely display of birds in free flight. The show's premise is a bit silly, but you can count on seeing falcons, vultures, hawks, and toucans demonstrating their unusual talents. Several members of the audience, including kids, are invited onstage to interact with the birds. Showtimes are noted on your entertainment schedule; be there 10 minutes before showtime to assure a good seat, 20 minutes during the on-season. Flights of Wonder is a good choice for the most crowded times of the afternoon.

Expedition Everest

Expedition Everest is the Animal Kingdom's most popular ride, and one of the most exciting attractions in all of Disney World. The premise is that your mountain train is chugging up the snowy mountainside when it suddenly encounters a break in the track. Uh-oh. The trip back down not only involves wild plunges and even wilder speeds, but you also meet up with the yeti that lives in the mountain, and, rumor has it, he's not in a good mood. Your train races both forward and backward through bamboo forests and glacier fields as you attempt to escape his rage. There are tight turns, and you take some of them going backward.

Helpful Hint

Expedition Everest draws major crowds and some very long lines. Although the ride does board quickly and the lines do move fast, come in the morning, or use Fastpass.

The ride is a huge hit with our readers, with almost 80% of them listing it as their favorite attraction in the Animal Kingdom. "I expected my 11-year-old to like it," wrote one mom from Arizona, "but to my surprise my 6-year-old loved it just as much. Even my father-in-law insisted on riding twice!"

The Scare Factor

Although Expedition Everest doesn't have the corkscrews and flips that are at Rock 'n' Roller Coaster, the yeti is indeed slightly more frightening than Steven Tyler. Also, the train moves at almost twice the speed of Space Mountain, which means the ride will probably be too intense for kids under 8. The height requirement is 44 inches.

Insider's Secret

The Animal Kingdom provides interactive entertainment throughout the park. Cast members are stationed with animals throughout the park, and kids are welcome to ask questions and have up-close encounters with the bugs, birds, reptiles, and small mammals. At the Dawa Bar in the Africa section you'll find storytellers, music, African drumming, and the amazing Karuka Acrobats.

And keep an eye out for DeVine, a moving human topiary, who can often be found literally hanging around the park. She blends in so well with the vegetation that she's been known to startle some guests.

Food Choices in the Animal Kingdom

Since the Animal Kingdom closes the earliest of all the parks—usually between 5 and 7 PM, depending on the season—people rarely eat dinner there. There are two sit-down restaurants: the Rainforest Café, which is just as you enter the park, and open for breakfast, lunch, and dinner and the Yak & Yeti, an Asian-fusion restaurant with table-service, a full bar, quick-service options, and a beer garden.

The Tusker House in Africa is the site of the Animal Kingdom's only character breakfast. Reserve before you leave home by calling 407/WDW–DINE. (After the character breakfast is over each day, the Tusker House serves buffets for lunch and dinner. It remains one of the few places in the Animal Kingdom where you can consistently count on finding fresh vegetables.) "The food at the Tusker House character breakfast was outstanding," said one mom of three. "We loved the Jungle Juice and the Mickey waffles. My daughter was so happy to finally meet Daisy Duck, and the characters do a little song that's really cute."

Pizzafari, near Camp Minnie-Mickey, and Flame Tree Barbecue, near the entrance to DinoLand, are also good lunch choices. All of the restaurants have outdoor patios, where you can take your food, find a pretty view, and really relax. These lush, shady eating areas in the Animal Kingdom help blur the line between fast-food and sit-down dining.

The Dawa Bar, adjacent to the Tusker House patio, offers alcoholic beverages and entertainment in the afternoon.

Tips for Your Last Hour in the Animal Kingdom

@ Why is there no big closing show at the Animal Kingdom? Most evening shows require fireworks, lasers, and other pyrotechnics, and all that noise and light would scare the animals.

@ Since there's no closing show, midday crowds drift out of the Animal Kingdom throughout the afternoon and early evening, and leaving isn't a problem. Return to the parking lot or bus station whenever it suits your schedule.

The Disney World Water Parks

Typhoon Lagoon

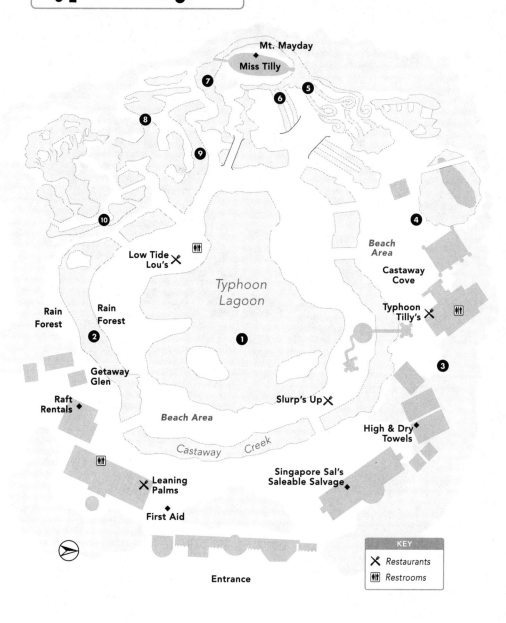

Mt. Mayday

Miss Tilly

7

5

6

8

9

4

Beach
Area

10

Castaway
Cove

Low Tide ✕ 🚻
Lou's

Typhoon
Lagoon

Typhoon ✕ 🚻
Tilly's

Rain
Forest

Rain
Forest

2

1

3

Getaway
Glen

Slurp's Up ✕

Raft
Rentals ◆

High & Dry ◆
Towels

Beach Area

Castaway Creek

🚻

Singapore Sal's
Saleable Salvage ◆

✕ Leaning
Palms

First Aid ◆

KEY
✕ Restaurants
🚻 Restrooms

Entrance

Getting to the Water Parks

On-site visitors can take the bus to both Typhoon Lagoon and Blizzard Beach, but expect a long commute. Getting to Typhoon Lagoon may involve sitting through three stops at Downtown Disney, and getting to Blizzard Beach often involves a stop at the Animal Kingdom. Plus, guests of the Magic Kingdom resorts (the Grand Floridian, Contemporary, Wilderness Lodge, and Fort Wilderness) have to go to the TTC and then transfer to a water park bus. In other words, bus travel can be a headache. If you have a car, drive to the water parks.

For off-site visitors a car is definitely the best option. If you don't have one, take a cab.

Try to arrive about 20 minutes ahead of the stated opening times for the parks, particularly if you're visiting in summer or during a major holiday. During midday and afternoon hours in peak seasons, the parking lots often fill to capacity.

During peak season, Extra Magic Hours allow on-site guests a little more time in the water parks. "Our extra magic evening at Typhoon Lagoon was the highlight of our entire week at Disney World," wrote one family from England. "It was a warm, starry night and perfect for swimming in the big wave pool."

Water Parks Touring Tips

- The water parks draw a rowdy preteen and teenage crowd, which means young kids and unsteady swimmers may get dunked and splashed more than they like. If your children are very young, stick to the kiddie sections (Ketchakiddee Creek in Typhoon Lagoon and Tike's Peak at Blizzard Beach), which are off-limits to older kids.

- Summer afternoons in Florida often mean thunderstorms, and even a rumble of distant thunder can lead to water park closings. If you're visiting in summer and want to make sure you have time to try everything, visit the water parks first thing in the morning.

- You can rent towels, but they're small so it makes more sense to bring your own. There are plenty of lockers ($10 small, $12 large, with a $5 refundable deposit), and the locker keys come on rubber bands that slip over your wrist or ankle, so you can keep them with you while you're in the water.

- If you arrive in the morning when a swarm of guests enters at once, getting a locker can be quite a hassle, with the rental lines sometimes 20 minutes long and the area around the lockers packed. Some families skip locker rentals altogether and keep vitals such as room keys,

Helpful Hint
Bring rubber beach shoes with nonskid bottoms if you have them. They'll protect the soles of your feet from the hot sidewalks.

charge cards, and a bit of cash in one of those flat plastic holders you wear around your neck. (They sell them in the water park gift shops for about $7.) That way they can grab the best lounge chair locations and dash straight to the rides while everyone else is still trying to get a locker.

@ You can also borrow life vests for free, although you have to leave your driver's license or a credit card as a deposit. Snorkeling equipment can be picked up for no charge at Hammerhead Fred's near the Shark Reef at Typhoon Lagoon. There's no point in bringing your own fins and floats; only official Disney equipment is allowed in the pools.

@ Because you're climbing uphill all day, half the time dragging a tube or mat behind you, the water parks are extremely exhausting. If you spend the day at one, plan to spend the evening in films or shows. Or take the night off.

@ There are fast-food restaurants at both water parks as well as places to picnic.

@ The Lost Kids Stations at both parks are so far away from the main water areas that it's unlikely your children would find their way there. Instruct them, should they look up

Helpful Hint

Trying to decide which water park to visit? We agree with this statement from a father of two from Michigan: "Last year with our extended family we visited both water parks and concluded that Typhoon Lagoon was the favorite of the adults and the younger children because it's very pretty with nice beaches and shallow places for little ones to swim. Family members age 10 to 25 preferred Blizzard Beach because of all the big slides."

and find themselves separated from you, to approach the nearest person wearing a Disney name tag. A cast member will escort the kids to the Lost Kids Station, and you can meet them there. Because both of the parks are full of meandering paths with many sets of steps and slides, it's easy to get separated from your party. Set standard meeting places and times for older kids.

@ Girls should wear one-piece swimsuits. More than one bikini top has been lost on the waterslides.

@ If you're visiting in summer, consider dropping by both Typhoon Lagoon and Blizzard Beach. They're very different experiences. Typhoon Lagoon has the better beaches and pools. Blizzard Beach is the pow! park, focusing on slides.

@ Typhoon Lagoon and Blizzard Beach are often closed for refurbishing in January and February, although it's rare for both to be closed at once unless the weather is truly cold or inclement. If you're planning a winter trip, call 407/824–4321 or visit www.disneyworld.com to see which will be open during the time you're in town.

@ Ride the slides and flumes in the morning and save the pools for the afternoon. Lines for the slides reach incredible lengths by midday.

Typhoon Lagoon

Disney calls its 56-acre Typhoon Lagoon "the world's ultimate water park," and the hyperbole is justified. Where else can you float through caves, take surfing lessons, picnic with parrots, and swim (sort of) with sharks? Typhoon Lagoon is the perfect replica of the perfect tropical isle—older kids can hit the thrill slides, younger kids can splash in the bays and dig in the sand, and parents can relax (at least in shifts) under a palm tree with a piña colada in one hand and a best seller in the other.

For anyone with a Water Park Fun & More option, entrance to Typhoon Lagoon is included. Otherwise, admission is $40 for adults and $34 for children 3 to 9, before sales tax.

Typhoon Lagoon Attractions

Crush 'n' Gusher
This thrill ride combines flumes, spillways, and steep drops, but the real kick is that you're hit so hard with pulsating streams of water that at one point in the ride your two-person raft is actually propelled back uphill. The concept behind the ride is that you're lost in an abandoned fruit-processing facility. There are three paths out—the Banana Blaster, Coconut Crusher, and Pineapple Plunger—each about 420 feet long with plenty of twists and turns along the way.

The Scare Factor
The Crush 'n' Gusher is not for the nervous. The height requirement is 48 inches; even if they're tall enough, you should probably warm up younger children on Keelhaul Falls before tackling Crush 'n' Gusher.

Humunga Kowabunga
With three enclosed waterslides that drop you a stunning five stories in a matter of seconds, Humunga Kowabunga is definitely a thrill. Riders reach speeds of up to 30 mph!

The Scare Factor

Humunga is an intense ride that fully deserves its height requirement of 48 inches. Part of the scare factor is certainly the drop, but falling in complete darkness makes the experience even more intense. Nonetheless, once people ride it and get over that initial trepidation, they usually climb right back up to do it again.

Storm Slides

The Storm Slides are curvier and thus a little tamer than a straight plunge down the mountain. Each of the three slides offers a slightly different route, although none is necessarily wilder than the others.

The Scare Factor

Kids of any age can ride the Storm Slides, but they need to be fairly confident in the water. Although the pool you land in at the bottom isn't deep, you do hit the water with enough force to temporarily disorient a nervous swimmer. Most kids 7 to 11 love these zesty little slides, and, if they're good swimmers, some kids even younger can handle the Storm Slides.

Mayday Falls and Keelhaul Falls

A Disney employee helps you climb into your inner tube and begin your winding journey down a white-water stream. The journey is fast, giggle inducing, and has enough turns that you often feel like you're about to lose your tube.

The Scare Factor

Keelhaul Falls is slightly milder than Mayday, so let younger children try it first. Cast members can provide some smaller inner tubes with built-in bottoms. Kids as young as 4 have reported loving this ride.

Gangplank Falls

You weather these white-water rapids in four-passenger rafts. Slower and calmer (but much bumpier) than Mayday or Keelhaul, Gangplank is a good choice for families with kids who are nervous about tackling a white-water ride on their own. Gangplank Falls does load slowly, however, and the ride is short, so hit it early in the morning before the line becomes prohibitive.

Surf Pool

In this huge and incredible 2.5-acre lagoon, guests can ride machine-made waves up to 6 feet high. The waves come at 90-second intervals and are perfectly sized for tubing and body-surfing. A foghorn blast alerts you to when a big one is on its

Insider's Secret

Families with preteens and teens should consider the surfing lessons offered in the Typhoon Lagoon wave pool before the park opens in the morning. The instructors are top-notch, and since you're learning to surf in a controlled environment, almost everyone manages to catch a wave by the end of the class. The cost is $150 per person for guests 8 and up. (Prices subject to change so confirm when you book.) For details or reservations, call 407/939–7529 (407/WDW–PLAY).

way; if you're bobbing around with young kids, stay in the shallow areas, where the swells won't be too overwhelming, and you can avoid the surfers.

Toddlers and preschoolers can safely splash around in two small, roped-off coves called Blustery Bay and Whitecap Cover.

Castaway Creek

Castaway Creek is a meandering 2,000-foot river full of inner tubes. You simply wade out, find an empty tube, and climb aboard. It takes about 30 minutes to lazily circle the rain forest, with a bit of excitement at one point when riders drift under the waterfall. There are numerous exits along the creek, so anyone who doesn't want to get splashed can hop out before the falls. In fact, Castaway Creek serves as a means of transportation around the park; savvy guests who don't want to burn their feet on hot pavement or waste energy walking around often hop in and float their way from attraction to attraction.

The Scare Factor

Castaway Creek is a fun, relaxing ride appropriate for any age. The water is 3 feet deep throughout the ride, however, so keep a good grip on young kids or those who can't swim.

Shark Reef

An unusual attraction, Shark Reef is a saltwater pool where snorkelers swim "among" exotic marine life, including small leopard and hammerhead sharks. The sharks are behind Plexiglas and aren't too numerous, so anyone expecting the *Jaws* experience will be disappointed.

Disney provides the snorkeling equipment and a brief orientation on how to use it. Only official Disney equipment is al-

The Scare Factor

Shark Reef isn't scary per se, but young kids some-times struggle with the equipment and panic when they either flood their masks or suck water through their snorkel. Swimmers need to be able to confi-dently cross a 60-foot pool twice, a task that might preclude the participation of some young kids who find this too physically demanding even with a floata-tion vest. If older kids want to suit up, younger sib-lings can watch from an underwater viewing area that gives you a good view of the marine life and the snorkelers.

lowed in the pool, so don't bother packing your own masks. If you want to snorkel, it's best to visit Shark Reef in the morning. By mid-afternoon, the pool can get crowded.

Ketchakiddee Creek

This is a water playground designed for toddlers and preschool-ers, with geysers and waterspouts in the shapes of crocodiles and whales, as well as pint-size slides, a grotto with a waterfall, and a small white-water raft ride. No kids over 48 inches are al-lowed inside, which keeps the area safe for the younger kids.

Blizzard Beach

Blizzard Beach may have the cleverest theme of any Disney park. The tropical ambience of Typhoon Lagoon seems natural for a water park, but who could have predicted a melting ski lodge?

Blizzard Beach is built on the tongue-in-cheek premise that a freak snowstorm hit Orlando and a group of enterprising businesspeople built Florida's first ski resort. The sun returned in due time, and for a while it looked like all was lost—until someone spied an alligator slipping and sliding down one of the

Blizzard Beach

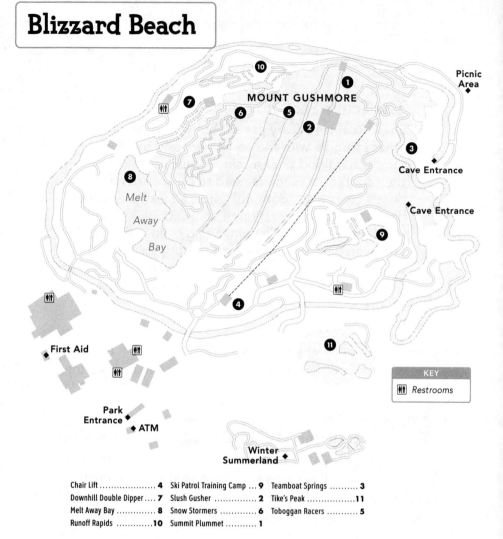

Picnic Area

MOUNT GUSHMORE

Cave Entrance

Cave Entrance

Melt Away Bay

First Aid

Park Entrance

ATM

Winter Summerland

KEY

🚻 Restrooms

slushy slopes. Thus Blizzard Beach was born. The snow may be gone but the jumps, sled runs, and slalom courses remain, resulting in a high-camp, high-thrill ski lodge in the palms. The motif extends into every element of the park: There are Plexiglas snowmen, a chalet-style restaurant, even ski marks running off the side of the mountain. And the original skiing alligator, Ice Gator, is the park mascot.

At the center of Blizzard Beach is "snowcapped" Mt. Gushmore. You can get to the top via ski lift (long line, short ride) or a series of stairs (big climb, short breath), but how you get down is up to you. The bold descend via Summit Plummet or Slush Gusher, but there are medium-intensity flumes, tube rides, and white-water raft rides as well.

Blizzard Beach was built in response to Typhoon Lagoon's popularity and has since become the busier of the two. There are big crowds in the morning, but showing up early is the only way you can ensure you'll get in at all. Like Typhoon Lagoon, Blizzard Beach is included in Water Parks and More; otherwise, admission is $40 for adults and $34 for children 3 to 9, not including sales tax.

Blizzard Beach Attractions

Summit Plummet
The icon of the park, Summit Plummet is 120 feet tall, making it considerably longer than Humunga Kowabunga at Typhoon Lagoon. From the outside, it looks like Summit Plummet riders are shooting out of the side of the mountain into midair. And in reality the ride is nearly as intense, with a 60-degree, 60-mph drop that's almost twice as fast as Space Mountain—and here you're not even riding in a car.

The Scare Factor
The height requirement for Summit Plummet is 48 inches. Although it's a very short experience—less than four seconds from top to bottom—the drop feels like free-fall and may be the most intense sensation in all of Disney World. In short, this flume is not for the faint of heart.

Slush Gusher
This is another monster slide, but with a couple of bumps along the way to slow you down. Akin in intensity to Hu-

Insider's Secret

If you're riding either Summit Plummet or the Slush Gusher, don't forget to cross your legs as you descend. Your bathing suit will still ride up, but at least you'll have some protection against the Mother of All Wedgies. And, women and girls should wear one-piece swimsuits unless they want their tops up by their ears as they land.

The Scare Factor

Kids must be 48 inches tall to ride Slush Gusher. Try it as a plunge test before you queue up for Summit Plummet.

munga Kowabunga at Typhoon Lagoon, Slush Gusher is so much fun that many kids insist on doing it more than once, despite the climb to the top and the long line.

Runoff Rapids

You take a separate set of stairs up the back of Mt. Gushmore to reach these three inner-tube rides. To start, you get to choose between tubes that seat one, two, or three people. Just remember, the heavier the raft the faster the descent, so don't assume that by piling all the kids in one raft you're toning down the experience. The rapids are great fun, and each of the slides provides a slightly different thrill so you can try it over and over. The only downside is that each time you have to troop up the seven zillion stairs (157, to be exact); visit early in the morning before your stamina fails.

Snow Stormers

This is a mock slalom run that you descend on your belly as you clutch a foam rubber "sled." The three slides are full of twists and turns that splash water into your face, and if you'd like, you can race the sledders on the other two slides to the bottom. It's so much fun that hardly anyone does it just once.

Toboggan Racers

Eight riders on rubber mats are pitted against one another on a straight ride down the mountain. The heavier the rider, the faster the descent so the attendant at the top of the slide will give kids a head start over adults. Not quite as wild as Snow Stormers, Toboggan Racers lets kids get used to the sensation of sliding downhill on a rubber sled.

Teamboat Springs

In one of the best rides in the park, the whole family can join forces to tackle the white water as a group. The round boats, which you board at the top of Mt. Gushmore, carry up to six people, and the ride downhill is zippy, with lots of splashes and sharp curves. Teamboat Springs draws an enthusiastic thumbs-up from all age groups, from preschoolers to grandparents. It's much longer, wilder, and more fun than Gangplank Falls, the comparable white-water ride at Typhoon Lagoon.

Downhill Double Dipper

On this individual tube ride, you race the rider in the other chute, going through water curtains and freefalls during your descent. At one point in the ride, you're completely airborne. The Double Dipper is fun and addictive, albeit a bit more jarring than some of the other rides at Blizzard Beach. Test the kids on nearby Runoff Rapids before you tackle it.

The Scare Factor

Downhill Double Dipper is a bit rougher than it looks and has a 48-inch height requirement.

Ski Patrol Training Camp

This special play area is designed for kids 5 to 11 who are too old for Tike's Peak but not quite ready for the big-deal rides. They can walk across icebergs, swing from T-bars, test their mountaineering skills, and ride medium-intensity slides.

Tike's Peak

This is where the toddlers and preschoolers gather to play on small slides and flumes, in igloo-style forts, and in a wading pool that looks like a broken ice-skating rink. No kids over 48 inches tall are allowed to play.

Chair Lift

The Chair Lift offers direct transportation to the top of Mt. Gushmore where Summit Plummet, Slush Gusher, and Teamboat Springs await. It's also a fun little diversion in itself, but lines can grow unbelievably long in the afternoon. Hiking up the steps is a lot faster. And while there's nothing scary about the ride, it's tough to hold on to a squirming toddler who's been slathered with sunscreen, so there's a height requirement of 32 inches.

Melt Away Bay

Unlike the huge Surfing Lagoon at Typhoon Lagoon, this swimming area is relatively small and offers mild swells instead of big waves. Fed by "melting snow" waterfalls, the pool is perfect for young kids and unsteady swimmers. There are plenty of chairs and shady huts nearby for relaxing but these tend to be claimed early in the day.

The Rest of the World

Downtown Disney

Village Lake

Cirque
du Soleil

**THE
WEST SIDE**

Disney
Quest

House of
Blues

Virgin
Megastore

Wolfgang
Puck Café

Bongo's
Cuban Café

PARKING

AMC Movie
Theaters

Planet
Hollywood

PARKING

Buena Vista Drive

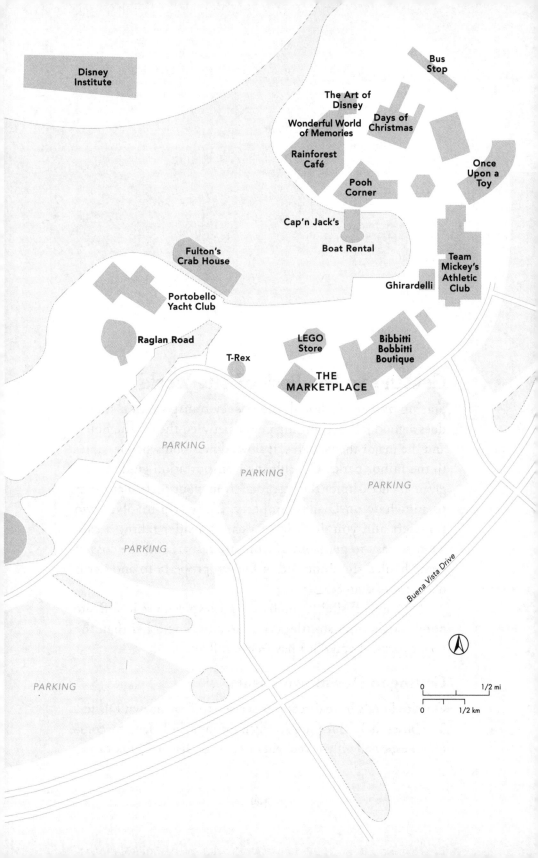

Getting to the Rest of the World

Staying on-site? Although the Disney transportation system does a good job of shuttling guests between the on-site hotels and the major theme parks, it slows down a bit when it comes to the minor parks. Consult the transportation guide you're given at check-in for the best route from your particular resort to anywhere on Disney property. If the trip involves two transfers and you don't have a car, consider taking a cab. They're easy to get from any on-site resort, and the cost of being hauled from one end of Disney property to another is never more than $20.

Staying off-site? If you have your own car, use it. Off-site hotels rarely offer shuttle service to anything other than the major parks. If you don't have a car, call a cab.

Getting to Downtown Disney

On-site hotels have direct bus service to Downtown Disney. The buses make three stops, which means a fairly lengthy commute, especially if you're trying to get to Disney Quest or the

Cirque du Soleil, both of which are at the final stop, in the West Side. Those staying at Port Orleans, Saratoga Springs, or Old Key West have boat service directly to the Marketplace, a pleasant way to get there.

In addition, on-site and off-site guests can drive directly to Downtown Disney. There's no charge for parking.

Getting to the Wide World of Sports

The fastest route is to drive your own car. Otherwise, buses are an option, but few run to this out-of-the-way location. Check your transportation guide for the best route from your resort; if more than two transfers are involved, take a cab.

Getting from One Resort to Another

On-site guests with their own car can simply drive to the new resort and inform the guard that they're visiting for dinner or some other activity. If you don't have your own car, your simplest option is to take a cab. Your cheapest option is to use the theme park that's closest to you as a transfer station. For example, if you're staying at the Grand Floridian and have dinner reservations at the BoardWalk, take the monorail to the Magic Kingdom and catch a bus to the BoardWalk from there.

Helpful Hint
Transportation options are always subject to change. To assure the best route, consult the transportation guide you're given at check-in or consult a concierge at the Guest Services (a.k.a. Guest Relations) desk of your hotel.

The Don't-Miss List for the Rest of the World

Character Breakfasts (if you have kids under 9)

Cirque du Soleil

DisneyQuest (if you have kids over 10)

Downtown Disney

Downtown Disney

The enormous entertainment, dining, and shopping complex known as Downtown Disney is packed at night. Families who'd like to visit when there are fewer crowds should show up in the afternoon and eat dinner relatively early, like at 5 PM.

"We didn't want to buy a ticket for our first day, since we were landing in Orlando around noon," reported one woman who visited with her husband and 14-year-old sister. "Instead we went to Downtown Disney, and we thought it was a great introduction to Disney World. We picked up our tickets at Guest Services, so we were all set for the following day, then we kicked off our vacation with a great meal at Fulton's Crab House and some shopping at World of Disney."

As part of a recent rehab that coincided with the closing of Pleasure Island, Downtown Disney is getting its own iconic attraction, a giant tethered balloon that will lift you 300 feet into the air, offering views of the surrounding area.

Insider's Secret

Downtown Disney is a great spot for the first night of your vacation. It doesn't require a ticket, but it still has plenty of Disney spirit.

Downtown Disney Marketplace

The Marketplace section of Downtown Disney, not surprisingly, is full of shops. A good place to start is the World of Disney, the largest Disney store on Earth, and the best place to find that perfect souvenir. Little girls will freak out at the sight of the Bibbidi Bobbidi Boutique (a.k.a. "the Princess Room"), where they can try on princess costumes, then have their hair, makeup, and nails done. Packages range from $55 for hairstyling and makeup to $205 for a complete photo portfolio and costume you can keep. Kids must be 3 and older to participate, and you can make appointments 180 days in advance by calling 407/939–7895 (407/WDW–STYL).

One word of warning: Once you've gone princess, it's hard to go back. "We were arriving in Orlando in the afternoon," wrote a mother from New York, "And as you suggested we went to Downtown Disney, so we wouldn't burn a day on our theme park tickets. We thought it would be cute to have our 5-year-old daughter Kate outfitted at Bibbidi Bobbidi Boutique to kick off her Disney vacation, but as it turns out, she was so enchanted with her new look that she refused to take down her

Helpful Hint

If you're trying to decide which boutique is best for your little princess, consider that the Magic Kingdom location—while undeniably more glamorous—requires theme park admission. To maximize your expensive tickets, it makes more sense to spend your day in the Magic Kingdom visiting attractions, not hanging out in a hair salon. Visit the Bibbidi Bobbidi Boutique at Downtown Disney on your day off, the first evening you arrive, or any other time when you're not burning a day on your ticket.

hairdo, change clothes, or wash her face for the next seven days. In pictures we took near the end of vacation, Kate looks like Belle on crack."

Another must-see is Once Upon a Toy, the ultimate shop for Disney-theme toys. Kids also enjoy Team Mickey's Athletic Club, which sells sporting equipment and clothes, and the Days of Christmas. The LEGO Store is just amazing, with enormous LEGO sea serpents, spaceships, and life-size people scattered around the lagoon, as well as a play area where kids can build their own models. Of course, without a budget, this can get out of control very fast. "I do have to take issue with your description of Downtown Disney as 'free,'" wrote one mother from Virginia. "We ended up spending more there than we did in any of the theme parks!"

If money is no object, visit the Art of Disney, where you can find limited-edition cels and other collectibles. Scrapbook hobbyists will enjoy Disney's Wonderful World of Memories next door, which offers Disney scrapbook supplies.

Hidden Mickey
Look closely at the fountains near the entrance to the Marketplace. Does the shape look familiar?

The Rainforest Café is great fun because birds and fish (real) and rhinos and giraffes (fake) surround your table while you eat. Check out the bar stools with their flamingo and zebra legs. The new restaurant T-Rex with its dinosaur theme (duh) is also oriented towards families. You're greeted by a life-size T-Rex as you enter and walk through a prehistoric environment with waterfalls, geysers, and a fossil dig site.

The part of Downtown Disney known as Pleasure Island was closed in late 2008 to make way for more shops and restaurants and will reopen in stages throughout 2009 and 2010. This will mean new shops, new restaurants, and a revamp of existing restaurants.

Insider's Secret

The Marketplace has a small play area with a few simple rides and neat interactive splash fountains to keep younger kids entertained. You can also find the world's largest—and possibly only?—perikaleidoscope (a cross between a periscope and a kaleidoscope).

Insider's Secret

Although the area formerly known as Pleasure Island is undergoing a major rehab, some shops and restaurants—including the popular Irish pub Raglan Road—are still open.

Downtown Disney West Side

The West Side is home to a variety of shops and restaurants, a 24-screen AMC theater, and a Virgin Megastore, which sometimes has concerts out front. You can also find two of Disney World's hottest attractions: DisneyQuest and Cirque du Soleil.

Bongos Cuban Café offers an Americanized version of Cuban dishes, a wild tropical decor, and throbbing Latin music.

The House of Blues serves up Cajun and Creole cooking along with live jazz, country, and blues music. The Gospel Brunch at 10:30 AM and 1 PM on Sunday is an especially good choice for families. The price is $34 for adults and $18 for kids 3 to 9. Tickets can be purchased by calling 407/934–2583 (407/934–BLUE).

Wolfgang Puck Café serves terrific pizzas and sushi downstairs. Request the upstairs dining room for a tonier adult dining.

The giant blue globe of Planet Hollywood holds props from a variety of movies, and even the menus—printed with high school graduation pictures of stars—are entertaining. Film clips run constantly on giant screens and the atmosphere is loud and cheerful.

Insider's Secret

Is there a birthday boy or girl in the group? Goofy's Candy Company has added a special room to allow families to host some pretty sweet birthday parties.

DisneyQuest

Most people call DisneyQuest an arcade simply because there isn't another name that could identify this totally unique type of play environment. Within its five levels, you will, indeed,

Helpful Hint

DisneyQuest is large and loud, and each play zone has steps leading to other levels. In other words, it's easy to lose your kids. If you're going to let older kids and teens explore on their own, pick a designated time and place to regroup.

find classic arcade games. But you'll also find high-tech inter-active experiences that almost defy description.

Favorite games include Pirates of the Caribbean, where you take the deck to battle phantom buccaneers, and Virtual Jungle Cruise, an exhausting river-raft ride in which you paddle through the rapids of a prehistoric world. During your stay you can also battle comic book villains, rescue settlers from an uprising on an alien planet, shoot foam balls at your competitors in a bumper-car war, and become a human joystick in a hockey-style pinball game.

Helpful Hint

No strollers are allowed inside DisneyQuest, and there are a lot of stairs. Plan accordingly.

The centerpiece attraction of DisneyQuest is Cy-berSpace Mountain. Bill Nye the Science Guy helps you design your own virtual roller coaster. You can build in as many flips, spirals, and hills as time and distance allow; program in the speed of the car; and even get to name the sucker. When you're finished, your coaster is given a scariness rating from 1 to 5, meaning that you can either design a gentle, rolling grade-1 coaster suitable for kids or a flip-you-over, slam-you-down grade-5 coaster. (If your coaster gets a rating that's too mild or too wild, you can always redesign it.) Then you enter a booth where you're strapped into a capsule, and you ride a virtual re-

Time-Saving Tip

DisneyQuest can become overwhelmingly crowded in the evening, on weekends, and on rainy days. To make sure you have the chance to try out every-thing, visit at opening time on a weekday morning.

creation of the coaster you just designed, complete with spins and flips.

Needless to say, preteens and teens can get hooked on this stuff very fast, and DisneyQuest is primarily designed for the age 10–20 set. (Some parents drop off teens at the arcade while they relax at one of the West Side restaurants.) But there's entertainment for younger siblings as well, and any age can enjoy the gentle arcade games like Skeeball or the Create Zone where you can design your own toy or learn to draw a Disney character.

DisneyQuest usually opens at 10:30 AM during the on-season and 11:30 AM during the off-season. A single entry price ($40 for adults, $34 for kids 3 to 9) lets you play as long and as much as you like—an alarming thought for the parents of a 12-year-old boy. Admission is also included with the Water Park Fun & More option.

Cirque du Soleil

After a week at Disney World, probably the last thing you're itching to do is to buy an expensive ticket to watch an acrobatic show. But the Cirque du Soleil show La Nouba positively wowed the families we surveyed.

Although the athleticism and agility of the troupe will amaze you, it's their ability to use props, sets, costumes, and their bodies to set a mood and tell a story that makes Cirque du Soleil so unique. Don't expect any elephants or people being shot out of cannons—Cirque performances are more like theater than traditional circuses. Cirque du Soleil can best be appreciated by kids ages 8 and up.

Cirque du Soleil has a multitiered pricing structure. General tickets range from $53–$117 for adults and $43–$94 for kids ages 3 to 9. The 90-minute show normally runs Tuesday through Saturday twice daily (usually at 6 and 9 PM). For reservations, details, and specific pricing for the dates you'll be visiting, visit www.cirquedusoleil.com or call 407/939–7600.

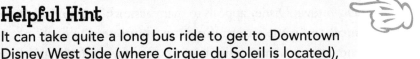

Helpful Hint

It can take quite a long bus ride to get to Downtown Disney West Side (where Cirque du Soleil is located), even from an on-site hotel. Since the resorts often share buses to Downtown Disney, and since the West Side stop is last once you get there, you'll have to sit through several stops before you arrive. The moral? Drive if you can, but if you're taking a bus to Cirque du Soleil leave your hotel an hour and a half before showtime.

BoardWalk and the ESPN Club

Not up for the sprawl of Downtown Disney? At night, the shops, restaurants, and nightclubs in front of the BoardWalk Resort take on a whole new glitter. You can find plenty of low-key entertainment—face painting, hair braiding, midway games, and sometimes comics and magic acts—along the waterfront. Eat dinner at the Flying Fish Café if you're feeling fancy, then rent a surrey bike ($19 to $25 for 30 minutes, depending upon bike size) for a lap around the lagoon.

The ESPN Club is a good stop for sports enthusiasts. The center contains a broadcast and production facility (meaning celebrity athletes are sometimes on hand) and serves up—and I quote—"the best ballpark cuisine from around the country." This bold claim translates into sandwiches, salads, and burgers, all sized for hearty appetites.

Two BoardWalk clubs are open strictly to adults 21 and older. The Atlantic Dance Club changes format frequently but is presently offering DJ-spun Top 40 dance music without a cover charge. Jellyrolls is a sing-along piano bar with lots of audience participation.

The fact that the BoardWalk isn't as vast and crowded as Downtown Disney appeals to many visitors; you can have a good meal and some entertainment without getting back into the mouse race. And at night, with the glowing Yacht and Beach Clubs visible across the water and the fireworks of Epcot in the distance, the BoardWalk ranks as one of the most beautiful spots in Disney World. Pull up a rocker and let the world go by.

On-site guests can take monorails or buses to any theme park and then transfer to the BoardWalk bus. If you're staying at the Yacht and Beach Clubs, the Swan, or the Dolphin, just walk. Off-site guests can either park in the BoardWalk lot or pay for the $10 valet parking, which is worth it on weekend evenings when the regular lot is crowded.

Disney Extras

Dinner Shows and Character Breakfasts

Book any dinner shows you would like to attend before you leave home by calling 407/939–3463 (407/WDW–DINE). Reservations are accepted up to 180 days in advance and are especially important for the Hoop-Dee-Doo Musical Revue, which requires a lot of hoop-dee-doo just to get tickets. The on-site dinner shows include the following:

- *The Hoop-Dee-Doo Musical Revue* plays three times nightly (at 5, 7:15, and 9:30 PM) at Pioneer Hall in Fort Wilderness campground. You can dine on ribs, fried chicken, and strawberry shortcake while watching a lovably hokey show that includes lots of audience participation. The cost is $51–$59 for adults, $26–$31 for children 3 to 9.

- *The Spirit of Aloha* is presented seasonally at 5:15 and 8 PM in the open-air theater in Luau Cove at the Polynesian Resort. The luau features hula dancing, traditional music, and a "Polynesian feast," which translates as fruit, chicken, pork ribs, and pineapple bread. The cost is $56–$61 for adults and $27–$32 for children 3 to 9. "The Polynesian is a beautiful setting," wrote one family from Connecticut, "But we expected more of a traditional luau. Just be aware that this show has a modern story line."

@ *Mickey's Backyard Barbecue* is presented seasonally on se-lect nights at Fort Wilderness and features a country band, line dancing with the characters, and picnic food such as barbecued ribs, roast chicken, and corn on the cob. The price is $45 for adults, $27 for children 3 to 9. The bar-becue is decidedly rowdier than other Disney dinner events. A mother of four from New York wrote, "The closest we came to a never-again moment was Mickey's Backyard Barbecue. It was a free-for-all with characters and kids running loose on the dance floor. On the other hand, the Polynesian luau was a delight, with plenty of en-tertainment for the kids but a much calmer atmosphere."

Money-Saving Tip

Unlike regular restaurant reservations, which can be canceled at the last minute or simply ignored, making reservations for dinner shows and character meals requires a credit card guarantee. If your plans change, and you fail to cancel your reservation at least 48 hours in advance, you'll be charged the full amount.

Character Dining

The character meals are time-consuming and expensive, but families with young kids give them very high marks. It's not about the food, which is usually fine, it's about the chance to have the characters actually visit your table so that there's plenty of time for pictures, hugs, and autographs. Breakfasts run $23–$33 for adults and $19–$35 for kids 9 and under, with lunches and dinners running $34–$47 for adults and $25–$38 for kids.

Helpful Hint

Kids under 3 get into the parks for free, but what's the deal with character meals? Historically the buffets are more liberal than the sit-down venues about comping the under-3 set, but don't assume: Anytime you book a character meal, ask the restaurant to spell out its policy about who, if anyone, eats for free.

The princess breakfasts in Cinderella Castle are the priciest, partly because they include a photo, but mostly because Disney realizes parents are willing to pay pretty much anything to get their daughters inside the castle. Reservations can (and should) be arranged 180 days in advance by calling 407/939–3463 (407/WDW–DINE). Any character meal that takes place inside a theme park requires theme-park admission.

Character meal times, places, prices, and the characters featured change often, so call to confirm the information before you book the meal. If your child has his heart set on meeting a

Insider's Secret

If you're going to a princess character breakfast, it's only fitting that little girls dress for the occasion. If you think the full princess outfit is a little too much for a day in the parks, change your girls back into casual clothes after the meal.

particular character, be sure to verify that the character will actually be there when you visit.

Insider's Secret

Since dining will take about two hours, try to book the first character breakfast of the day. Families who have scheduled character breakfasts on the last day of their visits have also noted that a long breakfast coincides well with the usual 11 AM check-out time at most Orlando hotels.

In the Resorts

- Cape May Café, Beach Club Resort—Seaside picnic breakfast buffet with Goofy, Donald, and Minnie.

- Chef Mickey's, Contemporary Resort—Party with Mickey, Minnie, Donald, Pluto, and Goofy for breakfast and dinner.

- My Disney Girl's Perfectly Princess Tea Party—For the ultimate princess experience, pull out your wallet, take a deep gulp, and head to the Grand Floridian for the Perfectly Princess Tea Party. Held daily from 10:30 to noon, the tea party includes a meet and greet with Princess Aurora from *Sleeping Beauty*, plus storytelling, sing-alongs, and a princess parade. (Needless to say, all little girls wear their princess gear for this one.) Tea-party guests receive a ribbon tiara, bracelet, and special princess scrapbook. The cost for one child and one adult is $225, additional children are $150 each, and additional adults are $75. Lunch is served, but with all the excitement, don't be surprised if no one eats it. Reservations can be made at 407/939–3463 (407/WDW–DINE).

- 1900 Park Fare, Grand Floridian—Breakfast with Mary Poppins, Alice in Wonderland, the Mad Hatter, and Pooh and dinner with Cinderella, Prince Charming, the Evil Stepmother, and the Stepsisters. This is a rather girly-girl character dining option and a good choice for anyone who can't get a reservation at Cinderella Castle in the Magic Kingdom.

- 'Ohana, Polynesian Resort—Luau breakfast with Lilo and Stitch, as well as Mickey and Pluto.

Insider's Secret

The fact that the 'Ohana breakfast is (at least at present) the only character meal featuring that prankster Stitch makes it especially lively—and an especially good choice for boys who may have seen one princess too many. "Stitch took my brother's Buzz Lightyear gun and engaged Pluto in a stickup," one boy happily reported. "It's a memory my family will cherish forever."

In the Magic Kingdom

- Cinderella's Royal Table in Cinderella Castle—Medieval banquet breakfast with princess characters such as Snow White, Aurora, the Fairy Godmother, and a couple of princesses to be named later (Disney rotates them). Crystal Palace—Breakfast, lunch, and dinner buffets with Pooh and friends.

Insider's Secret

The princess breakfast at Cinderella's Royal Table is so popular with swooning little girls that it's nearly impossible to book. For dates in summer, it often sells out within minutes of the reservation line opening. Your best bet is to call exactly 180 days in advance at precisely 7 AM. Call 407/939–3463 (407/WDW–DINE). Otherwise consider the equally regal Princess Storybook Dining at Akershus in the Norway pavilion at Epcot or 1900 Park Fare at the Grand Floridian, which also features Cinderella and her entourage.

In Epcot

@ Akershus in Norway—Breakfast, lunch, and dinner buffets in a castle setting. At present Snow White, Mulan, Mary Poppins, Belle, Aurora, and Jasmine show up at breakfast. At lunch and dinner you'll meet Belle, Jasmine, Aurora, Alice in Wonderland, Pocahontas, and Ariel—who, we're happy to report, is walking just fine in a ball gown. The princesses are sometimes reshuffled, so if your child has a preference, confirm who's expected to appear.

Helpful Hint

If you like to spend your mornings in the theme parks, plan your character meal for lunch or dinner, when you'll welcome the chance to rest during a leisurely meal.

In Hollywood

@ Hollywood & Vine—Stars from Playhouse Disney meet and greet during breakfast and lunch.

In the Animal Kingdom

@ Tusker House—Mickey, Donald, Daisy, and Goofy appear at breakfast.

Money-Saving Tip

When you enter a character meal, you'll probably be ushered into a line where families are waiting to have their pictures taken with the characters by a professional photographer. These shots can be added to your PhotoPass or if you want to save a few bucks (not to mention the wait in line), ask to be shown directly to your seats. There will be plenty of time later for you to take your own pictures with the characters as they visit your table. Note: pictures are included in the price of some princess-themed meals.

Special Holiday Parties and Events

Mickey's Very Merry Christmas Party

Disney World is at its most magical during the holidays. Hours are extended, special parades and shows debut, and the parks and hotels are beautifully decked. If you fantasize about seeing it snow on Main Street, this is your chance. (We're talking real snow here—generated from the rooftops along Main Street and billowed down on the crowd below.)

The week between Christmas and New Year's is the absolute busiest of the year at WDW, but it's possible to celebrate the holidays at Disney without being caught in the crush. Decorations go up just after Thanksgiving, and the special shows and parades debut shortly thereafter. The first two weeks of December are among the least crowded of the year and thus the perfect time to celebrate Christmas at Disney (assuming, of course, that your child's school schedule can accommodate the trip).

Each resort puts up its own theme decorations as well—a nautical tree for the Yacht Club, seashell ornaments at the Beach Club, Native American tepees and animal skulls for the Wilderness Lodge, an enormous Victorian dazzler at the Grand Floridian. The resort-theme decorations, in fact, are so gorgeous that holiday tours of the Disney hotels are popular among Orlando locals.

Christmas at Disney World is lovely all on its own, but Disney also offers a special ticketed party event on select evenings in the Magic Kingdom. Tickets for Mickey's Very Merry Christmas Party ($56 adults, $50 kids 3–9) should be purchased well in advance, either online at www.disneyworld. com or by calling 407/934–7639 (407/W–DISNEY).

Mickey's Not-So-Scary Halloween Party
On selected evenings during September and October, the Magic Kingdom hosts Mickey's Not-So-Scary Halloween Party. As the name implies, this celebration is geared toward younger kids with fortune-tellers, face painters, and trick-or-treating throughout the park; parades featuring the characters in costume; and a special fireworks finale. Be sure to bring along everyone's Halloween costumes.

Advance tickets for Mickey's Not-So-Scary Halloween Party are a must, so visit www.disneyworld.com or call 407/934–7639 (407/W–DISNEY) before you leave home. The party is offered on up to 20 dates throughout September and October, but the October 31 party always sells out first. Tickets cost $60 for adults and $54 for kids 3–9.

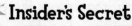

Insider's Secret

If you have preteens and teens who are up for a gorier scene, check out the super scary Halloween Nights event at Universal Studios.

In the past, events called the Pirates and Princess Parties have been offered in the Magic Kingdom on select evenings in January and again from mid-August through mid-September. There are special parades and fireworks, treasure hunts for chocolate doubloons, and the characters are on hand for meet and greets. But the parties haven't proved as popular as Disney hoped—nowhere close to the crowd swells at Christmas and Halloween—so Disney may be dropping them. If you're visiting during the off-season check to see if the parties are scheduled at www.disneyworld.com or call 407/934–7639 (407/W–DISNEY).

Money-Saving Tip

Both Mickey's Not-So-Scary Halloween Party and the Pirate and Princess Party offer discounts ($5 to $7 per ticket) on advance ticket sales for select evenings. Be sure to look for discount dates when you call or visit the Disney Web site.

Tours for Kids and Families

Most of Disney's behind-the-scenes tours require that guests be 16 and up to participate, but there are two programs at the Grand Floridian that are created specifically for kids and one tour in the Magic Kingdom that was designed for families.

These programs are not only great fun for the kids, but are also, when you consider they include lunch and a couple of hours of child care, a bargain. Reserve your child's place before you leave home, preferably at the same time that you make reservations for your meals.

Pirate Adventure

This rollicking two-hour boat tour takes kids on a treasure hunt across the Seven Seas Lagoon with stops at all the Magic Kingdom resort marinas. Counselors help kids collect clues and complete a map that ultimately leads them to buried treasure. It's a good choice for active kids in the 4 to 10 age range. Lunch is served on the pontoon boat after the last stop, and everyone leaves with a goody bag of treasure. "My 6-year-old son loved the Pirate Adventure at the Grand Floridian," reported one mom from New York. "It's very reasonably priced, and since I'm a single parent, I have to confess it was wonderful to just have a couple of hours to lie by the pool while he was on tour."

The Adventure currently departs the Grand Floridian marina at 10 AM on Monday, Wednesday, and Thursday. Kids ages 4 to 10 may participate in this child-only event that costs $30. For reservations, call 407/939–3463 (407/WDW–DINE) 180 days in advance.

Helpful Hint
It's essential to book the Pirate Adventure a full 180 days before you arrive. It fills up fast.

Wonderland Tea Party

Kids join Alice in Wonderland and the Mad Hatter for a tea party held at 1900 Park Fare in the Grand Floridian. The table is festively decorated and a full lunch is served, but this is a tea party in reverse, so naturally the

Insider's Secret

Looking for a way to kill an hour or two while the kids participate in one of the Grand Floridian programs? The spa is just around the corner.

children start with dessert. Afterward, the characters lead them in a variety of games, and each child leaves with a souvenir photo of him- or herself with the characters.

The Wonderland Tea Party is served weekdays from 1:15 to 2:30 PM for kids ages 4 to 10 (no moms!), and the cost is $40. For reservations, call 407/939–3463 (407/WDW–DINE) 180 days in advance.

Family Magic Tour in the Magic Kingdom

Everyone gets into the act on this tour; although the activities are geared to kids ages 3 to 10, parents and both younger and older siblings can come along. The only rule is that you have to be willing to act silly.

Your tour guide meets you at Guest Services in the Magic Kingdom and sets up the premise of the tour. Perhaps Peter Pan has stolen Captain Hook's favorite hook, and the captain is so furious that his band of buccaneers is threatening to take over the whole Magic Kingdom. To stop him, you must follow a map that takes you around the park—hopping, skipping, hiding, and keeping an eye out for each new clue.

At the final stop of the tour, you meet up with a character or two for a closing surprise. The tour is a great option for families who have been to the Magic Kingdom several times and are looking for a new spin. It's less appealing for first-time visitors who are itching to get on the rides.

The Family Magic Tour is held daily from 10 to noon, and the cost is $27 per person, regardless of age. Call 407/939–8687 (407/WDW–TOUR).

That Sportin' Life: On Water

Most on-site hotels have lovely marinas with a variety of water-craft for rent, but the major water recreation area of WDW is the Seven Seas Lagoon in front of the Magic Kingdom. Marinas at the Grand Floridian, Polynesian, Contemporary, Fort Wilderness, and Wilderness Lodge all service the lagoon, and you don't have to be a guest of the resort to rent watercraft. (Although you'll need to show either a driver's license or a resort ID.)

Reservations are a good idea, especially in the on-season, and it also never hurts to confirm prices before you go. Call 407/939–7529 (407/WDW–PLAY) for more information.

Water-sport options include the following:

Boat Rental

The Disney fleet includes mini-speedboats called Sea Raycers, canopy boats, sailboats, pontoons, pedal boats, and kayaks. The marina staff can help you decide which watercraft best fits your needs.

Insider's Secret

By far the best place to rent the Sea Raycer mini-speedboats is the Seven Seas Lagoon. You have plenty of room to explore and can really pick up some speed. The boats are for rent at the marinas in the Contemporary, Polynesian, and Grand Floridian resorts or Wilderness Lodge. At present prices are $32 for 30 minutes. Drivers must be at least 14 years old and 5 feet tall, although kids of any age will enjoy riding along with Mom or Dad.

Fishing

Fishing equipment is for rent at Coronado Springs, Fort Wilderness, and the Port Orleans Resort, Riverside section. If you'd like more action than simply dropping a line, two-hour fishing tours for parties of up to five people—including special excursions for kids 6 to 12—depart from numerous water locations throughout WDW. Reservations can be made up to 180 days in advance; call 407/939–7529 (407/WDW–PLAY) for exact times, locations, and prices.

Surfing

Surfing lessons are offered at Typhoon Lagoon on select mornings before the park opens. Participants must be at least 8 years old and strong swimmers. For those up to the challenge, this clinic ($150 per person) is one of the most fun things to do in all of WDW. Because the waves are controllable and the instructors are top-notch, almost everyone can ride a wave by the end of the class. Call 407/939–7529 (407/WDW–PLAY) for details. Always confirm prices when booking.

Parasailing and Waterskiing

Another high-thrill activity is parasailing. Excursions leave daily from the Contemporary Resort marina and the 10-minute flights cost $95 for one person or $170 for two riders in tandem. At your top height of 600 feet above the lake you can see all four parks. The Sammy Duvall Watersports Center also offers waterskiing, wakeboarding, kneeboarding, and tubing. The $170 price covers up to five people and includes the boat, a driver, and an instructor for an hour. For reservations and more information call 407/939–0754.

Specialty Cruises

Two of the greatest ways to spend an evening in Disney World are watching the Magic Kingdom fireworks or the pyrotechnics of IllumiNations at Epcot. And there's no classier viewing spot than aboard your private boat. "We called before we left home and rented a pontoon boat to see the Epcot fireworks," wrote one father. "What a treat. We had a great captain who drove us around then 'parked' under the bridge so we could see the show. It was great floating there, sipping a drink, while others were jam-packed in the park waiting for the show, and probably trying to figure out how they were going to exit along with thousands of others."

The Premium Cruise is a pontoon boat, which holds up to 10 people for $300. It includes the piped-in music from the Magic Kingdom fireworks or Epcot's Illuminations. When you factor in how many people can participate in the experience, the specialty cruises are actually a (somewhat) cost-effective way to create a memorable evening for the whole family. Just be sure to reserve 90 days in advance by calling 407/939–7529 (407/WDW–PLAY).

That Sportin' Life: On Land

Biking

Bikes are for rent at most on-site hotels at a cost of $8 an hour or $22 a day; helmets are included.

Golf

There are six courses on WDW grounds with greens fees running anywhere from $125 to $135 for Disney World resort guests and $135 to $145 for day guests. Twilight rates start at

$75. With such pricey fees, anyone planning to try out the courses should consider a package that includes golf. Instruction is also available for kids and adults. Visit www.waltdisney world.com or call 407/939–4653 (407/WDW–GOLF) to reserve tee times and confirm rates.

Health Clubs and Spas

The Contemporary, Grand Floridian, Swan, Dolphin, Yacht and Beach Clubs, BoardWalk, Animal Kingdom Lodge, Coronado Springs, Old Key West, and Saratoga Springs resorts all have health clubs. The rates average about $20 a day, with reduced length-of-stay rates. The most complete workout facility is at Saratoga Springs.

There are full-service spas at the Grand Floridian, Saratoga Springs, and Animal Kingdom Lodge. "My 7-year-old daughter had her first manicure at the Grand Floridian spa and was in heaven," a mom from New York wrote. "She felt very grown-up, and the manicurist was the sweetest cast member I've ever met—even at Disney World, where everybody is nice!"

Horseback Riding

Guided trail rides leave the Fort Wilderness grounds four times a day. Children must be at least 9 to ride; the horses are gentle and the pace is slow.

Younger kids can ride the ponies at the Fort Wilderness Petting Farm while older siblings are on the trail ride. Children 2 and over and up to 80 pounds are welcome. If the whole family would like to get into the cowboy act, Fort Wilderness also offers horse-drawn wagon rides that depart from Pioneer Hall at 7 PM and 9:30 PM nightly.

Miniature Golf

Fantasia Gardens, just across from the Disney's Hollywood Studios, is real eye candy—an 18-hole mini golf tribute to the movie *Fantasia* with dancing hippos, orchestrated fountains, and the Sorcerer's Apprentice running the whole show. A second course, Fantasia Fairways, is a miniature version of a real golf course, with sand traps, water hazards, and roughs. Although you play with a putter, the holes are 100 feet long and difficult enough to drive a veteran golfer to curses.

Helpful Hint

Fantasia Fairways is too tough for golfers under 10, and even Fantasia Gardens is a fairly difficult course. Winter Summerland is a better choice for the preschool and grade school set.

The second miniature golf complex at Disney World is Winter Summerland (beside Blizzard Beach), where you're greeted with the question "Would you like to play in snow or sand?" Your first clue that there's strange weather ahead is that Santa, his sleigh pulled by flamingos, has crash-landed on the roof and skidded through a snowbank–sandbank into the wackiest campground on earth. You can opt to play either the icy white "greens" of the winter course, where you can find a hockey rink, a snow castle, and slalom ski runs, or the sandy shores of the summer

Insider's Secret

While both of the Winter Summerland courses are child-friendly, the summer course is the harder of the two. Must be all those sand traps.

course, where the Beach Boys serenade you amid pools, waves, and barbecue pits.

Rates at Fantasia Gardens, Fantasia Fairways, and Winter Summerland are $12 for adults and $10 for kids ages 3 to 9. Reservations aren't necessary.

Running

Trails cut through the grounds of nearly every Disney resort. Consult Guest Services for ideas on the best route around your particular hotel. Wilderness Lodge, with its invitingly shady trails, is an especially good choice if you're visiting in summer when even morning runs can be steamy.

Tennis

Several on-site resorts (the Contemporary, the Grand Floridian, the Yacht and Beach Clubs, BoardWalk, Old Key West, Saratoga Springs, the Swan, and the Dolphin) have tennis courts, and the Contemporary also offers clinics for guests 10 and older. There's considerable variation in rental rates and reservation policies, so call 407/939–7529 (407/WDW–PLAY) for details.

Disney's Wide World of Sports

This multimillion-dollar sports complex hosts competitions and tournaments, with facilities to accommodate 25 different kinds of sports. It's the spring training camp of the Atlanta Braves and the summer training camp of the Tampa Bay Buccaneers. You can also find a branch of the All Star Café, a huge sports bar with multiple screens and interactive games.

Activities at the Wide World of Sports vary widely, so call 407/939–4263 or visit www.disneyworldsports.com before you leave home to find out what will be going on during your visit. If there's something that catches your fancy, admission is $12

Helpful Hint
Visit the Wide World of Sports only if there's a specific event going on that interests you. Otherwise, save your time and money. There isn't a whole lot to do here.

for adults, $9 for kids ages 3 to 9. Getting to the Wide World of Sports is tricky. There's no direct bus service, so the trip, with transfers, can take about 90 minutes each way. Drive if you can; if you don't have a car, consider calling a cab.

CHAPTER

11

Dining
at Disney

Full-Service Restaurants at Disney

You've come to ride, but you also need to eat. The good news is that the variety and quality of the on-site restaurants have vastly improved in the 20 years I've been doing this guide. The bad news is that the size of the crowds has also increased, making it more of a hassle to get into the restaurants.

Unless you want to eat fast food for every meal, you should make your dining reservations before you arrive, preferably when you book your hotel. Sure, there's a chance you can get a last-minute reservation if you're visiting during the off-season and if you're not picky about the time and the place and if you reserve early enough on the day of. But who wants to waste precious morning time—the best time of day to ride the rides—trying to navigate the reservations system? Your best bet is to make advance reservations so you don't have to think about where you're eating every night.

The basic Disney Dining Plan includes one table-service meal, one quick-service meal, and one snack per person per day. It's certainly possible to upgrade to the deluxe or wine-and-dine

Insider's Secret

The Disney Dining Plan has been a runaway success—so much so that it's more important than ever to make advance reservations for full-service restaurants. The reason is this: All families on the plan will be eating at least one full-service meal each day, which in itself means more dining demand since in the past many budget-conscious families stuck to counter-service meals. Additionally, the fact that the system allows guests to combine meals if they want to try a signature dining venue means that people who otherwise wouldn't have considered the California Grill or other upscale spots are trying to get in. The result? Guests on the Disney Dining Plan are flooding the full-service restaurants in such great numbers that all guests—including those who aren't on the plan or who aren't staying at Disney hotels—are feeling the squeeze.

Consider the experience of this grandmother from Rhode Island. "We have visited Disney World many times and have certain restaurants we know we enjoy. For our upcoming visit we decided against the dining plan but imagine my surprise when I called for reservations two months in advance and found that we could not get into 8 of our 10 favorites. Some of them were giving us ridiculous times like 10 PM for dinner, and others were simply saying there was nothing available at all. We were crushed!"

plans, but if your kids are young it's unlikely you'll want to spend that much time in restaurants. "In order to make sure our investment in the deluxe plan paid off, we scheduled lots of table-service meals," wrote one mother. "By the second day my husband was complaining that he felt like a slave to all of our reservations and we ended up canceling quite a few, which was disappointing. But we decided as first-time visitors we'd be better off spending that time in the parks."

Even if you're on the basic plan, it's still possible to have plenty of culinary adventures. You can use two of your table-service credits in order to experience (a) a character dining; (b) a dinner show; or (c) one of Disney's signature restaurants, such as Citricos, the Flying Fish, or the California Grill. When you purchase the Dining Plan you'll receive a brochure outlining all of your options.

Helpful Hint

The dining plan is loaded into your ticket/resort ID card, and the system keeps track of how you're doing—in fact, each time you use the card your server will give you a receipt showing the remaining balance of your meals. Give the balance a glance each time; mistakes are rare but a couple of families have reported they got to their last day with no meals left.

Making Reservations

The system works like this: a reservation doesn't hold the restaurant to a specific time for seating you but rather guarantees you the next available table after you arrive. Let's say you made advance reservations for four people at 7 PM. When you show up at 7, your table won't be waiting with your name on it, but you will be given the next available table for four. Waits average between 10 and 30 minutes, but it's still far better than walking in with no prior arrangement.

So how do you make reservations? You call 407/939–3463 (407/WDW–DINE) up to 180 days in advance of the day for which you want reservations. Admittedly, this requires some planning. Ideally, you'll sketch out a general schedule for each day and evening of your vacation, so you'll know that on Tuesday you're having dinner at Epcot and on Saturday you're having a character breakfast.

Helpful Hint

If you're worried that the kids will get antsy during a full-service dinner, rest assured that Disney is all about getting the food out fast. The kiddie menus have games and puzzles, and waiters will bring out crayons, crackers, and drinks with lids to keep the kids busy while you wait.

Helpful Hint

If you really can't plan out your schedule ahead of time, take the safe route and book your dinners at restaurants in your on-site hotel. That way you'll be ready for an early bedtime and an early morning the next day. If you get a last-minute reservation at another restaurant, you can always cancel your first reservation.

If you've arrived at Disney without dining reservations, you can try to get last-minute slots by calling 407/WDW–DINE as soon as you know where to eat. Call with your cell phone while you're in line for a ride, or, if you're staying at an on-site hotel, you can also press the dining button on your hotel room phone. You won't get Saturday night seating at California Grill by waiting until you get there but if you're flexible about where and when you eat, finding last-minute reservations is possible.

You can make multiple reservations for different restaurants at the same time, although it's bad form not to cancel the others once you've made up your mind which restaurant to attend. Also, there's no penalty for not showing up for a reservation, except at some experiences like the dinner shows or character meals, where a credit card deposit is required. As a rule, it's better to overbook than underbook, especially if you're traveling at a busy time.

You can also try to reserve in person at the restaurants or at dining reservations booths throughout the parks. Since many

Helpful Hint
Restaurant hours are sometimes changed or shortened during the off-season, but signature restaurants are always open.

people overbook their meals, on any given day about 20% of the people with reservations will be no-shows, offering a window of opportunity for people who prefer to make last-minute dining decisions. There's no guarantee, but you might get lucky.

Prepared to roll the dice? At Hollywood drop by the reservations booth at the corner of Sunset and Hollywood. At the Animal Kingdom check with Guest Services (a.k.a. Guest Relations). At the Magic Kingdom, go to the restaurant itself or City Hall. At Epcot, which offers the best shot of getting into a restaurant at the last minute thanks to the sheer number of them, go to Guest Services at Innoventions Plaza, to the left of Spaceship Earth as you enter. At Downtown Disney, go directly to the restaurant where you want to dine, or stop by Guest Services.

There are quite a few buffets at Disney World and, for families, they solve certain problems, i.e., you get the food fast (as in, immediately) and there are plenty of options for picky eaters. But consider working some full-service venues into your week as well. As one mother from Oregon wrote, "The fast-food and buffet venues have the same hectic atmosphere as the parks—you still have to stand in a line, carry things, and try to keep an eye on the kids in the meantime. And they're so loud, especially the character meals! We had an elegant, wonderfully relaxing lunch at the Brown Derby one day, and my husband said it was the perfect getaway from theme-park chaos—almost as if we'd gone back to our hotel room for a break."

Helpful Hint

A mom from New Jersey offers this council: "Get to your reservation a few minutes early. There may be several people with 6 PM reservations, for example, and they'll seat you in the order that you arrive and check in. And also, don't expect too much in terms of food quality from the character meals. You're paying for the fun, not the food."

Finding Healthy Food

Disney has removed trans fats from all of its meals, making it easier to feel good about grabbing a snack on the run. You'll

Best Fast-Food Options for Families

IN THE MAGIC KINGDOM: COSMIC RAY'S STARLIGHT CAFÉ

There's plenty of seating, the line moves fast, and they have sandwiches and salads in addition to the usual hamburgers and chicken fingers. (Cosmic Ray's is also one of the few counter service restaurants to offer kosher alternatives.)

AT EPCOT: SUNSHINE SEASONS

Several cuisines are served at various counters, so each family member can choose a completely different meal and then meet up at the same table.

AT DISNEY'S HOLLYWOOD STUDIOS: TOY STORY PIZZA PLANET

Good pizza, fast service, and an arcade combine to keep the kids happy.

IN THE ANIMAL KINGDOM: TUSKER HOUSE

The most health-conscious buffet in Disney World, with plenty of flavor to boot.

also find health-conscious choices in the kids meals—fruit instead of chips and milk or water instead of soda, for instance.

And guests give Disney chefs major (trans-fat-free) brownie points for their willingness to address specific dietary needs. The chefs at full-service restaurants prefer advance warning (you can note any special dietary requests when you make your reservations) but are also pretty adept at meeting guest needs with shorter notice, as evidenced by this New Jersey mother's story. "I've been on a weight-loss plan for several

Best Restaurants for a Parents' Night Out

The popularity of the Disney dining program means you may be seeing more kids in the upscale restaurants, but these three remain relatively adult-oriented.

CALIFORNIA GRILL

Real foodies love this sleek restaurant in the Contemporary Resort with a view of the Magic Kingdom fireworks show.

JIKO

Exquisite contemporary African food paired with fabulous South African wines make this Animal Kingdom Lodge restaurant one of the best in Orlando.

VICTORIA AND ALBERT'S

Pure elegance and flawless cuisine make this posh restaurant in the Grand Floridian Resort perfect for a special celebration.

months and am happy to have lost 50 pounds. But the very thought of going to Disney World terrified me. I pictured nothing but grease and sugar. Our very first meal was at the Brown Derby restaurant in Hollywood, and when I asked the server a question about how something was prepared she said 'Just a minute.' Almost immediately the chef came out and he practically created a new entrée for me on the spot. After that, I asked to speak to the chef every time we sat down for a meal. My son started calling me 'The Dining Room Diva.'"

Another mother wrote, "Both of my sons, ages 4 and 7, are allergic to dairy, eggs, and nuts, and dining out is usually a

Quick Guide to Full-in the Magic

Restaurant	Description	Location
Cinderella's Royal Table	Dine in the castle with the princess characters	Fantasyland
The Crystal Palace	Buffet dining with Winnie the Pooh and friends	Main Street
Liberty Tree Tavern	Thanksgiving-style feast	Liberty Square
The Plaza Restaurant	Don't miss the sundaes	Main Street
Tony's Town Square Restaurant	*Lady and the Tramp* theme and Italian classics	Main Street

challenge for us. We had reserved a character dinner at the Crystal Palace, and after I spoke to the chef about our dietary restrictions, he couldn't have been more wonderful. He walked me through the buffet pointing out which foods would be safe and which were risky, and he made a special batch of pasta just for our boys. For dessert he brought them banana splits using the same soy ice cream we buy at home. They were in their glory!"

Rating the Disney Restaurants

The restaurant descriptions that make up the bulk of this chapter cover only full-service sit-down restaurants. Let's face it, most fast-food places are pretty similar, and there's only so

Service Restaurants Kingdom

Rating	Price	Advance Reservations	Suitability for Kids	Meals Served
★★	$$$	Necessary	High	B, L, D
★★★	$$	Necessary	High	B, L, D
★★	$$	Recommended	High	L, D
★★	$$	Recommended	Moderate	L, D
★★	$$	Recommended	High	L, D

much you can say about burgers, fries, and soft-serve ice cream. Therefore, we decided not to overwhelm you with full descriptions of all of the 100-plus food service venues throughout Walt Disney World and to focus on restaurants where you're apt to be spending more time and more money and will thus have higher expectations.

Helpful Hint
To find your best bets for healthy fast-food dining, stop by Guest Services in each park as you enter for a healthy dining guide. There will be at least one low-fat and one vegetarian entrée at every full-service restaurant.

Definition of Quick-Guide Ratings

Food Quality

★★★ Exceptionally good
 ★★ Tasty food
  ★ Okay in a pinch

Price for an Adult Meal Comprising a Main Course and an Appetizer

$$$ Expensive; about $25 and up
 $$ Moderate; about $15–$25
  $ Inexpensive; about $15

Advance Reservations

Not Offered: This restaurant doesn't accept advance reservations unless you have a party of 10 or more. You can show up at an off-time and get a beeper, then shop nearby while you wait for your table.

Recommended: This restaurant draws average-size crowds. In high season, it will fill to capacity, so you should make reservations at least several days in advance. If you're touring in the off-season or dining at off-hours, you should be able to walk in and get a table.

Necessary: This is a popular restaurant. If you haven't made advance reservations, you'll probably be closed out.

Suitability for Kids

High: The restaurant is informal, with food choices designed to appeal to kids. There may be some sort of entertainment going on, or perhaps the setting itself is interesting.

Moderate: This restaurant is casual and family-oriented.

Low: This is one of WDW's more adult restaurants with sophisticated menu choices and leisurely service.

Meals Served

B is for breakfast, L is for lunch, and D is for dinner.

Magic Kingdom Restaurants

Cinderella's Royal Table ★★

High amid the spires of Cinderella Castle in Fantasyland, this restaurant is the most glamorous in the Magic Kingdom. The food is also elegantly presented—although rather expensive for what you get—and getting in for lunch or dinner isn't as hard as you might expect.

But breakfast—that's a totally different story. Cinderella's Royal Table is best known as the home of the extraordinarily popular princess character breakfast, the toughest ticket in all of Disney World. A mother of two from Virginia reported, "It took us three days to get through the phone line for the princess breakfast in the Magic Kingdom, but it was well worth it! My 4-year-old daughter wore her Cinderella dress, and she loved all the special attention she received. It was a year ago and she still talks about it." "Too magical for words," agrees the mom of a 5-year-old in Maine.

The Crystal Palace ★★★

Winnie the Pooh and friends circulate among diners . . . and everybody agrees that that's cool, but there's a real split of opinion on the quality of the food. Consider this report from a Texas mother of two: "In general I dislike buffets, but the food here was far better than I expected and our children absolutely

Quick Guide to Full-

Restaurant	Description	Location
Akershus	Authentic Norwegian cuisine and princess character buffets	Norway
Biergarten	Rousing, noisy atmosphere and live entertainment	Germany
Bistro de Paris	Classic French cuisine— very elegant, very adult	France
Le Cellier	Great steaks, excellent salmon, huge desserts	Canada
Les Chefs de France	Like a Paris sidewalk café	France
Coral Reef	Great views of the Living Seas tank	Living Seas pavilion
Garden Grill Restaurant	American dishes and the Disney characters	Land pavilion
Marrakesh	Exotic food and surroundings, belly dancers	Morocco
Nine Dragons	Cuisine representing every region in China	China
Rose & Crown Pub & Dining Room	Pub atmosphere and live entertainment	United Kingdom
San Angel Inn	Beautiful, romantic setting	Mexico
Teppan Edo	Dining room chefs slice and dice before your eyes	Japan
Tutto Italia	Upscale Italian, lively service	Italy

Service Restaurants at Epcot

Rating	Price	Advance Reservations	Suitability for Kids	Meals Served
★★★	$$	Necessary	High	B, L, D
★★	$$	Recommended	High	L, D
★★★	$$$	Necessary	Low	D
★★★	$$$	Recommended	Low	L, D
★★	$$$	Necessary	Moderate	L, D
★★	$$$	Necessary	High	L, D
★★	$$	Recommended	Moderate	D
★★	$$	Recommended	Moderate	L, D
★★	$$	Recommended	Low	L, D
★★	$$	Recommended	Moderate	L, D
★★	$$	Recommended	Moderate	L, D
★★★	$$$	Necessary	High	L, D
★★	$$$	Necessary	Moderate	L, D

loved the ice-cream sundae bar. (Even though things got so messy that we did have to change their shirts after lunch!) The Crystal Palace would be a good choice even if it didn't have the Pooh characters." But a mother from Florida was less pleased, writing, "You might want to reevaluate your rating on this one. We showed up starving but hardly anyone, including the children, found anything on the buffet they were willing to eat."

Liberty Tree Tavern

In Liberty Square and decorated in a style reminiscent of colonial Williamsburg, the Tavern serves salads, sandwiches, and New England clam chowder at lunch. The evening menu is an all-you-can-eat Thanksgiving-style feast with turkey and stuffing, flank steak, mac and cheese, and other family favorites.

The Plaza Restaurant

The salads, sandwiches, and burgers served at the Plaza are very filling—and very bland. The restaurant is best known for its wide selection of ice-cream treats, which are trotted over from the Ice Cream Parlor next door.

Tony's Town Square Restaurant

Located in the Main Street Hub, this thoroughly enjoyable restaurant is dedicated to Lady and the Tramp, with scenes from the film dotting the walls and a statue of the canine romantics in the center. The cuisine, like that of the café where Tramp wooed Lady, is classic Italian, and the portions are generous.

Epcot Restaurants

Akershus   ★★

The Norwegian buffet at Akershus (which one parent described as "all the herring you can eat") never really caught on, so this lovely castle-like restaurant in the Norway pavilion has shifted its buffet menu to include more American staples.

Even better, Akershus has princess-theme character dining at breakfast, lunch, and dinner. This takes some of the pressure off the popular Cinderella Castle breakfast in the Magic Kingdom, but you'll still need to make reservations 180 days in advance.

Biergarten   ★★

There's plenty of room to move about in this German beer hall where yodelers and an oom-pah-pah band get the whole crowd involved in singing and dancing. The all-you-can-eat buffet features traditional Bavarian dishes: bratwurst, spaetzle, and salads.

Bistro de Paris   ★★★

The Bistro is quieter, calmer, and more elegant than its sister, Les Chefs de France, located below it. It's also a tad too civilized for kids under 12. Expect classic French cuisine, a wonderful wine selection, and Continental service.

Coral Reef   ★★

One whole wall of this restaurant is glass, giving you a remarkable view of the Living Seas tank. Watching the fish keeps the kids entertained while parents browse the menu, which features, naturally, upscale seafood dishes.

Quick Guide to Full-
at Disney's

Restaurant	Description
'50s Prime Time Café	Want to star in a 1950s sitcom?
The Hollywood Brown Derby	Elegant and lovely with upscale cuisine
Hollywood & Vine	Large, attractive buffeteria
Mama Melrose's Ristorante Italiano	Good food, good service, wacky ambience
Sci-Fi Dine-In Theater	Campy; you eat in cars at a drive-in theater

The Garden Grill ★★

Easily recognizable American dishes, served family style, make this a good choice for younger children. The restaurant is on a revolving platform, allowing you to observe scenes from the Living with the Land boat ride below.

Le Cellier ★★★

Le Cellier is one of the most popular restaurants in Epcot, perhaps because there are relatively few steak houses in Disney World. The steaks here are excellent, as is the salmon, and the desserts are as big as the prairies of Alberta.

Service Restaurants Hollywood Studios

Rating	Price	Advance Reservations	Suitability for Kids	Meals Served
★★	$$	Recommended	High	L, D
★★★	$$$	Recommended	Low	L, D
★★	$	Recommended	High	L, D
★★	$$	Recommended	Moderate	L, D
★★	$$	Recommended	High	L, D

Les Chefs de France ★★

Modeled after the sidewalk cafés of Paris, this restaurant bustles pleasantly. The classical French menu is a bit hit-or-miss in quality, but the waiters are charming, and you can gaze out at the World Showcase action.

Marrakesh ★★

Ready for exotic surroundings and unusual entertainment? Kids enjoy the belly dancers, and the ladies sometimes invite them to enter into the act. The unfamiliarity of the food may pose a

Quick Guide to Full-
in the Animal

Restaurant	Description
Rainforest Café	Large and lively
Tusker House	Buffet with great variety, character breakfast
Yak & Yeti	Asian fusion, complete with bar and beer garden

problem, but if the kids can be persuaded to give it a try, they can find that roasted chicken tastes pretty much the same the world over.

Nine Dragons

Another revamp is underway, and this one should lift Nine Dragons from being one of the sleepier restaurants in the World Showcase to one of the most dramatic. The new restaurant (with a new name) will take the idea of an exhibition kitchen to new levels, featuring five separate cooking stations where guests can interact with the chefs.

Service Restaurants Kingdom

Rating	Price	Advance Reservations	Suitability for Kids	Meals Served
★★	$$	Not accepted	High	B, L, D
★★★	$$	Necessary for character meals; otherwise suggested	High	B, L, D
★★	$$	Suggested	Moderate	L, D

Rose & Crown Dining Room ★★

This charming bar and restaurant has live entertainment, friendly service, and upscale pub grub such as fish-and-chips and meat pies. If you eat on the patio, you have a great view of the World Showcase Lagoon.

San Angel Inn ★★

A beautiful location inside the Mayan pyramid of the Mexico pavilion, with the Rio del Tiempo murmuring in the background, makes this restaurant a charming choice. The service is swift and friendly and older kids can browse among the market stalls of the pavilion or even ride the Gran Fiesta Tour while waiting for their food.

Teppan Edo

In the Japan pavilion, the revamped Teppan Edo offers grilled specialties at large tables, in front of which the chefs slice and dice in the best Benihana tradition. Upscale options such as Wagyu and Kobe beef are available. It's terrifically entertaining for the kids—the chefs often jazz up the presentation even more in their honor—and the stir-fried, simply prepared food is a hit with all ages. A father of four from Ohio wrote a rave review: "Japan is a good choice if you want to eat out in Epcot with kids. The chefs toss food and catch it in their hats, make silly jokes like throwing the butter and saying 'butterfly.' And one time when we were in, they had a lady making origami animals for the children. Plus, since they cook at the table, you get your food really fast."

Tutto Italia ★★

Expect authentic Italian food, equally authentic waiters, and a lovely setting, which, since it's tucked away in the far reaches of the Italy pavilion, actually feels a little secluded. At least by Disney World standards.

Restaurants at Disney's Hollywood Studios

'50s Prime Time Café

With its kitsch decor and ditzy waitresses dressed like June Cleaver, this restaurant is almost an attraction in itself. Meat loaf, macaroni, milk shakes, and other comfort foods are served in a 1950s-style kitchen, while dozens of TVs blare clips from classic shows in the background.

"Hi kids," says your waitress, pulling up a chair to the Formica-top table. "You didn't leave your bikes in the driveway, did you? Let me see those hands." Assuming you pass her clean-fingernails inspection, "Mom" will go on to advise you on your food choices. "I'll bring peas with that. Vegetables are good for you." The camp is lost on young kids, but they nonetheless love the no-frills food and the fact that Mom brings around crayons and coloring books, then hangs their artwork on the front of a refrigerator with magnets. But it's the baby-boomer parents, raised on the sitcoms that the restaurant spoofs, who really adore this restaurant. "You just have to get in the mood of the place," advised a mother of one from Illinois. "The whole routine about being on a TV show is very corny and very funny and the servers are great. We liked the food (chicken, pot roast, steak, salads, the basics), but when we left, my 8-year-old daughter said 'That was a good show,' and I think that's exactly the way you need to think of it."

The Hollywood Brown Derby ★★★

A signature Cobb salad as well as veal, pasta, and fresh seafood are served at the Derby, where, just as you'd expect, caricatures of movie stars line the walls. The food is quite sophisticated considering that you're inside a theme park, and the restaurant itself is elegant and lovely, like stepping back into Hollywood at its heyday. The wine program, which offers suggested pairings by the glass with each entrée, is one of the best in Disney World.

Hollywood & Vine ★★

This large, attractive, art deco "buffeteria" offers classic American dishes at breakfast, lunch, and dinner. Lines move quickly and the variety makes this a good choice for families. This is the

Quick Guide to Full-
in the

Restaurant	Description	Location
Artist Point	Fine dining in a rustic setting	Wilderness Lodge
Big River Grille & Brewing Works	Casual restaurant and brewpub	BoardWalk
bluezoo	Fine seafood in a sleek, upscale setting	Dolphin
Boatwright's Dining Hall	Southern dishes and tame Cajun	Port Orleans, Riverside
Boma	African-inspired buffet and great breakfasts	Animal Kingdom Lodge
California Grill	The best of all	Contemporary
Cape May Café	Character dining at breakfast, clambakes in the evening	Beach Club
Captain's Grille	Cheery and bright—a cut above a coffee shop	Yacht Club
Chef Mickey's	Character dining while the monorail zooms by	Contemporary
Citricos	Gourmet cuisine and an outstanding wine list	Grand Floridian
Coral Café	Buffets in the evening	Dolphin
ESPN Club	The perfect place to watch the big game	BoardWalk
Flying Fish Café	Excellent seafood and steaks	BoardWalk
Grand Floridian Café	Great variety, southern classics	Grand Floridian
Gulliver's Grill at Garden Grove	Whimsical decor, basic food	Swan

Service Restaurants
WDW Hotels

Rating	Price	Advance Reservations	Suitability for Kids	Meals Served
★★	$$$	Recommended	Low	D
★	$$	Not accepted	Moderate	L, D
★★	$$$	Necessary	Low	D
★	$$	Recommended	Moderate	B, D
★★★	$$	Recommended	Moderate	B, D
★★★	$$$	Necessary	High	D
★★★	$$	Recommended	High	B, D
★★	$$	Recommended	Moderate	B, L, D
★★	$$	Necessary	High	B, D
★★★	$$$	Necessary	Low	D
★	$$	For large parties only, recommended	Low	B, L, D
★	$	Not accepted	Moderate	L, D
★★★	$$$	Necessary	Low	D
★★	$$	Recommended	Moderate	B, L, D
★★	$$	Recommended	Moderate	B, L, D

(continued)

Quick Guide to Full-
in the

Restaurant	Description	Location
Jiko	African-influenced cuisine, South African wines	Animal Kingdom Lodge
Kimonos	Sushi in an elegant setting	Swan
Kona Café	Pacific Rim food with a tropical emphasis	Polynesian
Maya Grill	Latin American–inspired cuisine	Coronado Springs
Narcoossee's	Great fresh seafood; view of MK fireworks	Grand Floridian
1900 Park Fare	Buffet-style character dining	Grand Floridian
'Ohana	Family-friendly, with island entertainment	Polynesian
Palio	Gourmet Italian in a colorful setting	Swan
Shula's	Linebacker-size steaks in a dignified atmosphere	Dolphin
Shutters	Casual island fare	Caribbean Beach
Victoria & Albert's	The most elegant restaurant on Disney property	Grand Floridian
The Wave	Innovative regional cuisine	Contemporary Resort
Whispering Canyon Café	Comfort food, family-style service	Wilderness Lodge
Yachtsman Steakhouse	One of the premier steak houses in Disney World	Yacht Club

Service Restaurants
WDW Hotels

Rating	Price	Advance Reservations	Suitability for Kids	Meals Served
★★★	$$$	Recommended	Moderate	D
★★	$$	For large parties only, recommended	Low	D
★★	$$	Recommended	Moderate	B, L, D
★	$$	Recommended	Low	B, D
★★	$$$	Recommended	Low	D
★★	$$$	Necessary	High	B, D
★★	$$	Recommended	High	B, D
★★	$$$	Recommended	Moderate	D
★★★	$$$	Recommended	Low	D
★	$$	Recommended	Moderate	D
★★★	$$$	Necessary	Low	D
★★	$$	Recommended	Low	L, D
★★	$$	Recommended	High	B, L, D
★★	$$$	Recommended	Low	D

only character dining venue in Disney World to feature characters from Playhouse Disney.

Mama Melrose's Ristorante Italiano

This restaurant is tucked away near the Muppet*Vision 3-D plaza and the out-of-the-way location means that you can sometimes squeeze in without advance reservations. Expect a casual New York feel and quick service. The restaurant serves gourmet flatbreads from a wood-burning oven and a wide variety of pasta dishes; the penne alla vodka is a favorite.

Sci-Fi Dine-In Theater   ★★

At least as campy as the '50s Prime Time Café, the Sci-Fi seats you in vintage cars while incredibly hokey movie clips run on a giant screen. Offerings range from drive-in staples like milk shakes and popcorn all the way to seafood and St. Louis–style ribs. Older kids adore the setting and the funny waiters; in fact they often get so absorbed in the old movie clips that they sit quietly while parents relax in the backseat. Younger kids, in contrast, might be spooked. "Only okay food but really very fun," said one mom, while another wrote, "My 4-year-old was so freaked out by the atmosphere we had to leave early."

Animal Kingdom Restaurants

Rainforest Café

The jungle motif and large aquariums make the Rainforest Café great fun for kids. The food is nothing special, but tasty enough, with an emphasis on appetizers and other simple meals, like burgers, sandwiches, and huge salads. There are locations at both the Animal Kingdom and Downtown Disney.

Tusker House

The Tusker House is a favorite with families, offering buffets with a lot of variety and a popular character breakfast in the morning. "We tried this character breakfast when we got closed out of the ones at the Magic Kingdom," said one dad, "But it turned out to be a real treat. Good food, cute character presentation, and it moved fast—everything we needed."

Yak and Yeti

This Asian-fusion restaurant in the Asia section offers full-service dining, casual outdoor dining, a full bar, and a beer garden. The food is quite good, and the setting is the most adult and relaxing of all the Animal Kingdom restaurants.

Restaurants in the WDW Hotels

Artist Point

The most upscale of the Wilderness Lodge eateries, Artist Point offers Pacific Northwest–theme food in a casual, almost rustic, setting. The salmon is the house specialty, and the wine list highlights excellent selections from the Pacific Northwest.

Big River Grille & Brewing Works

WDW's only on-site brewpub is a good place to sample new beers and a couple of specialty ales. The food—mostly sandwiches and salads—is pedestrian, but the pleasant patio allows you to take in the action of the BoardWalk while you sip your beer.

bluezoo ★★

Famed chef Todd English brought this sleek contemporary seafood restaurant to the Dolphin. Although it's far too tony in atmosphere and eclectic in menu for most kids, bluezoo is a good spot for drinks or a parents' night out. The menu changes regularly but tends to feature unusual seafood dishes, such as the butter-poached Maine lobster with truffle-potato ravioli.

Boatwright's Dining Hall ★

The only full-service restaurant in Port Orleans is this casual dining hall in the Riverside section. The Cajun cooking is very tame, and classic American dishes round out the menu. The room isn't walled, and as it's beside the food court, it's always noisy.

Boma ★★★

This large family restaurant in the Animal Kingdom Lodge offers one of the best breakfast buffets in all of WDW. You can find the usual American classics, like eggs and pancakes, plus excellent grilled sausage and an outstanding selection of breads and pastries. The dinner buffet features African-inspired dishes, including wonderful grilled meats. You get plenty of value for your money. "This is by far the best food deal in Disney World," agreed a mom from Georgia. "The food was fresh and beautifully prepared. Both the kids and the adults loved it."

California Grill ★★★

Widely acknowledged to be the best restaurant in all of Disney World, the California Grill is very popular and always crowded. (One clue to the quality: Disney executives dine here.) "We used two Dining Plan table-service credits," reported one mother of three from Alabama, "But it was totally worth it. The only problem is we ate our first meal there and it set the bar so high that nothing else compared. We spent the rest of the vacation saying 'It's okay, but it's not the California Grill.'" Not only is the food excellent and stylishly presented, but the views from the top of the Contemporary are unparalleled, especially during the Magic Kingdom fireworks.

Cape May Café

Our readers give high marks to this bright and airy eatery in the heart of the Beach Club. It has an excellent seafood buffet at dinner, featuring shrimp, clams, mussels, and a couple of landlubber choices. The breakfast buffet, during which the characters, dressed in adorable old-fashioned bathing attire circulate among the diners, is very popular. Consider this report from a grandmother of four from Ohio: "We wouldn't consider it a trip to Walt Disney World without a stop at the Beach Club's Cape May Café. It's a family tradition, and the food is wonderful. We always leave the theme parks in the afternoon to take a nap, and Cape May is the perfect place to eat dinner before you go back into Epcot to see IllumiNations."

Captain's Grille

This restaurant, off the main drag in the Yacht Club Resort, serves fish, chicken, and beef in a pleasant nautical-theme room. The enormous breakfasts offer hearty eaters the chance to load up for a day of touring.

Chef Mickey's

The Contemporary Resort is one of the best places in Disney World for a character breakfast or dinner. As Mickey and the crew wander among the diners, the monorail whisks by over-head. The buffet has classic American breakfast food in the morning and family-pleasing standards like pasta, chicken, and roast beef in the evening, plus a sundae bar for the kids. A father of three from New Jersey echoed the reports of many of our readers: "Chef Mickey's is definitely the way to go if you want to see the basic old-fashioned Disney characters like Mickey and Goofy. The buffet was great, and the characters spent plenty of time with our sons."

Citricos ★★★

Citricos offers Mediterranean cuisine in the Grand Floridian, and the restaurant is known for its outstanding wine list. Up to 20 labels are available by the glass, with a specific wine paired with each appetizer and entrée on the menu. A beautiful setting with consistently delightful cuisine, Citricos is a real treat for a parents' night out.

Coral Café ★

With breakfast and dinner buffets as well as an à la carte menu, the Coral Café is the largest restaurant in the Dolphin Resort. Picture an upscale coffee shop with long hours and casual food and you have the idea.

ESPN Club ★

Anchoring one end of the BoardWalk, the ESPN Club is better known for broadcasting sports events than for its food. "Our teenaged sons loved going to the ESPN Club on a Sunday during football season," wrote one mom of three from Pennsylvania. "The place was packed with people from all over the country, all wearing jerseys and screaming for their teams. We

should have packed our Eagles jerseys—next time we'll know!"
Menu choices include buffalo wings, burgers, nachos, and, of
course, plenty of beer. There's an arcade next door to entertain
the kids.

Flying Fish Café

The zany art deco decor is by Martin Dorf, who also designed
the California Grill and Citricos. The menu is updated frequently but generally includes wonderful seafood, delicious
steaks, and excellent risottos. If you haven't made reservations,
you can always dine at the bar and watch the chefs at work.

Grand Floridian Café

If you'd like a good solid meal of traditional favorites, simply
served, with a pretty view of the Grand Floridian grounds,
this café is for you. The menu tilts to the south—fried chicken,
local fish, and key lime pie.

Gulliver's Grill at Garden Grove

This is the largest restaurant in the Swan, and it has a bit of a
split identity. In the morning and at lunch, it's an upscale coffee shop. In the evening it becomes Gulliver's Grill, with more
elaborate dining. Sometimes characters are on hand to entertain
the kids; check the character schedule when you make reservations.

Jiko

Jiko (Swahili for "cooking place") is the flagship restaurant of
the Animal Kingdom Lodge, and the menu features contemporary African cuisine with an emphasis on fresh vegetables,
grains, and game. Two wood-burning stoves simulate the effect

Quick Guide to Full-in the Rest

Restaurant	Description	Location
All-Star Café	Ultimate sports bar with cool games for the kids	Disney's Wide World of Sports
Bongos Cuban Café	Americanized versions of Cuban dishes	Downtown Disney West Side
Fulton's Crab House	Fine dining on a riverboat	Downtown Disney
House of Blues	Cajun and Creole cooking with live music	Downtown Disney West Side
Planet Hollywood	Always fun, film clips run constantly	Downtown Disney West Side
Portobello Yacht Club	Northern Italian cuisine	Downtown Disney
Raglan Road	Upmarket Irish Pub with music and dance	Downtown Disney
Rainforest Café	Fun and funky atmosphere	Downtown Disney Marketplace
T-Rex	Casual dining with a dinosaur theme	Dowtown Disney Marketplace
Wolfgang Puck Café	Terrific salads, pizza, and sushi	Downtown Disney West Side

Service Restaurants of the World

Rating	Price	Advance Reservations	Suitability for Kids	Meals Served
★★	$$	Not accepted	Moderate	L, D
★	$$	Not accepted	Moderate	L, D
★★★	$$$	Recommended	Low	L, D
★★	$$	Not accepted	Moderate	Sunday brunch, L, D
★★	$$	Recommended	High	L, D
★★	$$	Recommended	Low	D
★★	$$	Recommended	Low	L, D
★★	$$	Not accepted	High	B, L, D
★	$$	Not accepted	High	L, D
★★★	$$$	Only upstairs, recommended	Moderate	L, D

of cooking in the open bush. The interesting wine list is exclusively South African. "Very exotic with wonderful food and a lovely setting," reported a father of two from New York. "Our server was extremely knowledgeable about the South African wines. We'll be back!"

Kimonos ★★

If you love sushi and sashimi, you'll adore this elegant restaurant in the Swan Resort.

Kona Café ★★

The Kona Café offers Pacific Rim food with a tropical emphasis. The crab cakes are delicious, and the desserts alone make the Kona worth the trip. Situated in the Polynesian, this is also one of the best places among all the Magic Kingdom resorts for breakfast.

Maya Grill ★

The Maya Grill serves steak, pork, chicken, and seafood with a nuevo Latin touch. Many of the entrées are grilled over an open fire. Sadly, the quality doesn't match the variety.

Narcoossee's ★★

Inside the white octagonal building on the water at the Grand Floridian, Narcoossee's offers exceptionally pretty views as well as fresh seafood. As a bonus, you can see the Magic Kingdom fireworks.

1900 Park Fare ★★

This large, pleasant Grand Floridian restaurant is appealing to families because it offers character dining and large buffets with kid-pleasing food. Be forewarned—this place is always loud, even when the characters aren't in attendance.

'Ohana ★★

A fun, family-friendly place—the name, in fact, means "family" in Hawaiian—in the Polynesian Resort, 'Ohana specializes in skewered meats, teriyaki- and citrus-based sauces, and tropical fruits and vegetables. The food is prepared in a large, open-fire pit, and there's often some sort of activity, such as limbo contests, to keep the kids entertained. "This place is a blast," a mom from North Carolina wrote. "The food is good, and they get it out fast, but the really nice thing is all the activities for the kids, like crazy relay races and hula lessons. We sat down at the table, ordered some of those big tropical umbrella drinks, and just relaxed and watched the kids have a ball. The only bad thing was that there was so much going on our youngest son never got around to eating his dinner. The nice waitress said this happened all the time and boxed it for him to take back to the room."A mom from Massachusetts confirms, "The service here is excellent. Our waiter was so busy trying to keep our 1-year-old entertained it was almost like having a babysitter."

Palio ★★

The Swan is home to this trattoria, which serves wonderful pasta in a pleasant, open setting. Palio is Italian for "flag," and, indeed, many brightly colored flags hang from the rafters.

Shula's ★★★

The Dolphin's swankiest steak house is owned by former Miami Dolphin coach Don Shula. (Nice tie-in!) The restaurant is quite dignified, despite the football theme, and you'll need an NFL-size appetite to finish the 48-ounce Porterhouse or

4-pound lobster. Note: This is not, repeat not, a family restaurant. The menu pointedly states, "No children's menu available."

Shutters ★

Shutters, in the Caribbean Beach Resort, is a casual island-theme restaurant serving prime rib, lamb chops, and jerk chicken. The food is nothing special, but if you just can't go to Florida without sampling a big, fruity rum drink, this is your kind of place.

Victoria and Albert's ★★★

Extraordinarily elegant cuisine and special attention to details, such as personalized menus, harp music, and roses for the ladies, are the hallmarks of this lovely restaurant. The only AAA five-diamond restaurant in WDW (and the most expensive), V&A is the ultimate spot for a parents' night out.

The Wave ★★

Located in the Contemporary Resort, The Wave serves breakfast, lunch, and dinner offering "bold American cooking with flavors from all over the world." The seasonal menu features local and regional products as well as organic beers, trendy cocktails, and an international wine list that literally offers a strange little twist. All of the wines have screw tops instead of corks.

Whispering Canyon Café ★★

Kids can saddle up and ride stick ponies to their table at this family-style eatery in the Wilderness Lodge. All-you-can-eat barbecue dinners are brought to the table in cast-iron buckets, or you can order à la carte. If you like home cooking in a casual atmosphere where the kids can get a bit rowdy, Whispering Canyon is a good bet.

Yachtsman Steakhouse

We're not sure how a yachtsman gets his hands on so much good beef, but this Yacht Club restaurant is one of the premier steak houses in Disney World. You can find a full selection of hand-cut steaks and chops with your choice of sauces, served up in a clubby dining room.

Restaurants in the Rest of the World

All-Star Café

This sports bar is the only full-service restaurant at Disney's Wide World of Sports complex. TVs broadcast sporting events from every wall and the mood is loud, cheerful, and raucous, with plenty of games for the kids. Expect pasta, pizza, sand-wiches, and burgers.

Bongos Cuban Café

Founded by singer Gloria Estefan, Bongos delivers an Ameri-canized version of Cuban dishes, such as black bean soup and grilled pork, along with a wildly tropical decor, and loud Latin music.

Fulton's Crab House ★★★

Fulton's, on the moored Empress Lilly riverboat, offers seafood flown in fresh daily from all over the world. The raw oysters are always a treat.

House of Blues

Dan Aykroyd's House of Blues serves up Cajun and Creole cooking while a nightclub attached to the restaurant serves up jazz, country, rock and roll, and, yes, blues music. The Gospel brunch on Sunday is an especially good choice for families. To find out who's playing or to purchase tickets call 407/934–2583 (407/934–BLUE).

Planet Hollywood

Planet Hollywood's giant blue globe holds numerous movie props, including the bus from *Speed,* which hovers menacingly overhead while you dine. Film clips run constantly and even the menus, which are printed with the high school graduation pictures of stars, are entertaining. The food is just what you'd expect.

Portobello Yacht Club

A recent revamp transformed the Portobello Yacht Club into a Tuscan country trattoria with an attractive interior and a wide variety of authentic Italian dishes. It's a bit quieter and more adult than many of the Downtown Disney restaurants. The patio is especially pleasant in spring and fall.

Raglan Road

A life-size bronze statue of Irish poet Patrick Kavanaugh sitting lost in thought on a bench greets you outside this Downtown Disney Irish pub. Inside are four huge wooden bars that were crafted in Ireland in the 19th century. There's often live music and, although there's no cost to get into the bar, the music and dancing bring a lot of excitement into the pub. As for the food, the classics go upscale, with Angus-beef shepherd's pie and Colorado lamb in a sophisticated port wine sauce. A dive bar this is not—a pint of Guinness will cost you $6.50. But Raglan Road is a favorite with locals and visitors alike.

Rainforest Café

This sister restaurant to the Animal Kingdom location serves casual food in a jungle-theme atmosphere. Most kids love the Rainforest Café, but the music can get very loud, which may bother babies and toddlers. Waits can be long in the evening and advance reservations are not presently available, so take a buzzer and shop around the Marketplace while you wait.

T-Rex

Managed by the same company that runs the Rainforest Café, T-Rex offers casual, family-friendly dining in the form of pasta, pizzas, seafood, and salads, plus giant audio-animatronic dinosaurs, geysers, waterfalls, and a fossil dig site.

Insider's Secret

A new (and as yet unnamed) restaurant will be opening in Downtown Disney in 2010 featuring Central and South American cuisine, specialty drinks, and live Latin music.

Wolfgang Puck Café

There are three parts to this restaurant: the ultracasual Express, which offers salads, sandwiches, and such; the inside restaurant, which provides Puck's signature pastas and pizzas, as well as outstanding sushi; and, upstairs, the formal dining room, serving the best Puck has to offer. Needless to say, the first two locations work best for families, and the latter is best reserved for a parents' night out. "The best meal we had during our entire time in Orlando was downstairs at Wolfgang Puck," said one father of two. "The kiddie food was a cut above average, and the adults thought the sushi was great." A father of three concurs that the inside restaurant is the perfect middle ground between the express and formal options and that, "the Hoisin BBQ ribs are worth coming back for."

CHAPTER
12

Disney After Dark

Disney World After Dark with the Kids

Is there life in Disney World after 8 PM? Sure there is. The crowds thin, the temperature drops, and many attractions are especially dazzling in the dark. During peak seasons the major theme parks run extra-long hours, so it's easy to have fun at night. But, needless to say, the particular kind of fun you'll have depends on whether the kids are with you.

Evening Activities for the Whole Family

The Evening Parade in the Magic Kingdom

Disney's ever-popular evening parades blend lasers, lights, and fireworks for a dazzling display. Tinker Bell's Flight begins a few minutes before the fireworks, so be sure to look to the castle to watch her descent.

The parade runs every night during the on-season and twice a night on holidays and especially crowded days. In the off-season it runs only on selected evenings, so plan your schedule to ensure you'll be in the Magic Kingdom on one of the nights it's slated to run. If you miss the parade, you can still get

Insider's Secret
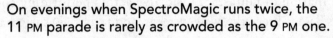
On evenings when SpectroMagic runs twice, the
11 PM parade is rarely as crowded as the 9 PM one.

to see the *Wishes* fireworks since it always closes the evening.
Times and dates are listed on your entertainment schedule; you
can get this information in advance by calling Guest Services
(a.k.a. Guest Relations) at your hotel or visiting www.
disneyworld.com.

The Electrical Water Pageant

If you're staying on-site, the Electrical Water Pageant may actually float by your hotel window, because it's staged on the
Seven Seas Lagoon, which connects the Polynesian, Contemporary, Grand Floridian, and Wilderness Lodge resorts. A much
shorter and simpler show than SpectroMagic, the Electrical
Water Pageant is a charming progression of moving multicolor
sea images whose sparkling lights are reflected in the dark water.

IllumiNations

IllumiNations fully ranks with Fantasmic! and SpectroMagic as
a fantastic closing show that appeals to all ages. It can be viewed
nightly from anywhere around the World Showcase Lagoon at
9 PM.

Helpful Hint

Electrical Water Pageant times vary with the season,
so contact Guest Services for the exact time the
parade is scheduled to float by your resort. If you're
not staying at a Magic Kingdom resort but would
like to see the parade, plan to have dinner at one of
the resorts in question, then wander out to the
beach area at showtime.

Fantasmic!

This nightly closing show at Hollywood is a must-see. The combination of fantastic music, live actors performing cool stunts, lasers, fireworks, water screens, and favorite Disney characters makes for one spine-tingling show. Showtimes vary so check your entertainment schedule.

Downtown Disney

Downtown Disney keeps hopping long after the theme parks shut down. Some families wait to shop and eat until late at night.

BoardWalk

Lively and gorgeous after dark, the BoardWalk is a hub of family-style activity. Eat dinner, then rent a surrey bike for a quick lap around the lagoon. There are also two clubs here, but they're strictly for adults 21 and over.

Miniature Golf

Evening is often the most comfortable time to check out Fantasia Gardens or Winter Summerland, especially in summer.

Night Swimming

Blizzard Beach and Typhoon Lagoon run extended hours in summer, and evening swimming can be a delight during the hottest weeks of the year. You don't have to worry about sunburn, and the crowds are much lighter. Hotel pools stay open late as well, many until after midnight.

Disney World After Dark without the Kids: Finding a Sitter

Why would any decent parent seek a sitter while on a family vacation? Consider this scenario: Meaghan's sucking the inside of her mouth. Loud. Mom keeps making everyone stop while she readjusts the strap of her shoe to accommodate the blister she picked up halfway around the World Showcase Lagoon.

You spent $272 to get through the Magic Kingdom gates—and Devin spends two hours feeding quarters into the same arcade game that's in the mall back home. Dad has been singing the first line—and only the first line—of "Zip-a-Dee-Doo-Dah" since Thursday. You've asked to see the kiddie menus from nine different restaurants in nine different Epcot countries, and you end up at the American pavilion fast-food joint because Kristy won't eat anything but a hot dog. It's 108 degrees, this trip is costing $108 an hour, and that infernal sucking sound is getting on your last nerve.

Although it may seem un-American to suggest building time apart into the middle of a family vacation, the truth is that everyone will have more fun if you occasionally break up the group for a while. Even the most devoted of families aren't accustomed to being together 24 hours a day—for every meal, every ride, every potty stop. Every minute.

Some of the hotels in Orlando have responded with programs designed to get the kids involved with other children while parents have a night on the town. The idea is that everyone returns refreshed and recharged, with some happy stories to tell, and you can start the next day actually glad to be together again.

Quite a few off-site hotels have their own kids' clubs. Visit and tour the club before you drop your children off and make sure that the place seems clean, safe, and has an appropriate child-to-caregiver ratio.

On-Site Kids' Clubs

The following on-site hotels have kids' clubs (all numbers begin with area code 407):

Animal Kingdom Lodge	938–4785
BoardWalk	939–5100
Contemporary	824–1000

Dolphin	934–4241
Grand Floridian	824–1666
Polynesian	824–2000
Wilderness Lodge	824–3200
Yacht and Beach Clubs	934–8000

The clubs generally run in the evening for kids ages 4 to 12, and they're most interesting for the 4–8 set. The older the child, the more likely he or she is to be bored. The clubhouses are well stocked with toys, computers, video games, and large-screen TVs. Make reservations by calling Guest Services at the appropriate hotel; on-site guests get first crack at the available slots, but if the clubs don't fill up, space is available to off-site visitors. Note that children must be toilet trained.

Helpful Hint

Prices, policy, and planned entertainment change quickly at the kids' clubs, so confirm everything when you make your reservations.

The clubs usually open at 4 or 5 PM and closing time varies. Obviously, if you'll be dining at a Disney resort, it makes sense to try to book your kids into that hotel's child-care program so that you can just drop them off, go on to your restaurant, and return to pick them up later. Parents are given pagers in case of emergencies, so you can truly relax while you enjoy your time alone. Rates are usually around $12 per hour, and a credit card guarantee is

Insider's Secret

The Polynesian offers the most elaborate kids' program: the Never Land Club, with buffet food and entertainment for the youngsters.

required when you make your reservation; if plans change, be sure to cancel or you'll be charged.

In-Room Sitters

Kids' clubs aren't always the way to go. You'll need to arrange for an in-room sitter if any of the following conditions apply:

- @ You have a child under the age of 4. That's the cutoff point for most group programs.

- @ You plan to be out after midnight. Most kids' clubs close down before then, some as early as 10 PM.

- @ Your kids are exhausted. If you know in advance that you plan to employ an all-out touring schedule or your kids fall apart after 8 PM, hire an in-room sitter who can make sure they're in bed by their usual time. Most of the kids' clubs try to put preschoolers down in sleeping bags by 9 PM but this involves moving them, and probably waking them, when parents return.

- @ You have a big family. Even with the add-on per-child rate, you can come out cheaper with an in-room sitter than you will if you book four kids into a group program.

For those staying on-site, Kids' Night Out provides trained sitters for all the Disney hotels; call 407/828–0920 at least eight hours in advance. And prepare for sticker shock. The rate is $15 an hour for one child, plus $3 per hour for each additional child, with a four-hour minimum. A $10 transportation fee is also common, meaning that in-room sitting for two kids for four hours can run $75 or more. Not cheap, but for many parents it's well worth the cost under the circumstances.

If you're staying off-site, contact your hotel for help with in-room sitting. Most Orlando properties have relationships with reputable services. Not only does this save you a bit of hassle, but the person at the Guest Services desk is also apt to know a lot more about who to call than you; if former guests haven't been pleased with a sitter, the hotel was undoubtedly the first to hear about it, so most family-oriented hotels use the same services over and over.

Dining without the Kids

The following five restaurants are especially adult-oriented and a good choice when the kids aren't along.

Insider's Secret

No matter what child-care option you choose, the key point is to make your plans in advance. If you suddenly get an urge for fine dining at 4 PM on a Saturday in July, it will be hard to find a sitter or get into a kids' club. But if you've checked out your options and reserved space in advance, planning an adult night out is a breeze.

Bistro de Paris

The Bistro, upstairs from Les Chefs de France and accessible by a back staircase, is so lovely and secluded that you might forget you're in a theme park. The wine list is one of the best in Epcot and the classic French fare is fabulous.

California Grill

Not only does the California Grill offer marvelous cuisine with stylish preparation, but the views from the top of the Contemporary are unparalleled. In terms of the quality and variety of the food, it's superb. A mom from New York agreed: "I'm a caterer so I know food, and I consider the California Grill to be by far the best restaurant in Disney World."

Citricos

Citricos, in the Grand Floridian, is excellent, but because of its proximity to Victoria & Albert's, the restaurant can be sometimes overlooked and is thus easier to get into. The menu features Mediterranean cuisine and is updated frequently. The wine selection is noteworthy.

Jiko

The "cooking place," as the name means in Swahili, serves truly innovative, sophisticated, well-spiced food based on African

Insider's Secret

Couples who are dining late may find themselves leaving a resort restaurant after the transportation system has closed down. You can either drive your own car or use Downtown Disney (whose buses run until 2 AM) as a transfer station. Your best bet, especially if you've had wine with dinner, is to let the valets at your resort or restaurant call you a cab.

cuisine. A collection of the unusual and tasty appetizers can make a meal, or your server will help you pair your main course (maize-crusted halibut, for example), with a superb South African wine. Jiko has roomy booths and a cooking island whose seats afford views of the busy chefs.

Victoria & Albert's

Where Disney has built a reputation on providing entertainment to the masses, this 60-seat, AAA five-diamond restaurant in the Grand Floridian proves that there's also room in Disney World for highly individual service. At Victoria & Albert's, harp music plays, candles flicker, menus are personalized, ladies are presented with roses, and people still dress up for dinner.

The six-course prix-fixe dinner presently costs $115 per person, or $175 if you have wine paired with each course, but it's an experience so elaborate that you'll be talking about it for years afterward. For example, on the evening we visited, the salad was a floral arrangement in a crouton vase—until our

Insider's Secret

What's more special than an evening at Victoria & Albert's? An evening at the chef's table. You're seated inside the kitchen where executive chef Scott Hummel treats you as his private guests. The chef's table is the proverbial "once in a lifetime" gourmet experience and you must reserve months in advance. Call 407/939–3463 (407/WDW–DINE) for details.

server, who called herself Victoria in keeping with the theme, tapped the side of the crouton with a spoon. It then broke, releasing the greens into a fan-shaped pattern on the plate. We were nearly hypnotized by the ceremony. This is by far the most elegant and refined restaurant you'll find on Disney property.

The Cruise Vacation Package

Disney is now entering its 12th year in the cruise line business, and their family-oriented cruise packages are more popular than ever. At present Disney has two ships, the Magic and the Wonder, but two more are on order and will debut in 2011 and 2012.

The most basic cruise is a Caribbean route with three- and four-day runs to Nassau and Disney's private island, Castaway Cay. These shorter cruises can be combined with a three- or four-day stay at Walt Disney World as part of a land-and-sea package.

If you'd like to cruise the Caribbean for a whole week, you have a choice between four-, five-, and seven-day itineraries—each with various ports of call. Up for a longer and more glamorous cruise? Disney offers specialty cruises to the Mediterranean and northern Europe, including transatlantic crossings. You can check out all the upcoming offerings at www.disneycruise.com.

The key thing about these cruises is that the activities and the attitude are decidedly geared toward families. There are no casinos on board, entertainment is wholesome, drinking and carousing are de-emphasized, shore excursions tend toward kid-friendly pursuits like snorkeling and dolphin swims, and there are excellent (in fact, award-winning) child-care options on board the ship. Disney cruises are perfect for the family that needs a bit of everything in the course of a one-week vacation: time for the adults to relax alone and time together as a family. Families whose kids vary in ages are especially sold on the cruises. Because there are so many kids on board and the age categories in the youth programs are tight, it's equally likely that your 3-year-old and 13-year-old will each have found a friend by the end of the first day. Let's face it—nothing beats a vacation where everyone is happy.

You can order a free vacation-planning DVD and brochure at www.disneycruise.com or by calling 800/951–3532. "We booked online but ordered the brochures just as a way to double-check everything," reported one father of three from New York. "We were glad we did because they're really cute and child-friendly and helped our kids visualize in advance what the ship would be like. The DVD is great, too—almost like a free Disney movie."

The Land-and-Sea Package

Many first-time Disney cruisers opt for the Land-and-Sea package, which combines a stay at Walt Disney World with a three- or four-day cruise. (The only itinerary difference between the two is that the longer cruise has a full day at sea.) It's a good way to get the best of both worlds.

Most families begin their trip at Walt Disney World. You're met at the Orlando airport and escorted directly to your resort, where you can find all the documentation you need for the entire week. After the theme-park segment of the trip is over, you're transported by a special Disney Cruise Line (DCL) bus to the ship, which waits in Port Canaveral harbor, approximately 90 minutes from Orlando.

Helpful Hint

Although it's possible to reverse the order, most families like touring first and cruising last. That way the relaxing cruise segment follows the more exhausting theme park segment of the week.

Disney does everything possible to make the transition "seamless"; the key to your Orlando hotel room is also the key to your stateroom on the ship and you can use it as a charge card both at Disney World and on board the ship. Your bags are picked up from your hotel room and transferred directly to your room on the ship. In short, the logistics of checking in and checking out, arranging transportation, and lugging baggage are all handled for you.

Cruise-Only Packages

If you've already visited Disney World, you might want to opt for a cruise-only package. It's certainly possible to take just the three- or four-day cruise, or you can upgrade to one of the seven-day cruises.

Approximate Costs

Calculating the exact cost of your cruise depends on several factors: the time of year, the size of your family, and the level of cabin or stateroom you choose. It's probably a little too late to do anything about the size of your family, but the other two factors are within your control.

If you look at the price charts in the brochure, it seems that off-season savings aren't very significant. But the brochure is deceptive because it doesn't list specials—and DCL actually offers some very interesting discounts during the off-season. These deals are available via www.disneycruise.com, travel agents, organizations like AAA, and independent travel Web sites like www.mousesavers.com. In other words, if you're going in the middle of summer or Christmas week, you'll probably end up paying close to the amount listed in the brochure. If you're going the third week of October, you should be able to snag some sort of discount and it may well represent a significant savings over the prices listed in the brochure.

Lodging also affects the bottom line. All staterooms on board are nicely appointed, designed for families, and therefore 25% larger than standard cruise ship cabins, so it's really just a matter of how much space you're willing to pay for and how posh a resort you want in Orlando. Guests booking a suite on the ship will stay at the Grand Floridian during the Orlando part of their vacation; families in an ocean-view stateroom with veranda will stay at a deluxe resort like the Polynesian or Beach Club; if you choose an inside or standard stateroom on the ship, you'll stay at one of the mid-price resorts like Port Orleans while in Orlando.

Your selection of resort and room has a major impact on the final price. For example, a family of four taking the full seven-day vacation in summer, and staying in a deluxe ocean-view stateroom with veranda during their cruise

Insider's Secret
When shopping for discounts leave no stone unturned— and make no assumptions. Although some families report that travel agents found them the best deals, others say that agents quoted higher rates than those given when they called Disney directly.

and the Beach Club Resort during the land segment of their vacation, will pay about $8,900. But do they need to go top-of-the-line? If that same family going that same week is willing to book a standard stateroom and stay at the moderately priced Port Orleans, the price drops to the $5,600 range.

And then there's the issue of timing, which can affect the bottom line even more. If this family of four were willing to travel during seven days in October, they could go deluxe for about $6,500, and moderate for about $4,000. In other words, by changing the level of your stateroom and the time of year you travel, you can cut the total price of the vacation package by more than half.

The most inexpensive option, as you might expect, is the three-day cruise without the time in Disney World. In July a family of four will pay $3,000–$4,400, depending on their level of stateroom. In October, they'll pay $2,300–$3,200 depending on their level of stateroom. (Note: These quoted prices do not include airfare. Adding it on is always an option, and the price rises accordingly, depending on where your flight originates.)

Get the picture? Prices vary dramatically and various contingencies can and will affect the bottom line. To estimate the price of your cruise, start by going to www.disneycruise.com and typing in the month you wish to travel, the itinerary, and

Money-Saving Tip

The ship is going to sail no matter how many people are on board, so cruise lines offer significant discounts as the time of departure approaches and staterooms remain un-booked. Disney is no exception to this rule, but be aware that the cheaper stateroom levels sell out first, so discounts are more likely to be available on the unsold premium-level staterooms. So last-minute travelers may not find lower prices, but they may well find more bang for their buck.

the number of people in your party. This will direct you to a page that shows all of your lodging options, from highest to lowest. Choose where you want to stay, and boom: the price of your cruise will pop up on the screen. You can fine-tune from there, and once you have a ballpark price, you can more intelligently comparison shop with a travel agent or on other Web pages. The Web site is also a great source of information on ports of call, shore excursions, and the layout of staterooms.

The glamorous northern European and Mediterranean cruises let you explore Europe as a family without the hassle of flying from country to country, dragging luggage, and checking in and out of hotels. In essence the cruises allow you to board the ship, unpack once, and let Europe come to you. With the exception of a couple of dreamy days at sea, most sailings are at night and each morning you wake up in a different port of call. An 11-night Mediterranean cruise for a family of four in May 2010, for example, will run between $9,000–$13,600, depending upon your choice of cabin.

Other Expenses

One of the beauties of cruising is that most of your expenses are included in your package price. Here's a list of what isn't included.

Alcoholic beverages
Arcade games
Child care for children under 3 at Flounder's Reef
Medical services
Merchandise bought on board or at ports of call
Palo, the adults-only restaurant on both ships, which charges a $15 per person cover
Photography
Ship-to-shore phone calls
Shore excursions

Spa treatments

Tipping (based on industry suggestions, this will be about $15–$20 a day.)

Lodging

Your cruise brochure and the Disney Cruise Line Web site contain renderings of all the staterooms, from the basic inside stateroom designed for three people to a two-bedroom suite that can sleep as many as seven. Most staterooms are in the deluxe ocean-view category, many of them with verandas, and most about 200–250 square feet. (In fact, nearly 75% of the cabins are outside staterooms, so if you're planning to save a few bucks by booking an inside stateroom, call early.)

Cruise veterans recommend that if you're doing the Land-and-Sea package you should focus more on the resort you'll be staying at in Orlando; on the short cruises you're so busy that you're rarely in your stateroom, so it's no big deal if you're a little cramped. In contrast, when you're taking the seven-day cruise you'll be at sea for three days, so the size and location of your stateroom are more important.

Insider's Secret

Palo, the adults-only restaurant, serves the best food on both ships and is very popular. So popular, in fact, that if you want to book a table, you need to either do so via the Internet before you leave home or immediately upon boarding the ship. There's a well-worth-it $15 surcharge for dinner or brunch and $5 for High Tea, which is available only on longer sailings.

Insider's Secret

When you book your cruise, you'll have to choose your meal times: either early or late. The early seating means you have dinner at 6, while the late seating is at 8:30. If you have young kids the early seating works best, although it does mean a crack-of-dawn breakfast time. But I've seen preschoolers literally fall asleep at the table at late seatings—active days bring about early bedtimes. Besides, if you want to sleep in, you can always skip the full breakfast and grab something light at the Topsiders buffet.

Dining

Disney makes dining on board very special. For starters you don't dine in the same restaurant every night. "We figured that a family on vacation wouldn't ordinarily eat at the same restaurant three nights in a row," says Amy Foley of the DCL. "So why would a family on a cruise ship want to eat in the same dining room every night?"

Instead, you experience "rotation dining," trying a different onboard restaurant each evening of your cruise. (Your server and tablemates rotate right along with you.) On *Disney Magic*, there's Lumiere's, which is decidedly French and the most elegant of the eateries, with a theme based on *Beauty and the Beast*. On *Disney Wonder*, your fine-dining option is Triton's, named for the Little Mermaid's father.

On both ships there's Parrot Cay, where the mood and the food are Bahamian and casual, but Animator's Palate is the real showstopper, an interactive dining experience in which the restaurant transforms into a brilliant palette of color as you dine. The meal begins in a room that is utterly black and white, right down to the framed animation sketches on the wall and

Helpful Hint

So where do the kids eat on the night Mom and Dad dine at Palo? First of all, make sure you don't schedule your Palo date night on the evening when you're scheduled for Animator's Palate. It's a thrill for kids and adults. Once you do choose a night and make a reservation at Palo, you have two options for the kids: sign them up for one of the kids' programs that includes dinner, or escort them to the Topsider buffet or one of the fast-food restaurants for an early meal. Afterward, drop them off at the kids' center and head upstairs to Palo.

the servers' somber attire. With each course, more color is added to the artwork, the walls, the table settings, and the servers' costumes. By dessert the whole room is glowing.

On both *Disney Magic* and *Disney Wonder,* adults have a fourth dining option, Palo, an Italian restaurant perched high atop the ship, offering a sweeping view of the ocean. Excellent wine-tasting classes are held there as well.

Not all the dining is formal. A breakfast buffet is available daily on the pool level for families that want to get an early

Time-Saving Tip

Once you book your cruise, reserve shore excursions via www.disneycruise.com or your travel agent. This guarantees you can get everything you want and also saves you from having to stand in line at the shore excursion desk on the first day of your cruise.

start. You can also find a casual buffet lunch daily, and, in case you don't want to take even a minute out of your fun, pizza, burgers, and ice cream are served all afternoon out by the pools.

Ports of Call

The three- and four-day cruises spend one day in Nassau, giving you a chance to shop, sightsee, or visit a casino. There are shore excursions designed for families (and kids of all ages are apt to enjoy a horse-drawn carriage ride), but, frankly, the Nassau stop exists mostly to placate the adults on board who miss the presence of a casino. If you do want to try your luck at the slots, or if your children are too young to comfortably take along on a shopping trip to the straw market, you can always leave them on board in the kids' programs.

The seven-day cruises offer family-friendly shore excursions at every stop such as sailing lessons, snorkeling, and submarine trips. The European cruises also offer shore excursions at every port of call, and the list of possibilities is staggering. A complete list of all shore excursions for every port of call can be found at www.disneycruise.com.

Castaway Cay

All the Caribbean cruises stop at Castaway Cay, a private island where you disembark at the pier (cutting out the time-consuming tendering process often required when a large ship stops at a small island) and stroll onto a beautiful beach. Once there you can hike, bike, play volleyball, take a banana boat ride, rent sailboats or sea kayaks, or simply sun yourself. Organized excursions for families include kayaking, speedboating, a stingray swim, or snorkeling tours. Lunch is cooked right on the island, and there's a small shop in case you find yourself in need of beach toys, towels, or sunscreen.

The children's programs go full force on the island, so after you've played a while as a family, you can drop the kids off

Insider's Secret

Disney has planted a few cute "shipwrecks" and a hidden Mickey or two along the snorkeling paths of Castaway Cay, but the water there is sometimes cloudy, and there are so many people in a small space it can be overwhelming to kids. "I got kicked in the head," reported one 8-year-old from Texas. The snorkeling is generally better on the shore excursions, especially at Grand Cayman on the western Caribbean itinerary and St. John on the eastern one. Most kids 8 and older, assuming they're reasonably capable swimmers, can master the mask and tube. Everyone wears life jackets so you can periodically bob and rest.

and have a little adult time. Counselors lead youngsters on scavenger hunts, "whale excavations," and sand castle–building contests; older kids participate in boat races or bike trips

Helpful Hint

Castaway Cay is so popular that some itineraries stop there twice. If you'd like a lot of beach time on your cruise, consider one of those sailings.

around the island with the counselors; teens have their own beach Olympics and *Survivor*-style games.

Meanwhile, adults can escape to the separate mile-long quiet beach called Serenity Bay, where they can sip a piña colada or have an open-air massage in a private cabana.

Kids' Programs Onboard

Flounder's Reef is the nursery, with play areas for children between 3 months and 3 years of age. It doesn't run the extensive hours of the other children's programs but is open daily to give the parents of infants and toddlers time to relax together or play with their older kids. There's a cost of $6 an hour for one child; for any siblings it's $5 per hour each.

Disney's Oceaneer Club for kids ages 3 to 7 occupies a huge play area complete with a re-creation of Captain Hook's pirate ship. The well-trained and upbeat counselors lead the kids in games and crafts, including dancing with Snow White, and a "lab" where kids learn to make flubber. Highlights of the longer cruises include a party with Peter Pan, and Goofy's PJ Party, a sleepover with games and storytelling. On the first evening aboard the ship, counselors meet with the parents to explain the program and help ease the kids in.

Kids ages 8 to 12 hang out in the Oceaneer Lab where they can learn to make flubber, draw animation cels, and race cars carved from soap. There's also plenty of outdoor action, from games on the sports deck to water activities in the sports pool.

The activities at Oceaneer's Club and Oceaneer's Lab run throughout the day and night. Whenever you drop your kids

Money-Saving Tip
Child care–entertainment is free for kids over 3 but you'll pay dearly to arrange child care for younger kids. For this reason some families wait until their youngest is past that crucial three-year mark before taking the cruises.

Insider's Secret

Children, already overwhelmed by the size and newness of the ship, often suffer a bit of separation anxiety the first time they're dropped off at one of the programs. Try to persuade them to join the activities that first evening, when everyone is new and fast friendships are made. The counselors are trained to look out for shy or nervous children and help them make a smooth transition into the group activities.

off, you're given a pager so that you can be reached at any time. If the kids are in the programs during meal times, they'll be escorted to the Topsiders Buffet by counselors.

Teens ages 13 to 17 have their own spaces: a private haven called Aloft aboard the *Wonder* and The Stack aboard the *Magic*. The spaces look like a combination coffeehouse–dorm room. Teens are pretty much given the run of the ship—coun-

Insider's Secret

The Disney Magic also features a scaled replica of the ship's bridge called Ocean Quest where kids in that tough "neither here nor there" 10–14 age range can chill and watch movies, play video games, or do their own age-appropriate arts and crafts.

selors lead them in ship-wide scavenger hunts, video game tournaments, and pool parties. Glow Jam, a nighttime sport involving glow-in-the-dark bracelets, and the Wildside Adventures on Castaway Cay, are especially popular.

Insider's Secret

The onboard spa offers a range of services, including some designed exclusively for couples. Just hanging out in the beautiful sauna and steam area is a great way to kill an afternoon. If you want to book a massage or facial, especially on a day when the ship is at sea, go immediately to the spa after boarding the ship to make an appointment. The best times get snatched up early.

Onboard Entertainment

There are three pools on board: one, shaped like Mickey, with a pint-size tube slide for little kids; a second "sports pool" for games and the rowdier activities of older children; and a third "quiet pool" for adults, complete with large, elevated hot tubs. In addition, the ship has a sports deck, a full-service spa, an exercise room, and several shops.

The cornerstone of onboard entertainment is the 975-seat Walt Disney Theater, one of the most technologically advanced theaters in the world and certainly the most remarkable on any cruise ship. Here DCL showcases Broadway-style shows, some of them new and some based on Disney classics. Must-see productions include Toy Story: The Musical; the Golden Mickeys, a tribute to classic animated films; and the stunning Disney Dreams, which always seems to bring half the audience to tears.

Studio Sea, a family lounge, provides dance music, parties, and participatory game shows starring the audience. The Mickey Mania trivia game is a real blast. The Buena Vista Theater shows a variety of Disney movies daily and, come nightfall, a jumbo screen allows you to watch movies outdoors on the

Helpful Hint

Of course the characters are sailing right along with you. They turn out for deck parties—including the welcome-aboard and farewell bashes—and also appear around the ship. Check your daily onboard newsletter, the Personal Navigator, for times and locations.

deck, a good way to coax wound-up kids to calm down and give way to sleep.

One of the definite highlights on the longer cruises is the Pirates of Caribbean party. Passengers dress like buccaneers and convene for a rollicking deck party with the characters. Smee and Captain Hook show up and try to cause trouble but, not to worry, Captain Mickey prevails, and a good time is had by all. The evening rounds out with fireworks, music, and dancing.

Insider's Secret

More and more, large families are meeting up on cruises, where everyone can be together but still go off and do their own thing. Consider this report from a mother of three from Michigan: "My sisters and I have a family reunion at Disney World every other year. When we get all the kids and spouses together, there are 14 of us, with a wide range of ages. Last year for the first time we took the cruise and found that worked great. Those with babies could go back to their cabins whenever someone got cranky or tired, those with school-age kids could just keep going, and those with older kids could let them go to the pools and arcades on their own."

After the shows wind down, adults can congregate in the entertainment districts, dubbed Beat Street on *Disney Magic* and Route 66 on *Disney Wonder.* Expect a dance club that alternates between rock and country music, a sports pub, and a piano bar.

CHAPTER

14

Universal
Orlando

Universal Studios

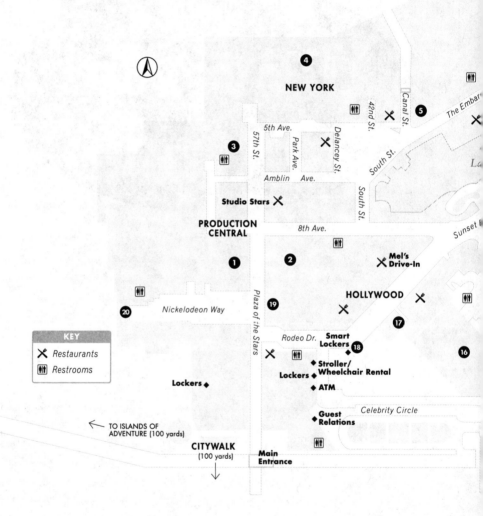

NEW YORK 4

5 Canal St.

The Embar

42nd St.

5th Ave.

Park Ave.

Delancey St.

South St.

La

3

57th St.

Amblin Ave.

Studio Stars

South St.

PRODUCTION CENTRAL

8th Ave.

Sunset

Mel's Drive-In

1

2

HOLLYWOOD

20

Nickelodeon Way

19

17

16

Rodeo Dr.

Smart Lockers 18

♦ Stroller/ Wheelchair Rental

Lockers ♦

♦ ATM

Lockers ♦

Celebrity Circle

← TO ISLANDS OF ADVENTURE (100 yards)

♦ Guest Relations

CITYWALK (100 yards)

Main Entrance

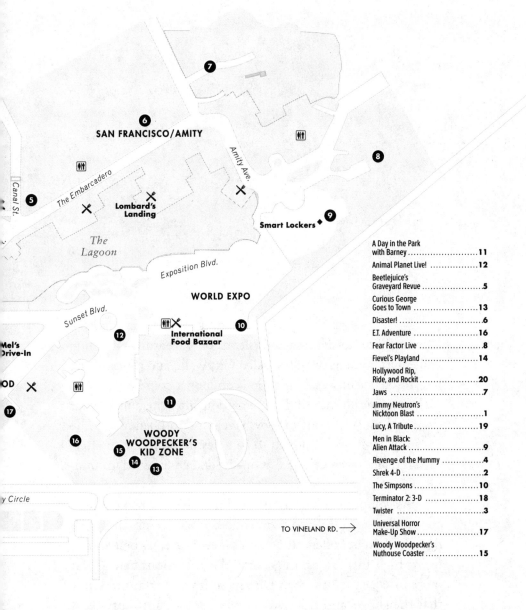

SAN FRANCISCO/AMITY

Canal St.

The Embarcadero

Amity Ave.

Lombard's
Landing

Smart Lockers ◆ **9**

5

6

7

8

*The
Lagoon*

Exposition Blvd.

WORLD EXPO

Sunset Blvd.

International
Food Bazaar

Mel's
Drive-In

OD

12

10

17

11

16

15

14

13

**WOODY
WOODPECKER'S
KID ZONE**

y Circle

TO VINELAND RD. →

With two full theme parks—Universal Studios Florida and Islands of Adventure—a dining and entertainment complex called CityWalk, and three on-site resort hotels, Universal Orlando is no longer content to be the park you visit on the last day of vacation, after the bulk of your time and most of your money have gone to Disney. On the contrary, Universal is poised to be a destination, not an afterthought, aiming to keep guests on-site and entertained for multiday stays.

As you prepare a touring plan for Universal, make sure to choose the best rides and shows for your particular family. Although Universal offers attractions for every age, it's best known for its high-thrill rides. In general, the attractions here are far more intense than those at Disney, so it's important to know that the shows and rides you choose are age appropriate. A mother of one from Missouri agrees: "The first time we went to Universal Studios our daughter was 4, and there wasn't too much she could ride or enjoy at such a young age. The next time we went back she was 8, and she loved it. Kids have to be a bit older to really get into the Universal Studios style of ride."

On the other hand, if you have teenagers, you may want to spend more time at Universal than at Disney. Consider this report from a father of three: "My children love roller coasters (the wilder the better) and prefer Universal to Disney. So we do the opposite of most families, staying at Universal and driving over for a day at Disney."

Universal Orlando is off Interstate 4 at Exits 74B and 75A. Road signs to the complex are well marked. For more information visit www.universalorlando.com or call 407/363–8000.

Helpful Hint

Just as many people confuse Walt Disney World and the Magic Kingdom, Universal's expansion has led to some confusion regarding the names of its parks. The entire complex, consisting of two theme parks, three hotels, and CityWalk, is called Universal Orlando. Universal Studios Florida refers to the original theme park, which has attractions based on the movies that Universal Pictures has produced over the years. Islands of Adventure is the second theme park.

Should We Stay On-Site?

Whether you decide to stay at one of Universal Orlando's three on-site resorts—the Portofino Bay Hotel, the Hard Rock Hotel, and the Royal Pacific Resort—depends on how much you're willing to spend for certain conveniences and privileges extended only to on-site guests. The on-site resorts, managed by Loews Hotels, are all luxurious, with the ultimate in amenities and price tags to match. Depending on the resort and the season, rates average between $200–$350 a night.

There are plenty of resorts on International Drive and other roads that flank the park, but Universal draws high-spending visitors by offering lots of perks for on-site guests.

Advantages of Staying On-Site

As you can see by the following list, staying on-site definitely makes your vacation more seamless.

- By far the biggest advantage is that resort guests can use the Express system, which is much like Disney's Fastpass, on an unlimited basis. Just show your resort ID, that is, your room key card, and you'll be admitted into the Express ticket line on any ride you choose at any time you choose. This virtually eliminates having to wait in line and it's a huge, huge perk. It's also a $20–$60 per person value—the cost of an Express pass.

- Resort guests get priority seating in restaurants and can make reservations in advance.

- Complimentary water taxi and bus transportation between your resort and the theme parks is included. (All three of the on-site hotels are linked to the two theme parks and CityWalk by a series of scenic waterways.) Not only does the transportation system make it easier for you to return to your room for a midday break, but it saves you the time, effort, and expense of driving to the theme parks.

- Complimentary package delivery of in-park purchases to guest rooms.

Helpful Hint

For information about and reservations for all three of the on-site hotels, call 888/273–1311 or visit www.universalorlando.com.

@ Resort IDs allow you to charge merchandise, food, and tickets to your hotel room.

On-Site Hotels

Hard Rock Hotel   407/363–8000

Fun, flashy, and funky, the 650-room Hard Rock Hotel has a broad and eclectic collection of rock memorabilia. If you like the idea of a 7 AM serenade from Elvis, you can even ask for a rock star wake-up call in the morning. Music plays continually throughout the beautifully landscaped grounds and sophisticated lounges. The dramatic pool area has a 260-foot waterslide, plus a 12-speaker underwater sound system, so you can get your aural fix even while taking a swim. There are three bars and two restaurants, including an Orlando version of the well-known Palm Restaurant, as well as a gym and activity center with children's programs, which are open year-round in the evenings with extended daytime hours during the on-season.

The Hard Rock Hotel is the perfect choice for families with older kids and teens who can appreciate the hipper-than-thou ambience. Rates range from $234 to $334 per night, and around $500 for a kids' suite. If money isn't an object you can live like the King in the $1,350-per-night Graceland Suite, whose flamboyant amenities include a piano.

Helpful Hint

All three of the Universal resorts are within walking distance of the Universal parks, about a 20-minute drive from Walt Disney World, and about a 10-minute drive from SeaWorld.

Portofino Bay Hotel   **407/363–8000**

The Portofino Bay, Universal Orlando's first hotel, is modeled after the Italian seaside village of Portofino. From the outside you see quaint, colorful row houses that are actually all connected on the inside. The 750 elegant rooms include 18 children's suites.

Portofino Bay has eight restaurants and lounges; a full-service spa; three swimming pools; and Campo Portofino, a supervised children's activity center, which is open in the evenings year-round with extended daytime hours during the on-season.

Like all the on-site properties, this is a Loews resort, so the service is top-notch. Of the three resorts, Portofino Bay is the most posh with the most amenities geared to adults who want to relax in a beautiful environment. Rates for regular rooms range from $274 to $399 a night, while suites, including the roomy kids' suites, are higher, averaging about $500.

Royal Pacific Resort   **407/503–3000**

The Royal Pacific is the largest of the three Universal resorts, with 1,000 guest rooms on 53 acres. The lush grounds, thickly planted with tropical plants and trees, have a distinct South Pacific flair, and they're connected to CityWalk and the theme parks via water taxi and a series of winding, well-manicured pathways. There are two restaurants and two lounges, plus a luau party area, a fitness center, a children's activity center, and a massive pool area.

Perhaps most significant, the Royal Pacific is Universal's convention hotel, with 80,000 square feet of meeting space. This doesn't mean the resort won't be comfortable for families—the enormous pool and the children's center indicate that the resort is family-friendly—but you may find a lot of businesspeople mixed in with the vacationing crowd.

Rates range from $219 to $334 a night, making the Royal Pacific the most affordable of the three on-site resorts.

Helpful Hint

To check out Universal packages, visit www. universalorlando.com. If none of the packages exactly suits your needs, you can type in the specifics you require and the system will tally up the cost, in essence allowing you to create your own package.

Money-Saving Tip

Traveling during the off-season? You can find major bargains at the Universal Resorts on select value days. The Royal Pacific starts at $150, the Hard Rock at $161, and Portofino Bay at $189.

What Kind of Tickets Do We Need?

Universal offers several ticket options. Prices below are for tickets purchased at www.universalorlando.com; they go up anywhere from $8 to $12 per day if you buy them at the gate.

Time-Saving Tip

Ordering your theme-park tickets online can save you money and, if you pick your tickets up at a kiosk, time. But, if your money-saving deal requires you to pick up your tickets at Guest Services (a.k.a. Guest Relations) think twice. The Guest Services booths at both Universal Studios and Islands of Adventure are nightmarish experiences in what are otherwise well-run parks; slow-moving lines forcing 20- to 30-minute waits are standard in the morning.

One-Day, One-Park Ticket

Admits holders to either Universal Studios or Islands of Adventure for one day.

- Adults and children over 9: $67 ($75 at the gate).

- Children ages 3 to 9: $56 ($63 at the gate).

One-Day, Two-Park Ticket

Admits holders to Universal Studios and Islands of Adventure for one day.

- Adults and children over 9: $90 at the gate.

- Children ages 3 to 9: $80 at the gate.

Two-Day, Two-Park Ticket

Admits holders to both Islands of Adventure and Universal Studios for two days.

- Adults and children over 9: $95 ($120 at the gate).

- Children ages 3 to 9: $95 ($110 at the gate).

Flex Ticket

Admits holders to Universal Studios, Islands of Adventure, Wet 'n' Wild, Aquatica, and SeaWorld for 14 consecutive days.

@ Adults and children over 9: $234 at the gate.

@ Children ages 3 to 9: $195 at the gate.

Money-Saving Tip

If you buy your tickets online, the savings can be significant. Specials vary with the season, but there's nearly always a reward for buying early, such as Universal's latest deal: three days' admission for the price of two.

You can also save money with the Universal Meal Deal, especially if you have big eaters in the party. The Meal Deal basically offers you all the food you'd like from a variety of counter-service options throughout either Universal Studios or Islands of Adventure for a base price of $21 for adults, $11 for kids 3–9. If you're visiting both parks, the one-day price is $25 for adults and $13 for kids. And the add-on drink option of unlimited soft drinks for $9 a person is a definite bargain considering the price of theme park beverages.

Tips for Your First Hour at Universal Studios

@ The parking garage is in New Jersey (it seems that way, anyhow), so arrive at least 30 minutes before the main gate opens. Parking costs $12 per car, $17 if you opt for the closer, preferred parking.

@ If you arrive before the main turnstiles open, you'll have time to pose for pictures with and get the autographs of some of the Hanna-Barbera and Nickelodeon characters. This is your chance to meet SpongeBob SquarePants.

@ Several rental options are available upon entry. Strollers are $13 for a single, $21 for a double; wheelchair rental is $12; and electric convenience vehicles are $35. Lockers are also available for $8.

@ You're generally allowed through the main turnstiles and partway down Plaza of the Stars and Rodeo Drive about 20 minutes before the official opening time. If you want to ride The Simpsons, Jaws, Men in Black, or E.T. Adventure first, go down Rodeo Drive as far as you're allowed. If you'd rather see Jimmy Neutron, Shrek 4-D, Twister, Revenge of the Mummy, or Disaster! first, go down Plaza of the Stars until the ropes stop you. Families who haven't had breakfast may have time for a pastry at the Beverly Hills Boulangerie before the ropes drop.

@ Since Nick Studios has closed, there are rarely shows taping, but if you'd like to see if anything important is going

Helpful Hint

Do you want to sleep in? Visit in the off-season when crowds are light and lines are short. You can arrive at the park at 10 AM and still comfortably do everything.

Time-Saving Tip
You can avoid waiting in lines with the Universal Express Pass. The price ranges from $20–$60 (depending on several factors, including season), but guests of Universal Resorts get Express Pass benefits for free.

down on the lot, drop by the Studio Audience Center on the right as you enter the park. Tickets are usually free but there is sometimes a minimum age for children attending tapings.

@ In the off-season, some attractions open at 9, some at 10, and some (mainly the shows) start even later. Adjust your touring plan to take in the rides as they open. Times are all marked on your touring map.

Time-Saving Tip
As soon as you can in the morning, ride The Simpsons; Revenge of the Mummy; and, if the kids are up to it, the Hollywood Rip, Ride, and Rockit. Then head directly to *Shrek 4-D*.

Universal Studios Touring Tips

@ If you're not an on-site resort guest and you didn't opt for the Express pass, try to visit the major attractions—Revenge of the Mummy; Men in Black; the Simpsons; Twister; Jaws; Shrek; E.T. Adventure; Disaster!; and Hollywood Rip, Ride, and Rockit—in the morning or in the evening. Take in the theater-style attractions in the afternoon.

@ If you miss one of the major continuously loading attractions in the morning, hold off on it until two hours before the park closes. Midday waits of up to 60 minutes are common at popular attractions such as Men in Black and Revenge of the Mummy, but the crowds ease off a bit during the dinner hour.

@ If you plan to see Universal Studios in one day, it's unlikely you'll have time for an afternoon break. However, numerous theater-style attractions offer plenty of chances to rest up and let small kids nap. A lot of shows open

Helpful Hint

Few rides at Universal have height restrictions. You must be 48 inches tall to ride Revenge of the Mummy; 54 inches tall for Rip, Ride, and Rockit; 40 inches tall for The Simpsons; 36 inches tall for the Woody Woodpecker Nuthouse Coaster; and 42 inches tall for Men in Black. Just because your kids are tall enough to qualify, however, doesn't mean it's a good idea to let them into the attractions. Consult the ride descriptions for information about the scare factors.

Some attractions, such as E.T. Adventure and Jimmy Neutron, provide separate stationary seating for kids less than 40 inches, thus allowing families to go through the attraction as a group.

around noon and begin a second performance around 2 PM. Ride in the morning and then catch a midday show, have lunch, and see a second show.

@ Most of the kiddie attractions—the Woody Woodpecker Nuthouse Coaster, A Day in the Park with Barney, Curious George Goes to Town, Fievel's Playland, E.T. Adventure, and Animal Planet Live!—are in the same general area of the park. This means that you can park the strollers once and then walk from attraction to attraction.

@ The theaters that hold the Universal Horror Make-Up Show, and Terminator 2: 3-D are high capacity, so even if the lines look discouraging, odds are you'll still be seated. Consult your entertainment schedule or check the board at the attraction entrance for showtimes, and then put one parent in line about 20 minutes before the show is due to start. The other can take the kids for a drink or bathroom break.

@ Headed to The Simpsons; Rip, Ride, and Rockit; Men in Black; or another intense attraction? Universal employees will help families traveling with a baby or toddler do a baby swap.

The Scare Factor at Universal Studios

Some of the shows and tours are family-oriented and fine for everyone, but several of the big-name attractions are too frightening for preschoolers. The motion-simulation rides may induce queasiness, and rides and shows are generally very loud. The volume level at Twister and Terminator can practically jolt the fillings from your teeth.

Helpful Hint

Because the rides are based on movies, how your child reacted to the movie is a good predictor of how well your child will handle the ride. If *The Mummy* movie scared him, it's a safe bet he's not going to like the ride any better. Likewise a movie that was relatively tame in the theater may yield a ride that's more mild than wild. Note the "scare factor" described here for each of Universal's rides and attractions.

Universal seems to set its age rules based on how physically wild the motion of a ride is and, except for Revenge of the Mummy and Hollywood Rip, Ride and Rockit, none of the rides at the Studios bounce you around too much. They're psychologically scary, however, and a few minutes inside Twister may lead to more bad dreams than the wildest of roller coasters. Indeed, Twister, Terminator 2: 3-D, and the Universal Horror Make-Up Show have PG-13 ratings, indicating that they may be too violent and intense for younger children.

Read the ride descriptions to help you decide what's right for your child.

Universal Studios Attractions

Jimmy Neutron's Nicktoon Blast

This motion-simulation ride stars Jimmy Neutron and plenty of other characters from the Nickelodeon lineup, including the Wild Thornberrys and SpongeBob SquarePants.

In the preshow you're introduced to Jimmy's latest invention, a spy camera, but then, as so often is the case in the world of theme-park rides, something goes dreadfully awry. The audience is loaded into motion-simulation vehicles to help Jimmy defend the earth from an alien attack. The vehicles rise, tilt, and lurch in reaction to what's happening on the large screen in front of you, and while the actual movement of the "rocket" isn't much, the special effects combine to make you feel as if you're really hurtling through space.

The Scare Factor

The presence of familiar Nickelodeon heroes like Jimmy and SpongeBob will ensure that most kids, even many preschoolers, will be clamoring to ride. The action sequences shouldn't alarm kids raised on Saturday-morning cartoons, but the motion simulation may be another matter. If you're prone to queasiness or think it might be too intense for your kids, ask for the stationary seating. If that goes well, you can always return and ride in the motion simulators on your second time through.

Shrek 4-D

In the preshow you learn that vile little Lord Farquaad has plans to destroy Shrek from the great beyond. (Note the clever digs at Disney in the preshow area.) As you enter the main theater, you'll be given 3-D glasses, but what makes this show really

The Scare Factor

While Lord Farquaad is not exactly the most intimidating movie villain of all time, the special effects are extremely convincing and the whole show is very loud, which may be too much for preschoolers. Kids ages 8 and older should do fine.

Quick Guide to

Attraction	Height Requirement
Animal Planet Live!	None
Beetlejuice's Graveyard Revue	None
Curious George Goes to Town	None
A Day in the Park with Barney	None
Disaster!	None
E.T. Adventure	Separate seating for kids under 40 inches
Fear Factor Live	None
Fievel's Playland	None
Hollywood Rip, Ride, and Rockit	54 inches
Jaws	None
Jimmy Neutron's Nicktoon Blast	Separate seating for kids under 40 inches
Lucy, A Tribute	None
Men in Black: Alien Attack	42 inches
Revenge of the Mummy	48 inches
Shrek 4-D	None
The Simpsons	40 inches
Terminator 2: 3-D	None
Twister: Ride It Out	None
Universal Horror Make-Up Show	None
Woody Woodpecker's Nuthouse Coaster	36 inches

Scare Factor
0 = Unlikely to scare any child of any age.
! = Has dark or loud elements; might rattle some toddlers.
!! = A couple of gotcha! moments; should be fine for school-age kids.
!!! = You need to be pretty big and pretty brave to handle this ride.

Universal Studios Attractions

Speed of Line	Duration of Ride/Show	Scare Factor	Age Range
Fast	20 min.	0	All
Fast	25 min.	!	5 and up
N/A	N/A	0	All
Fast	15 min.	0	All
Moderate	20 min.	!	5 and up
Slow	15 min.	!	All
Fast	25 min.	!!!	7 and up
Moderate	n/a	0	All
Moderate	7 min.	!!!	8 and up
Moderate	10 min.	!!	7 and up
Moderate	15 min.	!	5 and up
Fast	n/a	0	All
Fast	25 min.	!!	7 and up
Moderate	15 min.	!!!	7 and up
Moderate	30 min.	!!	4 and up
Moderate	7 min.	!!	7 and up
Slow	25 min.	!!!	7 and up
Moderate	15 min.	!!	7 and up
Fast	20 min.	!!	7 and up
Moderate	1½ min.	!	4 and up

The Universal Studios Don't-Miss List

A Day in the Park with Barney (for kids under 6)

Curious George Goes to Town (for kids under 8)

E.T. Adventure

Hollywood Rip, Ride, and Rockit (for kids 8 and up)

Jaws

Jimmy Neutron's Nicktoon Blast

Men in Black: Alien Attack

Revenge of the Mummy

Shrek 4-D

The Simpsons

special and different from the other 3-D attractions around town is that you're seated in special chairs that will make the experience tactile as well as visual. What does that mean? You'll not only see and hear the action happening on the screen, you'll feel and smell some of it, too. (Mercifully, taste is the one sense not engaged in the show.) And the adventures of Shrek and Donkey are predictably hilarious as they rescue the hapless Fiona.

Helpful Hint
Shrek is often on hand for autographs and hugs as you exit the ride. Check your entertainment schedule for times he's due to appear.

Revenge of the Mummy

Revenge of the Mummy combines a high-speed roller coaster with the latest technology in robotics and pyrotechnic effects—no wonder it's billed as a "psychological thrill ride."

As the story begins, you walk through shadowy Egyptian catacombs on a tour of the on-location set of the next Mummy

Money-Saving Tip

Try not to let the kids stop to shop in the morning; not only should you keep moving between rides while the park is relatively uncrowded, but each ride empties out through a shop that sells souvenirs related to that attraction. In other words, the shops encourage the ultimate in impulse buying, but hold off purchases until late in the day when you've seen it all.

Insider's Secret

Revenge of the Mummy is hot (literally) and often has lines to match. Be sure to use an Express pass and visit it as early in the day as possible.

movie. Once you're in the coaster, the ride's magnetic-propulsion launch system thrusts you forward, backward, and forward again as you dodge vengeful ghosts, mummies, and other monsters. Yowza!

The Scare Factor

The Mummy scares the willies out of preschoolers and some school-age kids as well. Your child must be 48 inches tall to ride.

Men in Black: Alien Attack

Remember the scene in *Men in Black* when Will Smith tries out for the force? Think you could do better?

The premise is that guests are rookie agents riding through the streets of New York and armed with laser guns called "alienators." Like in Disney's Buzz Lightyear ride, you're

Time-Saving Tip

Families with older kids should head for Men in Black directly after trying out Rip, Ride, and Rockit, The Simpsons, and Revenge of the Mummy. This attraction draws long lines by mid-morning.

supposed to shoot the aliens, but unlike in the Buzz ride, these aliens can strike back, sending your vehicle into an out-of-control spin.

As you shoot at the 120 audio-animatronics aliens, the ride keeps track of your individual score and the collective score of the six people in your vehicle. You're not only fighting off aliens, but also competing against the team of rookies in the car beside you. Here's where it gets cute. Depending on how well you and your vehicle-mates shoot, there are alternate endings to the ride. Will you get a hero's welcome in Times Square or a loser's send-off?

Insider's Secret

Want to max your Men in Black score? Near the end of the ride (when you face the mega-alien in Times Square), you will hear Zed instructing you to push the red button on your control panel "now!" Whoever hits the button at this crucial point gets a whopping 100,000 bonus points. Take that, space aliens!

The Scare Factor

Most kids take the aliens in Men in Black in stride—especially if they've seen the movies and know what to expect.

Because you're actually in a video game, it makes sense that video game rules apply—the more you play, the better you get. Can you spell addictive? Come early if you want to ride more than once.

Helpful Hint

There are lockers outside Men in Black and Revenge of the Mummy where you can store purses and packages while you ride.

The Simpsons

The Simpsons have moved into the real estate formerly occupied by Back to the Future. The basic premise is that you and the Simpson family are inside Krusty the Clown's vision of an

The Scare Factor

The first moments of The Simpsons are by far the most jolting and it takes a minute or two to get used to the sensations of motion-simulation technology. If you feel yourself getting queasy, look away from the screen, either at something within your car or at the other cars riding alongside you. In terms of the story line, what's there to say? Any kid who is used to the cartoon knows what to expect: it's a little sinister, a little screwy, and more than a little tasteless.

amusement park and evil Sideshow Bob is, as usual, up to no good. You sit in a vehicle—not unlike the motion-simulation vehicles in the former Back to the Future ride—and watch the action on a giant screen. The show is funny, hitting pretty hard on both Disney and SeaWorld, but also fairly gross; at one point you get put into Maggie's mouth as if you were a pacifier.

Hollywood Rip, Ride, and Rockit

Universal's newest coaster is both a nod to the success of Disney's similarly themed Rock 'n' Roller Coaster and a totally exciting thrill ride of its own. You begin with a straight shot into the sky, sailing 17 stories up at speeds of up to 65 mph. The action never stops as you zoom over to the CityWalk lagoon and back, with six near-miss moments and a record-breaking loop.

The Scare Factor

With a height requirement of 54 inches, the Hollywood, Rip, Ride, and Rockit is off-limits to many kids, and too intense for most kids under 8, even if they're tall enough to ride. The coaster is really designed for the preteen and teen set.

The technology is pretty nifty, too. You get to choose your own music for the ride: LED boards in the queue area display song options from five genres (rock, rap, country, pop, and disco), or you can just let the coaster's digital sound system choose for you. The ride is taped, and after you get off, you can edit and customize the footage, then compile it into a music video—a fun souvenir for older kids.

Disaster!

The "musion" technology of the preshow, which transforms two-dimensional images into what appears to be three-dimensional images, is quite effective, creating a hologram of actor

Christopher Walken interacting with a person on stage. The ride itself puts you in the middle of a San Francisco subway car, where you become victims of an earthquake, complete with fires, broken water mains, and near-misses with falling debris. During the ride, your experiences are taped—because you're allegedly extras in a disaster movie—and played back to you in the form of a tongue-in-cheek preview.

The Scare Factor

Disaster! is dramatic, but most kids aren't too frightened. The noise level may unnerve toddlers. And be aware that the show has quite a few sexual innuendos that sail right over the heads of younger children but might be inappropriate for preteens.

Twister

After a taped intro by Bill Paxton and Helen Hunt, the stars of the film, you're led into the main show area. There, a five-story-high tornado is created right before your eyes. The tornado, along with accompanying fires and explosions, swirls through the building while you watch from two platforms. You'll feel the wind, the rain, and the rumbles; and yes, the flying cow from the movie comes along for the ride.

The Scare Factor

Twister is extremely loud. Some families routinely bring earplugs to theme parks, but if you don't have them, try placing your hands over your kids' ears. The experience is too frightening for small children, but most kids 6 and up will be fine.

Terminator 2: 3-D

Universal's most high-tech action show combines 3-D effects, live action, and movie clips. The best special effect is the way the actors seem to emerge from the screen and then later run back "into" the movie. The show is fast and dramatic, just like the film series it's based on, and the ending is explosive.

Helpful Hint

Because of the size of the theater, Terminator 2: 3-D is relatively easy to get into and is best saved for the afternoon.

The Scare Factor

Although not as violent as the film series, Terminator 2: 3-D has some startling effects that may be too much for kids under 7. Again, it is extremely loud.

E.T. Adventure

This charming ride begins with a brief preshow featuring Steven Spielberg and E.T. Afterward you file through a holding area where—and this seems rather mysterious at the time— you're required to give your name in exchange for a small plastic "interplanetary passport." Next you move on to the queue area, which winds through the deep, dark woods—it even smells and sounds like a forest. (As a rule, Universal does a bang-up job of setting the mood in queue areas; E.T. is designed to make you feel small and child-like.)

After handing "passports" to the attendant, children under 40 inches tall and anyone elderly, heavy, pregnant, or otherwise unsteady are loaded into flying gondolas. Others ride bicycles,

Helpful Hint

All the attractions for very young children are in the same area of the park. If you have preschoolers, hang an immediate right on Rodeo Drive after you enter the park and follow the signs to E.T. Adventure.

and the lead bike in each group has E.T. in the front basket. You rise up and fly over the forest in an effective simulation of the escape scene in *E.T.* the movie. After narrowly missing being captured by the police, you manage to return E.T. to his home planet, a magical place populated by dozens of cuddly aliens.

As you sail past E.T. for the final time, he bids you farewell by name. Magic? Not quite. When you give your name to the attendant before you enter the queue area, it's computer coded onto your plastic passport. As you give up the passport and join your group of bicycles, the cards are fed into the computer, which enables E.T. to say, "Good-bye, Jordan. Good-bye, Leigh. Good-bye, Kim . . ." and so on, as your family flies past.

Helpful Hint

Unfortunately, E.T.'s "personal good-bye" system frequently malfunctions, so I wouldn't mention it to the kids at all. That way, if it works, everyone is extra delighted, and if it doesn't, the ride is still an upbeat experience.

Jaws
As the people of Amity Beach learned, that darn shark just won't stay away.

The Scare Factor

Kids 7 to 11 give Jaws a strong thumbs-up, and the ride is popular with many kids under 7. The fact that you're outdoors in the daylight dilutes the intensity. The really brave should wait until evening, when the "shark in the dark" effects are much scarier.

The ride carries you via boat through a big outdoor set. The shark rises from the water several times quite suddenly, the unseen boat before you "gets it" in a gruesome way, and there are also grenade launches, explosions, and a fuel spill. There's tremendous splashing, especially on the left side of the boat, and most of the boat captains throw themselves totally into the experience by shrieking, shouting, and firing guns on cue. It all adds up to one action-packed boat ride.

Fear Factor Live

Building on the merger between NBC and Universal, this attraction is based on the former television reality show of the same name. In order to volunteer, you must show up 75 minutes before showtime, be 18 years old, pass certain height and weight restrictions, and sign a waiver saying you won't sue the park, no matter what. If you're chosen you'll compete in a

The Scare Factor

Some Fear Factor challenges are pretty creepy—there are scorpions, spiders, eels, and "mystery meat" on stage—and predictably, teens and preteens love it. But the show really isn't designed for young kids. It's gross, it's loud, and, at times, demeaning to both the contestants and the audience.

series of extreme challenges designed to test the physical and emotional limits of the contestants. The audience gets into the act, too, by blasting contestants with water and controlling obstacles on stage. At the end of the show, winners get prize packages of Universal-theme gifts and tickets.

Universal Horror Make-Up Show

This show opens with a bang—or, more specifically, the startling effect of a man running on stage with a knife protruding from his chest. Everything that follows is fast-paced and funny but a good deal edgier than anything you'd see at Disney. The actors illustrate special horror effects on stage including "cutting" off the arm of an (adult) audience volunteer, and you'll also see clips from *The Mummy, The Fly,* and *An American Werewolf in London,* which has an astounding man-to-beast transformation scene.

The Scare Factor

Although the movie clips and general gore level are too intense for preschoolers, most kids 8 and over can stomach the Universal Horror Make-Up Show. Better than adults, frankly. The show has a PG-13 rating because of the blood and a couple of risqué jokes.

Animal Planet Live!

This is an appealing show for all age groups, but younger kids will be especially drawn to the animal stars. Kid volunteers from the audience join the fast-paced and funny performance. Showtimes are printed on your map; because of the large size of the theater, this is a great choice for the most crowded times of the afternoon.

Fievel's Playland

Fievel's Playland is cleverly designed and filled with Wild West–style props, including a harmonica slide that plays notes as kids go down it; a giant talking Tiger the cat; canteens to squirt; cowboy hats to bounce in; spiderwebs to climb; and a separate ball pit and slide area for toddlers.

The centerpiece of the playground is a 200-foot water ride in which kids and parents are loaded into two-person rafts and swept through a "sewer." The ride is zippier than it looks, will get you soaking wet, and is so addictive that most kids clamor to get back on again immediately. The water ride loads slowly, so by afternoon the waits are prohibitive. If you come in the morning, it's possible to ride several times with minimal waits, but by afternoon, one ride is all you can reasonably expect. Note that the water ride is closed on cold days.

Time-Saving Tip

Fievel's Playland often opens an hour or two after the general park opening. If you ride the big-deal rides and then show up at the playground at the opening time indicated on your map, you'll be able to try the water ride without much of a wait.

A Day in the Park with Barney

Designed to appeal to Universal's youngest guests, A Day in the Park with Barney is actually an enclosed park-like setting with pop-art-style, colorful flowers and trees. Barney appears several times a day in a song-and-dance show, and there's also an interactive indoor play area for toddlers. This play area is far cooler and calmer than Fievel's next door, and the nearby shop and food stand are never crowded.

Helpful Hint
The Barney preshow is a little uncomfortable—
a standing venue with parents having to lift kids
up if they have a prayer of seeing the stage. But
once you get inside, the area is much more
family-friendly and designed to let little kids
romp and dance along with the music.

"The highlight of my 2-year-old daughter's day was the
Barney show," a mother of two from Illinois wrote to us. "The
kids sit so close to him and his friends, and the setting is beautiful. I loved watching my little girl sing along during the 'I
Love You' song at the end."

Woody Woodpecker's Nuthouse Coaster
Somewhat like Goofy's Barnstormer at Disney, the Nuthouse
Coaster is scarier than you'd guess and kids must be 36 inches
tall to ride. Watch it make a couple of runs before you line up
with your 4-year-old.

Curious George Goes to Town
Perhaps a better name for this attraction would have been "Curious George Goes to the Car Wash." This large interactive play
area is a simulated city that includes climbing areas, ball pits,
and lots of chances to get very, very wet. There are fountains in
the center and water cannons up above; many parents let their
kids wear bathing suits under their clothing so they can strip
down and really get into the spirit of the place. It's a great way
to cool off in summer, so save it for the warmest part of the
afternoon.

On the other hand, if you're up for a maximum splash, a
clanging bell over the Fire Department indicates that a big wave

Helpful Hint

In chilly weather the water is shut off and Curious George Goes to Town becomes a dry play area.

of water is under way. On a hot summer day this may be the highlight of the park for young kids, but parents of preschoolers and toddlers, beware: The wave hits with enough force to knock small children off their feet.

Beetlejuice's Graveyard Revue

This rock-and-rap show starring Dracula, the Wolfman, and Frankenstein and his bride is primarily aimed at preteens and teens. Beetlejuice is the host and he offsets the ghoulishness with plenty of goofy humor. Younger kids won't be too frightened of the monsters themselves, but the extremely high volume of the music coupled with pyrotechnics might upset preschoolers. The show plays several times in the afternoon so

Insider's Secret

Universal can really throw a party. The park is festively decorated for Christmas, and a special parade runs for the weeks around Mardi Gras.

But the best holiday celebration of the year is Halloween. Halloween Horror Nights are a time-honored tradition at Universal and very popular with Orlando locals. All the movie bad guys are out in full force with plenty of special stage shows and "interactive experiences." Teenagers will love this ultimate spook house, and kids under 7 definitely won't. If you have kids ages 7 to 11, just make sure to stay close to them. Separate tickets are required for this party and should be purchased in advance. Visit www.universalorlando.com for details.

getting in isn't hard; arrive about 15 minutes before showtime for good seats.

Lucy, A Tribute

Fans of *I Love Lucy* should take a few minutes to walk through this exhibit, which houses memorabilia from the famous TV show, including scale models of the Tropicana and the Ricardos' apartment; clothes and jewelry worn on the show; personal pictures and letters from Lucy and Desi's home life; and the numerous Emmys that Lucille Ball won throughout the years.

The "California Here We Come Game" is a treat for hardcore trivia buffs. By answering questions about episodes of *I Love Lucy*, game participants get to travel with the Mertzes and Ricardos on their first trip to California. They lost me somewhere in the desert, but perhaps you'll do better.

Insider's Secret

Check your entertainment schedule and, if time permits, stop to watch some of the street entertainers that play around the park throughout the day. The Blues Brothers, featuring Jake, Elroy, and a talented singer named Mabel, play in the New York section and offer one of the liveliest shows in the park.

Tips for Your Last Hour at Universal Studios

Crowds thin at night so it's a good time to revisit favorite attractions or drop by anything you missed earlier in the day. If you want to have dinner at CityWalk, leave Universal about an hour before the official closing time to avoid the mad rush of exiting guests. For more on CityWalk, Universal's dining and entertainment district, see Chapter 15.

Islands of Adventure

Islands of Adventure

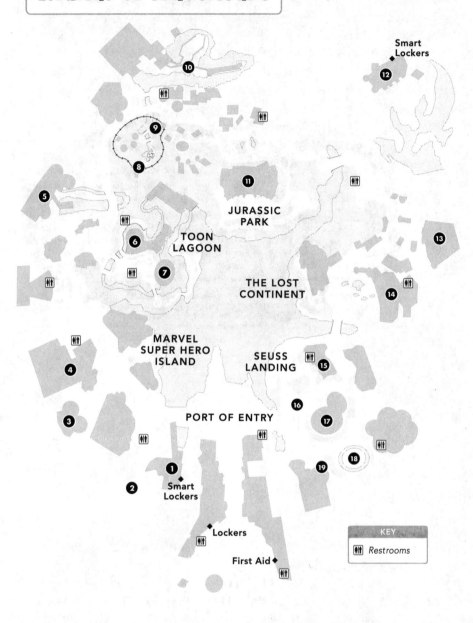

Smart
Lockers

12

JURASSIC
PARK

10

9

8

5

TOON
LAGOON

6

7

11

13

THE LOST
CONTINENT

14

MARVEL
SUPER HERO
ISLAND

SEUSS
LANDING

15

4

16

3

PORT OF ENTRY

17

18

1

Smart
Lockers

2

19

Lockers

First Aid

KEY

🚻 *Restrooms*

I slands of Adventure is all about rides: full sensory-immersion 3-D experiences, state-of-the-art coasters, watery descents that'll leave you dripping, and kiddie rides so cleverly designed that even the most cynical adults get totally into the spirit.

For information on tickets and multiday passes see Chapter 14 and note the financial advantages of buying online. Check for any price changes by calling 407/363–8000 or visiting www.universalorlando.com.

Money-Saving Tip

Are you a member of AAA? If so, you'll get a 10% price break on food and shopping throughout both IOA and Universal Studios. This can be quite a boon, especially if you're eating at a posh restaurant.

Getting Around Islands of Adventure

The layout of Islands of Adventure (IOA) is like a big lollipop, and you enter through the stick—the Port of Entry, which has shops, restaurants, and service areas. Port of Entry ends at the lagoon, and around the water are clustered the five islands of the theme park: Marvel Super Hero Island, Toon Lagoon, Jurassic Park, the Lost Continent, and Seuss Landing.

Insider's Secret

Big news! The Harry Potter "theme park within a theme park" is scheduled to open in 2010. It's an ambitious project, so don't expect it until late in the year or perhaps even 2011. Go to www.universalorlando.com for updates.

Because of IOA's essentially circular design, it's an easy park to tour. The sidewalks naturally lead you from one attraction to the next, with no crossroads or choices, and bridges connect each of the islands. The moods of the separate lands are quite distinct. As you walk into the mysterious and mythic Lost Continent, for example, you're greeted by the gentle tinkling of wind chimes; and to enter Jurassic Park, you walk through an enormous stone gate flanked with torches. Below your feet you'll see fossil prints in the sidewalk; and if you listen closely, you'll hear the rumbles and calls of dinos in the bushes.

We advise an early morning lap of the park to ride the big-deal attractions; an afternoon lap to check out the shows, play areas, water rides, and minor attractions; then a final circle in early evening to ride anything you missed—or revisit favorites. Sounds like a lot of walking, but in this user-friendly theme park, touring is a snap.

How Scary Is "Scary"? As Dr. Seuss Would Say, "Very!"

Nine of the 12 major attractions at Islands of Adventure have height restrictions—your first clue that this park is loaded with physically wild rides. Measure your kids before you leave home; there's no point in promising your kindergarten-age coaster warrior a trip on the Incredible Hulk if he's less than 54 inches tall. Here are the specific height restrictions:

The Amazing Adventures of Spider-Man	40 inches
Dr. Doom's Fearfall	52 inches
Dudley Do-Right's Ripsaw Falls	44 inches
Dueling Dragons	54 inches
Jurassic Park River Adventure	42 inches
The Incredible Hulk Coaster	54 inches
Popeye & Bluto's Bilge-Rat Barges	42 inches
Pteranodon Flyers	36 inches

In addition, a couple of the shows are atmospherically scary; Poseidon's Fury and the Eighth Voyage of Sindbad have frightened some preschoolers.

The bottom line? Read the ride descriptions carefully before you board. If the ride is outside (and many IOA attractions are), watch it make a couple of cycles before you decide. And if someone in your family panics while in line, inform the attendant you'll need to do a Baby Swap (or husband swap, as the case may be).

The Islands of Adventure Don't-Miss List for Kids 2 to 6

Camp Jurassic

Caro-Seuss-el

The Cat in the Hat

If I Ran the Zoo

Me Ship, the *Olive*

One Fish, Two Fish, Red Fish, Blue Fish

Popeye & Bluto's Bilge-Rat Barges (for older kids)

The Islands of Adventure Don't-Miss List for Kids 7 to 11

The Amazing Adventures of Spider-Man

Camp Jurassic

The Cat in the Hat

Dudley Do-Right's Ripsaw Falls

Dueling Dragons (older kids)

The Incredible Hulk Coaster (older kids)

Jurassic Park River Adventure

Popeye & Bluto's Bilge-Rat Barges

Poseidon's Fury

The Islands of Adventure Don't-Miss List for Kids 12 and up

The Amazing Adventures of Spider-Man

Dudley Do-Right's Ripsaw Falls

Dueling Dragons

Dr. Doom's Fearfall

The Incredible Hulk Coaster

Jurassic Park River Adventure

Popeye & Bluto's Bilge-Rat Barges

Poseidon's Fury

Helpful Hint

Confirm hours of operation by checking with your hotel or calling 407/363–8000.

Tips for Your First Hour at Islands of Adventure

@ Arrive 30 minutes before the stated opening time, which is generally 9 AM. Get tickets and maps, and take care of any business, such as locker or stroller rental.

@ Sometimes Port of Entry is open before the rest of the park. If so, browse the shops or have a quick breakfast at Croissant Moon Bakery, but be sure to be at the end of the street by the time the ropes drop.

@ The tip board will tell you which rides are running. During the on-season, most rides will open immediately; on less-crowded days, the rides may come online section by section.

Quick Guide to

Attraction	Location	Height Requirement
The Amazing Adventures of Spider-Man	Super Hero Island	40 inches
Camp Jurassic	Jurassic Park	None
Caro-Seuss-el	Seuss Landing	None
The Cat in the Hat	Seuss Landing	None
Discovery Center	Jurassic Park	None
Dr. Doom's Fearfall	Super Hero Island	52 inches
Dudley Do-Right's Ripsaw Falls	Toon Lagoon	44 inches
Dueling Dragons	Lost Continent	54 inches
The Eighth Voyage of Sindbad	Lost Continent	None
High in the Sky Seuss Trolley	Seuss Landing	34 inches
If I Ran the Zoo	Seuss Landing	None
The Incredible Hulk Coaster	Super Hero Island	54 inches
Me Ship, the *Olive*	Toon Lagoon	None
One Fish, Two Fish Red Fish, Blue Fish	Seuss Landing	None
Popeye & Bluto's Bilge-Rat Barges	Toon Lagoon	42 inches
Poseidon's Fury	Lost Continent	None
Pteranodon Flyers	Jurassic Park	36 inches
River Adventure	Jurassic Park	42 inches
Storm Force Accelatron	Super Hero Island	None

Scare Factor
0 = Unlikely to scare any child of any age.
! = Has dark or loud elements; might rattle some toddlers.
!! = A couple of gotcha! moments; should be fine for school-age kids.
!!! = You need to be pretty big and pretty brave to handle this ride.

Islands of Adventure Attractions

Speed of Line	Duration of Ride/Show	Scare Factor	Age Range
Moderate	15 min.	!!	7 and up
n/a	n/a	0	All
Slow	3 min.	0	All
Moderate	6 min.	0	All
n/a	n/a	0	All
Slow	2 min.	!!	7 and up
Moderate	8 min.	!!	7 and up
Moderate	7 min.	!!!	7 and up
n/a	25 min.	!!	8 and up
Slow	8 min.	0	All
n/a	n/a	0	All
Moderate	4 min.	!!!	8 and up
n/a	n/a	0	All
Slow	4 min.	0	All
Moderate	12 min.	!	4 and up
n/a	20 min.	!!	7 and up
Slow	80 sec.	!	4 and up
Slow	5 min.	!!	7 and up
Slow	3 min.	!!	All

Insider's Secret

Perhaps because most guests stay off-site and must rise, eat, drive, park, and undertake the substantial trek from the parking garage, Islands of Adventure is relatively empty in the morning and grows more crowded in the afternoon. The first two hours after opening are definitely your best chance to ride Spider-Man and other big-deal attractions.

Either way, Marvel Super Hero Island and Seuss Landing, the two islands adjoining Port of Entry, will be open.

@ If your kids are old enough to enjoy intense rides, veer left to Marvel Super Hero Island. Ride the Incredible Hulk Coaster, Spider-Man, and Dr. Doom's Fearfall in that order.

Helpful Hint

Rides are most likely to be closed for maintenance in winter. Check www.universalorlando.com to see if any attractions are scheduled for refurbishment during your visit.

@ If your kids are younger, veer right to Seuss Landing and start with One Fish, Two Fish and the Cat in the Hat.

Port of Entry

As the name implies, Port of Entry is where you enter Islands of Adventure. It's a visually charming area, meant to resemble an exotic Middle Eastern seaport, and it's a great place for a group snapshot.

Many of the park services are in Port of Entry: locker rentals ($8), Guest Services (a.k.a. Guest Relations), film developing stands, the lost and found, and an ATM are all here. You can rent a stroller ($13, $21 for a double) or a wheelchair ($12, $35 for an electric convenience vehicle).

In addition, there are shops and restaurants. The Universal Studios Islands of Adventure Trading Company is a store that's almost as big as its name, and, because it has merchandise from all five islands, it's a good place for wrap-up shopping on your way out of the park.

Pause for a second as you near the end of Port of Entry. There's a great view of the Jurassic Park Visitor Center across the water, and if you've seen the movie, the authenticity of the structure, especially from this vantage point, will get you reaching for the camera. To your left is the tip board, which gives you information on the opening sequence of the rides, approximate wait times, and upcoming showtimes. The tip board is staffed by an Islands of Adventure employee who can answer any questions.

Time-Saving Tip
Don't spend too much time shopping in the morning. The park is at its least crowded then, and you need to hurry on to the rides. You can always return to shop in the afternoon or evening.

Helpful Hint
Some IOA restaurants, including the Confisco Grille, close in the off-season. But Universal does a good job of estimating crowd flow, so there are always enough places open to serve everyone in the park.

Port of Entry also has several dining options. Confisco Grille, the only full-service restaurant in Port of Entry, offers pasta, fish, and steak as well as lighter fare such as salads and sandwiches. Adjacent to the Confisco is the Backwater Bar, which serves half-price drinks during the 3 to 6 PM happy hour.

Time-Saving Tip

Islands of Adventure has plenty of quick-service restaurants throughout, so finding food usually isn't a problem. But if you're visiting on a busy day, consider returning to Port of Entry for lunch. Crowds are usually lighter there.

The Confisco hosts character meals during the on-season, and a table is set up across from the restaurant where you can make reservations for either character dining or a meal at the park's other full-service restaurant, the excellent and elegant Mythos, in the Lost Continent section of the park.

Fast-food choices include the Croissant Moon Bakery, which offers bagels, pastries, and a variety of coffees—it's a great place for a quick breakfast as you enter the park. Later in the day sandwiches and desserts are added to the menu. The Arctic

Time-Saving Tip

Express passes are the way to go on crowded days, letting you into every Express line in the park on an unlimited basis. Guests of on-site hotels get this perk without having to pay for the PLUS pass—just show your resort ID. Otherwise, Express PLUS passes are for sale at ticket kiosks, Guest Services, and booths around the park.

Express offers funnel cakes and ice cream, while the Cinnabon next door offers the same gooey treats you find in malls and airports.

Marvel Super Hero Island

This is by far the wildest section of IOA, the island where superheroes fight bad guys, and you test your mettle on three high-thrill attractions. Most people are so busy dashing to the rides that they don't take the time to appreciate how well this section visually duplicates a comic book world. Signs are intentionally generic as in "Store," "Arcade," or "Café"; and colors are chosen to give everything a flat, grainy appearance.

The Amazing Adventures of Spider-Man

Spider-Man combines actual movement on a track, motion simulation, and 3-D effects. Unlike most 3-D shows, where you're sitting still and the action comes toward you, in Spider-Man you're moving from scene to scene through a comic book story. It feels as if everything is really happening, especially the 400-foot simulated drop at the end, yet the actual ride movement is very mild. In other words, young kids or people who freak out on coasters can enjoy the ride.

The concept is that the Sinister Syndicate, made up of such comic book villains as Doctor Octopus, Electro, Hobgoblin, and Hydro Man, have taken over New York City and stolen the Statue of Liberty. (Wonder why the bad guys never nab Boston or Omaha?) The plucky young photojournalist Peter Parker, alias Spider-Man, is nowhere to be found, and the city is in a panic. Chief Jameson, the bombastic newspaper editor, is "so desperate for the story that I might have to send a bunch of tourists out in the ScoopMobile." That's your cue.

Stay alert while you wait in line; the queue area effectively sets up the story, and the posters help you keep your bad guys straight. Thanks to Chief Jameson's utter disregard for the welfare of his cub reporters, even the instructional tape on how to load the ScoopMobile is hilarious.

As soon as you're loaded in you'll be stunned by the quality of the 3-D effects, which make you feel as if Spider-Man is on the hood of your car and that bricks are flying toward your face. The ending of the ride, in which you're "thrown" off the top of a New York skyscraper and caught in Spider-Man's net, is the biggest thrill of all.

Insider's Secret

The first row of the Scoop-Mobile has the best 3-D effects. The back row feels more of the spinning motion, and the middle row probably offers the most balanced experience.

The first time through, you're focused on sheer survival, but Spider-Man is an attraction that holds up through return trips. Pay attention to detail. For example, when Hobgoblin throws his fiery pumpkins at you, Spider-Man snares the first one in his web, but the second one goes awry and crashes through the wall and into the next scene.

The Scare Factor

Spider-Man has a 40-inch height requirement, which means quite a few preschoolers qualify to ride.

The actual ride movement has plenty of spins and bumps, but the infamous "drop" at the end is totally simulated, making it far more fun than scary. The real issue is the villains. The Sinister Syndicate throws everything it has at you, and the characters often appear very abruptly. If the in-your-face bad guys are too much for your kids, tell them to shut their eyes.

Money-Saving Tip

As you exit Spider-Man, you'll notice how Universal Orlando cleverly encourages souvenir shopping. While you're still excited about the ride, you exit through a shop full of Spider-Man merchandise. Remember this rule: No souvenir shopping until the afternoon, when you've tried out lots of rides and know what you really want.

Once you know a happy ending is guaranteed, a return trip through is a blast. Consider what this mother of two from California wrote to us: "Spider-Man is a wonderful ride and my husband's favorite. The first time we rode it with our kids (ages 9 and 11), the younger one was terrified by the fact that the bad guys land on the hood of the car and it really feels like they're reaching out for you. But once she got off the ride and walked around a while, she wanted to try it again."

The first time you ride Spider-Man, skip the Express and single-rider lines, and enter through the main entrance. The reason is that the walk-through to the ride is basically the preshow that tells you who you're fighting and why. Without it, you'll probably be wondering "Why are all these pieces of the Statue of Liberty lying around?"

The Incredible Hulk Coaster

This isn't your mother's roller coaster, on which you slowly crank up a hill getting ready for your first plunge. The Incredible Hulk Coaster is big, green, and mean—just like David

Time-Saving Tip

On a tight touring schedule? Spider-Man and Hulk are must-sees, but you can skip Storm Force and Dr. Doom.

The Scare Factor

The 54-inch height requirement eliminates many young kids, and Hulk is a pretty heart-thumping experience—probably too intense for any child under 10. Watch it make a few laps before you decide to ride.

Banner after he played around once too often with those gamma rays.

There's a separate line for those who want to sit in the front row, which has the best views, but the longest wait. The movement is slightly wilder in the back of the car. Note the word "slightly." Hulk is plenty intense no matter where you ride.

Those lockers at the Hulk entrance are there for a reason, and they're free to use. Store everything you can because seven big flips can send car keys and sunglasses sailing.

The ride opens with a "cannon" shot from a 150-foot tube, zooming from 0 to 40 mph during the first two seconds

Time-Saving Tip

Long lines? There are three ways to cut down on your wait:

- Purchase an Express PLUS pass.
- Stay at an on-site resort. Guests of Universal hotels are allowed Express-line access simply by showing their resort ID.
- Use the single-rider line. After you've gone through an attraction like Spider-Man at least once as a family, older kids might want to ride again on their own. The single-rider line moves much faster than the general-admission line.

Insider's Secret

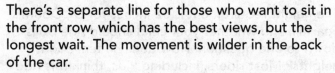

There's a separate line for those who want to sit in the front row, which has the best views, but the longest wait. The movement is wilder in the back of the car.

of motion, then immediately flipping over to give riders the sensation of going weightless. You'll make seven different inversions during the course of your ride, and twice disappear into a subterranean trench. Although the ride is wild, it's smooth, with very few jerky movements, and many coaster warriors swear that despite its awesome appearance, Hulk is the most user-friendly coaster in the park.

Dr. Doom's Fearfall

Dr. Victor von Doom is trying to defeat the Fantastic Four by sucking all the fear out of innocent citizens like you and using this collective fear to take over the world. (OK, so logic isn't the strong point of these rides.) The point is that you're strapped into outdoor seats, and shot 180 feet into the air. There's a bit of a yo-yo effect—you're raised and lowered several times—but the first five seconds of the ride are by far the scariest. Most riders report that once you're launched, you're fine.

Insider's Secret

If you like Dr. Doom in the morning, you'll love it at night when you have the added thrill of looking down at the glowing theme park lights and CityWalk.

The Scare Factor

The height requirement is 52 inches for Dr. Doom's Fearfall, and whether your child should ride boils down to one question: How does he feel about heights? Most riders, including kids, think this ride is over too quickly to get truly scary. As they say, "The waiting is the hardest part."

Storm Force Accelatron

This simple spinning ride—the cups spin individually and the discs that they're mounted on also move—is a cranked-up version of the Mad Tea Party at Disney World. It's a good way to entertain younger siblings while older kids tackle the nearby Hulk.

The Scare Factor

Storm Force Accelatron isn't scary, but the double spinning action makes some riders queasy.

Toon Lagoon

Like Marvel Super Hero Island, Toon Lagoon is also devoted to comic strip characters, but these are the stars of the Sunday funnies—such as Beetle Bailey, Betty Boop, Dagwood, and the kids of the Family Circus. Young kids have no idea who any of these characters are, but the true focus of the island isn't the toon, it's the lagoon; the attractions here are designed to splash you silly.

Dudley Do-Right's Ripsaw Falls

This log flume ride, in which you're helping Dudley and Horse save the perpetually pitiful Nell from Snidely Whiplash, culminates in a breathtaking 75-foot drop. The ride facade is so enormous that it serves as a park icon, and hardly anyone can walk by without stopping to gawk. The actual fall is even more dramatic than it looks; there's an explosion of light when the log enters the TNT shack at the bottom of the flume, followed by a second descent, in which you drop an additional 15 feet below the water level.

Needless to say, a descent of this magnitude isn't accomplished without a lot of splash. The water not only flies back in your face, but also sloshes into the log, puddling around your hips and feet. You'll enjoy the ride a lot more when you're ready to get wet—in other words, in the hottest part of the afternoon. This is also when you're likely to encounter long lines. Dudley Do-Right's Ripsaw Falls boards slowly and hour-long waits are not uncommon.

Insider's Secret

The ride facade obviously spoofs Mount Rushmore, but also keep your eye out for a clever jab at Disney's Pirates of the Caribbean just before you disembark.

The Scare Factor

Kids ages 7 and up name Dudley Do-Right as one of their favorite rides. The last drop is a definite squealer, so anyone with a fear of heights should think twice before getting in line. The height requirement is 44 inches.

Popeye & Bluto's Bilge-Rat Barges

If Dudley Do-Right is all about splashing, Popeye is about getting drenched straight through to your underwear. Parties of eight are loaded into circular rafts and sent on a wild and winding water journey. If through some miracle you manage to avoid the waves, the boat wash at the end of the ride spares no one. To add insult to injury, you're squirted with water guns by the kids aboard the nearby play area, Me Ship, the *Olive*.

For this reason, riding Popeye requires a bit of planning. Families in the know wear lightweight soccer-style shorts, don

The Scare Factor

Popeye & Bluto's Bilge-Rat Barges is one of the best big-deal rides for young kids, and parents with kids as young as age 5 report that they loved it. The height requirement is 42 inches. "Our 6-year-old daughter freaked out when she first saw Dudley Do-Right," wrote one father "and that big drop does look pretty intimidating, even to an adult. But after she'd gone on the Popeye boat ride—three times— she was totally over her fear and willing to go on Dudley Do-Right."

ponchos or plastic bags, or perhaps even bring a whole change of clothes. (If you were planning on buying a souvenir T-shirt anyway, hold off until after you ride when fresh, dry clothes are bound to feel great.) Leave cameras and valuables inside the nearby lockers and stow everything else that you can in the central pouch, including shoes and socks. A wet fanny can lead to momentary discomfort, but wet socks can lead to blisters and ruin your whole day.

Although there are some sizable dips and drops along the way, the fact that the whole family rides together in a circular raft somewhat dilutes the intensity, making this ride a good choice for kids who are not quite up to Dudley Do-Right's megadrop but still want to try a water ride. And because the rafts hold a fair number of people and load quickly, Popeye

Insider's Secret

The three major water rides—Dudley Do-Right and Popeye in Toon Lagoon, and the River Adventure in Jurassic Park—are fairly close together. Ride them all in a row, and you'll only have to dry off once.

never seems to have the daunting lines that are standard at Dudley. All in all, it's a good choice for the afternoon.

Me Ship, the Olive

This is a compact play area designed like a ship, with slides, climbing webs, and buttons that make tooting and beeping noises. Swee' Pea's Playpen is a separate play area for toddlers.

By far the most enjoyable feature of Me Ship, the *Olive,* is the water guns that allow you to take aim at the

Insider's Secret

Watch out—the squirt guns can squirt back!

occupants of Popeye & Bluto's Bilge-Rat Barges below. If you have a child too young to ride Popeye, take him aboard the *Olive* while you wait for the rest of the family to ride; he can seek revenge on his siblings as they pass.

Pandemonium Circus

A cartoon-character live show whose theme changes from time to time plays several times a day in the Pandemonium Circus Theater during the on-season. Showtimes are marked on your map. Although young kids enjoy these lighthearted shows,

Insider's Secret

Toon Lagoon is full of great photo ops. You can pose beneath the giant word bubbles, so that it appears you're saying or thinking such phrases as "It must be Sunday—we're in color!" and "I have the feeling people can read my thoughts!" The fountain on Comic Strip Lane is the hangout place for every cartoon dog you can think of and another fun place for a group snapshot.

they're pretty simple, so check them out only if you have preschoolers in tow. The characters pose for pictures with the kids afterward.

Jurassic Park

As you walk through the high stone entryway with its torches, note the distant rumbling of unseen beasts, and look down at the fossilized leaves and footprints in the sidewalk before you. The Canadian pines around Dudley Do-Right's Ripsaw Falls have given way to lush tropical vegetation, and the merry beat of Toon Lagoon slows to an ominous jungle rhythm. Is there any doubt you've entered Jurassic Park?

River Adventure

One of Islands of Adventure's premier attractions, the River Adventure starts out with a mild cruise through the habitats of gentle vegetarian dinosaurs. Hmm, do you think we'll stay on course? If you don't know the answer to that, you have to go back to Theme Park 101.

Sure enough, a playful dino bangs your boat, sending you drifting into a restricted zone, and once you're inside the dangerous containment area, your boat is pulled up a long ramp past vicious little raptors that leap around spitting at you. When the T-Rex at the top decides you'll make a good snack,

The Scare Factor

Eighty-five feet may sound like a T-Rex-size drop, especially in contrast to the 75-foot drop next door at Dudley, but because you're loaded into much larger boats, the fall doesn't feel that intense. Most families report that they found the River Adventure plunge less frightening than the one at Dudley Do-Right. There's some atmospheric scariness, however, in the form of some very real-looking dinos. It's key to let nervous youngsters know what to expect in advance—that is, you'll get pushed in with the raptors. If it's any consolation, this part of the ride is very short—less than two minutes from the beginning of the climb to the final plunge. Our surveys indicate that most kids 7 and up love the ride.

you escape via an 85-foot plunge—and that's one long, fast, steep descent.

Camp Jurassic

Of the three play areas in Islands of Adventure, this is the best one for kids ages 6 to 10. The setting is a group of posteruption volcanoes, with caves for hiding, and a multilevel, fairly rough terrain perfect for jumping, climbing, and exploring. There are slides, plenty of netting, and some take-no-prisoners water cannons. Because the Camp Jurassic play area is bigger and more spread out than Me Ship, the *Olive,* in Toon Lagoon and If I Ran the Zoo in Seuss Landing, it's easy for kids to get lost. Unless you're sure they can find their way back to one of the benches where Mom and Dad sit waiting, you may need to go with them.

Helpful Hint

Is there a gap in the ages of your kids? Or are some members of the family more risk-tolerant than others? You can always take the younger children to play areas while the older kids ride the scarier attractions. For example, Camp Jurassic is a good place for young kids to hang out while their older siblings try River Adventure.

Pteranodon Flyers

This aerial ride, in which children dangle beneath the wide wings of a gentle flying dinosaur, is the first thing you see when you enter Jurassic Park. Ergo, most kids insist on making a beeline there. It's indeed a pleasant 80-second flight around lushly landscaped Camp Jurassic, offering you great views of Islands of Adventure. The catch is that only three birds, each holding two riders, are on the track at a time. That adds up to lines that stretch all the way back to the Cretaceous period, even on days when the park isn't crowded. On busy days you can wait more than an hour, and there's no Express line. "It was not worth it," a dad from Florida confided to us. "We waited longer for Pteranodon Flyers than anything else in IOA and the ride doesn't last but about a minute."

In an effort to cut down on the line, Islands of Adventure has limited the ride to kids 36 to 56 inches tall, allowing one adult to ride with each child. In fact, the entrance signs al-

The Scare Factor

Pteranodon Flyers is fine for anyone who doesn't have a fear of heights, although there's a bit more swing to the Pteranodons than you'd guess.

Insider's Secret

Pteranodon Flyers generally opens around 10 AM. The tip board will give you exact times. If your kids are determined to ride, be at the entrance to Camp Jurassic as close to opening time as possible. Once Camp Jurassic is open, the line at Pteranodon Flyers can jump to a 20-minute wait within seconds.

most try to talk you out of riding, telling you that there are height requirements on both sides of the ruler and the ride lasts only 80 seconds. People flock to it anyway. Try to talk the kids out of riding unless you're there on a quiet day when the wait is less than 20 minutes.

Discovery Center

The Discovery Center is like a small, very hip museum. Little kids can make dinosaur sounds while the older ones X-ray eggs and guess which species is inside. The Dino DNA sequencing profile lets you superimpose your face onto a dinosaur, or you can test your scientific knowledge against two other contestants in a raucous game show called You Bet Jurassic.

The biggest kick is when a raptor hatches from an egg, a wonderful little treat in which an authentic-looking audio-animatronics baby pecks his way through the shell. The kids in the crowd get to name it. Being in the Discovery Center for a birth is a bit of a hit-or-miss proposition, but a honking noise alerts you that one of the eggs is getting ready to crack.

The center is cool and relatively uncrowded, making it a good place to drop by in the afternoon, when everyone's energy is flagging.

Insider's Secret

Successful touring depends on getting a midday rest. If you're visiting in summer, when the parks run long hours, you may want to return to your hotel for a swim and a nap after lunch, returning to the park in late afternoon. This is a snap if you're staying on Universal property and can take the boat back to your hotel. Families with a car may want to try it as well, especially if the commute between their hotel and Islands of Adventure is 20 minutes or less. Just save your parking receipt for reentry, and keep in mind that it's a pretty good hike to the parking garage.

The Lost Continent

The Lost Continent is probably the most thematically complex island in the park, encompassing three distinct sections. You begin in Merlinwood, which is based on the stories of Camelot and echoes medieval England with thatch-roof houses and Celtic music. This is where you can find Dueling Dragons, a roller coaster based on a legend so rich it takes Merlin himself to narrate the tale.

Within a few steps, the music and the mood change to indicate you're now in the Arabic section, home to the Eighth Voyage of Sindbad, and a jumble of tented, Middle Eastern shops in the marketplace known as Sindbad Village. There are fortune-tellers, and you can get your hair wrapped, your face painted, or your arm temporarily tattooed.

The last section of the Lost Continent is based on Atlantis. Here you can find the amazing-looking theater where Poseidon's Fury plays, and IOA's most elegant restaurant, Mythos.

Dueling Dragons

This double roller coaster, meant to emulate the battling Fire and Ice dragons, is the fiercest in the park, running at speeds of 55 to 60 mph. Two suspension-style coasters (that is, they hang beneath the track) operate at once, coming so close—within 12 inches of each other—in their mock battle that riders have the distinct impression they're going to crash.

Insider's Secret

Seeking the ultimate thrill? Dueling Dragons veterans say that riders in the outside seats are far more aware of how close the "close calls" really are. Or, if you want to have a good view of all the impending danger, queue up in the separate, longer line to wait for front-row seats.

The walkway to the ride is a long one, so there's plenty of time to establish the premise of how the Fire Dragon and the Ice Dragon have been fighting each other since time immemorial. As you wind through Merlinwood Castle, stained-glass windows tell the grim story of the demise of all who have approached the fierce dragons, and the muffled sound of their roars can be heard in the background. Merlin repeatedly advises you to turn back, but as you get closer to the ride, he accepts

Time-Saving Tip

If you want to ride Dueling Dragons twice to try out both Fire and Ice, try to ride in the morning. And as you exit, look for signs that say "Reentry to Ice" or "Reentry to Fire" so that you can loop back into the line without having to walk all the way out and back in again.

your determination and casts a spell to protect you. You're going to need it.

Dueling Dragons is a technologically complex ride; once you're loaded into one of the coasters, computers calculate the weight of your group of riders and make minute adjustments in speed to assure that the two dragons do indeed come within inches of each other at various points along the track. And in

The Scare Factor

Dueling Dragons is hands down the scariest ride in the park, as the 54-inch height requirement indicates. Children under 7 aren't allowed to ride, and it may even be too much for many kids 7 to 11.

terms of which dragon is scarier, our readers have a split of opinion, but it may come down to what you consider more un-nerving—plunging speeds or erratic motion. The red Fire Dragon goes about 5 mph faster, but the blue Ice Dragon, has more side-to-side movement.

Helpful Hint

Feeling queasy from your trip on Dueling Dragons? A first-aid station where you can sit and recover is among the shops of Sindbad Village.

The Eighth Voyage of Sindbad

This stunt show usually plays four to six times daily in the early afternoon and evening. (Showtimes are listed on your map.) The 25-minute show has every-thing you'd expect—fights, falls, drops, daring escapes,

The Scare Factor

Sindbad is another loud performance with lots of pyrotechnics including strobe lights and fog effects. In fact, there's so much fire on stage that those in the first three rows of the audience will feel the heat on their skin. If your kids are easily frightened and sensitive to loud noises, sit farther back.

and comedy in the form of an inept sidekick whose pratfalls are a lot more dangerous than they look. The theater is large, so you shouldn't have any trouble being seated as long as you show up 15 minutes before showtime. Sindbad is a good choice for afternoon, when you'll welcome the chance to sit down and rest for a while.

The Mystic Fountain

As you enter the theater where Sindbad plays, pause for a minute at the fountain in the courtyard. At various times throughout the day—including the periods just before and after a show—the mysterious spirit trapped within the Fountain of Knowledge will talk to you. The result is pretty funny as the spirit loves riddles, jokes, and questions and will gently tease any kids willing to step forward and enter the game. Encourage the kids to ask a question and be prepared for lots of punk attitude, as well as an occasional blast of water.

Poseidon's Fury: Escape from the Lost City

This 20-minute walk-through show takes place in one of the most impressive buildings in the whole theme park, a crumbling castle from the lost underwater city ruled by the water god Poseidon. The story line is established in the long, dark

Helpful Hint
You either walk or stand during Poseidon's Fury, so young kids in the back won't see much (this may be a blessing—see the Scare Factor). If you want a good view of the action, be sure to be among the first in your tour group to exit every room so that you can be in the front row in the next room.

Helpful Hint
Needing a little adult time? A glass of wine? A civilized menu? Decadent chocolate desserts? Just across from Poseidon's Fury is Mythos, a great place for a leisurely meal.

(and somewhat scary for kids) queue area, where we learn that we're on an archaeological dig at the ancient temple of Poseidon. But there's trouble—the power keeps flickering on and off, a professor is missing, and the sleep of an evil priest has been disturbed. He wants to find a powerful trident, and it's up

The Scare Factor
Poseidon's Fury is a walk-through show, not a ride, but the special effects are intense and the noise level is very high in places. Once you enter the castle, you're literally a captive audience; there are a couple of exit points along the way if children become frightened, but for most of the show you're in a series of darkened rooms. If your children are nervous, stand near the back, especially in the final room where the battle reaches its peak; viewers in the front will feel the fire-and-water effects more intensely than those in the rear.

Insider's Secret

The kiddie roller coaster known as the Flying Unicorn has been closed, and, in fact, the Lost Continent area is a bit torn up to make way for the new land based on the Harry Potter book series. Called The Wizarding World of Harry Potter, this "park within a park" is scheduled to open in 2010 and will be a completely interactive world where you can visit locations from the beloved book series, including Hogwarts, Hogsmeade, and the Forbidden Forest. (Author J.K. Rowling is serving as a creative consultant on the project, and the production designer from the film series is leading the creative design team to make sure the look is accurate enough to please even the most demanding fans.)

Although details are sketchy at this writing, you can expect a themed restaurant, immersive experiences, character meet and greets, plenty of merchandizing, and one gigantic centerpiece ride built around the stories of Harry Potter. To stay current on developments—and get the most accurate debut date—visit www.universalorlando.com.

to you, as the new archaeological team, to find the trident and restore it to its rightful owner, Poseidon.

You move from room to room, and there are some great special effects along the way. At one point you walk through a swirling tunnel of water. The final scene is a battle between fire and water, with plenty of splashing and pyrotechnics.

Seuss Landing

You'll find nothing but pastel colors and curved lines—even the trees are bent!—on this dream-like island, where everything looks like it popped out of a Dr. Seuss book. Almost everyone stops in their tracks at the sight of the amazing Caro-Seuss-el and the bright flying beasties of One Fish, Two Fish. But take your time strolling through—some of the best visual treats aren't so obvious.

One Fish, Two Fish, Red Fish, Blue Fish

One Fish, Two Fish is a circular thrill ride designed for young kids. Each fish has a joystick that controls the height of his flight, and throughout the ride you're given instructions such as "Red Fish fly high." If you opt to follow the instructions, that is, go "with the book," you stay dry. But if you disobey and go "against the book," one of the "bad fish" will spit on you. The idea is that this teaches kids to follow directions—I suspect it

Helpful Hint

One Fish, Two Fish can draw long lines in the afternoon. Come in the morning if you can.

The Scare Factor

One Fish, Two Fish is OK for any age. The joystick lets you keep it low for kids who dislike heights. Everyone flies high at the end of the ride for a few seconds, but by that time nervous kids have been aboard long enough to get used to the idea. The two-fish cars are big enough to let family members ride together.

really shows them how much fun it can be to rebel—but either way it's a terrific ride, and in the finale everyone aboard gets a spritz.

The Scare Factor

Expect some bumping and a few fast, tight spins of the car. Cat is designed to appeal to any age, however, and most kids love it.

The Cat in the Hat

This is a kiddie ride that's not just for the kiddies. A surprising number of kids from age 7 to 15 ranked Cat in the Hat as one of their favorites.

You board adorable couch-style cars to ride through 18 scenes taken straight from the well-loved book. The basic plot: Mom leaves, and the Cat in the Hat shows up with those well-known literary rowdies, Thing 1 and Thing 2. All sorts of mayhem results, sometimes enough to send your couch spinning wildly, and through it all the poor goldfish frantically tries to

Helpful Hint

Preschoolers will enjoy the Cat in the Hat ride, as well as the other Seuss Landing attractions, much more if they're familiar with the Dr. Seuss books. Read them on the trip to Orlando.

maintain order. The Cat in the Hat is like Spider-Man for the younger set. A lot goes on in a short time frame, and if you ride a second time you'll

Helpful Hint

Snapping the kids aboard the colorful Caro-Seuss-el is one of the best photo ops in the whole park.

notice even more clever details. The effects are so funny that any rider, no matter what the age, will exit with a grin on her face.

Caro-Seuss-el

The 54 mounts of this ultimate merry-go-round are all lifted directly from the stories of Dr. Seuss. While the up-and-down and round-and-round motion is familiar to any kid who has ever been on a carousel, the real kick is that you can make the beasties blink, flick their tails, and turn their heads.

High in the Sky Seuss Trolley

Once purely decorative, the little cars that circle Seuss Landing were eventually put into motion and are now part of a slow, gentle, trolley ride overlooking the attractions and at one point going through the Circus McGurkus Café. The 34-inch height

Insider's Secret

In terms of drawing long lines, the Trolley is a bit like Pteranodon Flyers: There are few cars and they move slowly, so board only if you have time to kill or the kids absolutely insist.

Insider's Secret

The emphasis on the big-deal rides makes many families automatically assume that Islands of Adventure is only for older kids. But the three play areas, and the attention to detail in all of Seuss Landing, show that Islands of Adventure has plenty to offer younger siblings as well.

restriction is more due to the construction of the cars than the intensity of the ride; shorter kids might be tempted to stand up just to be able to see out.

If I Ran the Zoo

IOA's third interactive play area was designed with preschoolers in mind, although older kids enjoy it, too. You can jump, climb, and squirt, as well as play tic-tac-toe with a Gak. Trap your friends in a cage of water or wait for the scraggle-foot Mulligatawny to sneeze—there's a silly surprise around every corner. A small water area gives younger kids a chance to cool off and splash around on a hot day.

Afternoon Resting Places

Families who'll be staying in the park all day need to build in afternoon rest stops to give everyone a chance to regroup. You basically have three options:

- *Restaurants.* Consider making lunch your big meal of the day. A sit-down meal, either at Confisco Grille, Mythos, or CityWalk is a chance to get off your feet and relax.

- *Shows.* The Eighth Voyage of Sindbad and the Pandemonium Circus shows give you a chance to sit down in a theater for a while. The Jurassic Park Discovery Center, although a museum-style attraction, is a quiet, calm, and cool place to catch your breath.

- *Play areas.* Sometimes kids just need to burn off their pent-up energy. If you suspect they need to climb, run, and play for a half hour, head for one of the three play areas.

Meeting the Characters

The times and places for character meetings are well marked on your map. The superheroes, including Spider-Man, appear in Marvel Super Hero Island; cartoon characters show up in Toon Lagoon; and the Seuss characters can be found, logically, in Seuss Landing. If you want to be guaranteed autographs and pictures without the elbow of some stranger from Michigan in each shot, make reservations for the character lunch at Confisco Grille.

Tips for Your Last Hour at Islands of Adventure

If you plan to have dinner at CityWalk, rest assured that 10,000 other people have the same good idea. Make reservations as you enter in the morning, if possible, or at least try to be sure you're out of the park at least an hour before it closes. If you're not planning to eat at CityWalk, it's still a good idea to be on your way 30 minutes before closing time, when a wave of people hits

Helpful Hint

Sometimes kids are overwhelmed by the characters, especially the Masked Marvels who show up on Marvel Super Hero Island, and the villains, such as Snidely Whiplash in Toon Lagoon and that nasty green Grinch in Seuss Landing. If your child appears nervous, don't push her forward; let her watch other kids pose for pictures for a while and she may loosen up. Asking for an autograph is a great way to break the ice.

the turnstiles at once, clogging the streets of CityWalk, and making the exit from the parking garage the wildest ride you've been on all day.

CityWalk

CityWalk is the dining, shopping, and entertainment complex that links Universal Studios with Islands of Adventure. A fun destination in its own right, CityWalk also provides more dining options than what's in the parks. If you'd like a break from touring, exit the park and head for lunch at CityWalk. Or stop there for dinner on your way home in the evening. CityWalk has shows and concerts every night, including a Blue Man Group production.

Good choices for family dining include:

@ *Bubba Gump Shrimp Co.* Shrimp . . . shrimp . . . and more shrimp in a casual, family-friendly environment. (Other types of seafood are on the menu as well, along with steaks and sandwiches.)

@ *Hard Rock Cafe.* The Hard Rock—and this is the world's largest, by the way—is munchie central, with indulgent

Helpful Hint
If you're staying on-site, make CityWalk dining reservations through Guest Services at your hotel. If you're staying off-site, you can make reservations at a well-marked booth as you enter CityWalk from the parking deck in the morning.

Money-Saving Tip

You can shop and dine at CityWalk without buying a ticket or paying a cover charge until around 8 PM when the club-hopping starts. And, once it does, if you want to visit several CityWalk clubs on a parents' night out, you can buy a one-price, all-clubs Party Pass for about $16. The cover charge for one club ranges $3–$7. The price of tickets for Hard Rock Live shows varies depending on the act. During the off-season you can frequently visit CityWalk for free with a multiday Universal Orlando theme park ticket.

snacks like potato skins, nachos, and the signature Pig Sandwich.

@ *Jimmy Buffett's Margaritaville.* The menu focuses on southern Florida and Caribbean foods, but you can also find Cheeseburgers in Paradise. The Volcano Bar erupts margaritas regularly, and entertainment consists of Buffett concerts on big-screen TVs and sometimes live music on the pleasant porch.

@ *NASCAR Sports Grille.* Expect good ol' boy cuisine such as ribs, steaks, and fried chicken. Race fans will enjoy the memorabilia scattered around the restaurant, the servers dressed like a pit crew, the rumble of race broadcasts on overhead TVs, and the NASCAR-theme games in the dedicated play area.

@ *NBA City.* It's a basketball-theme restaurant that serves Shaq-size servings of steak, pasta, and sandwiches, as well as hearty appetizers such as buffalo wings and quesadillas. Basketball games, both current and classic, play on giant screens throughout the sports bar and restaurant.

@ *Pastamore.* This Italian restaurant doesn't offer much entertainment, but the food is good and the lack of glitz makes it the easiest to slip into when CityWalk is crowded. Specialties include oven-roasted pizzas and excellent gelato.

Some CityWalk restaurants are more suitable for adults:

@ *Bob Marley's.* Modeled after Marley's home in Kingston, Jamaica, this restaurant serves island-influenced dishes like jerk chicken, plantains, and tropical fruit salads. The outdoor patio is the perfect spot for casual eating and drinking, especially at night when live reggae bands play.

@ *CityJazz.* Intimate and low-key, CityJazz offers live jazz music and a limited menu of tapas-style appetizers, as well as a martini bar and a wide selection of wines by the glass. During the off-season, the club is only open on weekends.

@ *Emeril's.* The most upscale and expensive option at City-Walk, Emeril's offers amazing food, such as crabmeat-crusted tournedos of beef and citrus-glaze duck. The

Insider's Secret

Emeril's is a popular restaurant, so you need reservations, at least for dinner, and it never hurts to make them before you leave home. Call 407/224–2424 to get your name on the list. If you don't have a reservation, it's easier to find a table at lunch.

restaurant is never stuffy or overly formal and is, in fact, the perfect spot for a parents' night out.

@ *The Groove.* The most high-energy dance club at City-Walk, the Groove hosts a variety of theme parties, including hip-hop, trance, retro, progressive, Top 40, and alcohol-free teen-oriented nights.

@ *Hard Rock Live.* A 2,500-seat auditorium adjacent to the Hard Rock Cafe, Hard Rock Live has a "state of the future" sound system and offers an impressive roster of musical acts. To check out who's playing while you're in town, visit www.universalorlando.com.

@ *Latin Quarter.* Some of the best food in CityWalk is served at Latin Quarter; examples of dinners include pork loin marinated in orange and cilantro, and broiled red snapper on yellow rice. Musicians play salsa and merengue music, while professional dancers and vacationing wannabes dance far into the night.

@ *Pat O'Brien's.* This New Orleans import has a casual dining menu but is really known for its huge fruit drinks—especially the Hurricane, so named because it's rumored to knock you level in two minutes flat. Enjoy your two minutes in the piano bar.

@ *Red Coconut Lounge.* Another enormous lounge and nightclub with dancing and drinks, this time in a more tropical setting.

@ *Blue Man Group.* The group plays Wednesday–Sunday in its own Sharp Aquos Theater next to Universal Studios. The 90-minute shows feature rock music, heavy percussion, audience participation, and lots of zany gimmicks, such as hurling food from the stage into the audience. The three Blue Men—who remain mute and eerily robotic with their shiny blue grease paint faces—anchor the show, which is popular with older kids. Prices start at $59 for adults, $49 for kids 3–9. Order tickets in advance at www.universalorlando.com or by calling 407/363–8000. (Oh, and don't worry—ushers pass out waterproof ponchos to guests in the "hurl zone.")

16 SeaWorld and Discovery Cove

SeaWorld

SeaWorld is a low-stress experience, and much less frenzied than the other Orlando parks. Easily toured in six or seven hours, it's laid out so that the crowds pretty much flow from one scheduled animal show to another, working in the smaller attractions along the way. SeaWorld is so beautifully landscaped that you often can't see one stadium from the other, and the sense of space is a welcome change after a week spent at Disney. But the openness also means that children up to age 5 will benefit from a stroller. Strollers are $11, $17 for a double. You can also rent wheelchairs for $10 and ECVs for $40.

SeaWorld admission is $70 for adults and $60 for children ages 3 to 9, excluding tax, but there's an incentive for buying your tickets online at least seven days in advance: the price drops to $60 for everyone. Parking is $10. Call 800/SEA–WORLD or visit www.seaworldorlando.com for more information.

If you're headed to the other SeaWorld parks, combo tickets are available. Two-park tickets for SeaWorld and Aquatica are $95 for adults and $85 for kids, a fairly significant savings.

If you'd like to add Discovery Cove and Busch Gardens to your ticket, the package prices begin at $287 regardless of age.

Shows

For years SeaWorld's claim to fame has been its animal shows, especially those that feature the dolphins, the sea lions, and the park icon, Shamu. These three classics plus Pets Ahoy!, a show starring a talented cast of dogs, cats, and other rescued animals, are the most fascinating. The shows are periodically updated to feature new technological advances, but most of this is window-dressing. It's hard to improve upon the grandeur and charm of the animals themselves. See them if you do nothing else.

The dolphin show, the sea lion show, and the Shamu show all take place in enormous open-air theaters, so touring SeaWorld is as simple as consulting your map for showtimes and being at the theater about 30 minutes early, 40 in the on-season. Sea-World does a good job of keeping tabs on crowding and providing accurate estimates on how early you need to be there.

Insider's Secret

Young kids love the dogs and cats of Pets Ahoy! and you can come up front and meet the animal stars after the show.

Insider's Secret

Be forewarned that if you opt to sit in the "splash zone"—the first 10 rows of the stadium—Shamu's good-bye wave will leave you drenched straight through to your underwear. Kids enjoy the blast of saltwater, at least on a summer day, but if you're touring off-season or catching a nighttime show, it's wiser to sit farther back and laugh at the unwary tourists down by the tank.

Rides

There are only three mainliner attraction rides, but they pack quite a punch. Plus, since the shows are the main attraction, the lines for the rides are shorter than at Disney and Universal. A mother of three from Michigan visited SeaWorld in the off-season and reported, "After all the time we spent waiting in line for rides at Disney and Universal, we were stunned to find that two of the rides at SeaWorld had practically no waits at all. The kids loved Kraken and were able to ride it several times with no wait."

Journey to Atlantis

SeaWorld's version of Splash Mountain, Journey to Atlantis takes you on a sometimes-gentle, sometimes-not water-flume ride through the lost city of Atlantis, then drops you down a steep incline to a great big splash below.

You start by boarding Greek fishing boats and are promptly lured by sirens into the depths of the lost city. The tiny boats twist, dodge, and dive through the water. For the first drop, the tracks come out of the front of the building, but the sirens pull you back for the second, unseen, 60-foot, S-shaped drop. The story line is weak and somewhat confusing compared with Splash Mountain, but the two drops near the end of the ride are totally thrilling.

Helpful Hint
If you have a rain poncho, bring it. This one's a soaker.

The Scare Factor
The height requirement is 42 inches. Kids 7 and up should be okay.

Kraken

Kraken reaches speeds of 65 mph with seven loops and three different points where it plunges underground into misty tunnels. We're talking major intensity. When I first read about Kraken, I suspected the name referred to the sounds your back and neck made as you rode. Not so. The motion of the ride is surprisingly smooth and the name actually refers to the great underwater dragon-monster of ancient Norse mythology.

The Scare Factor

The height requirement for Kraken is 54 inches. Kids under 8 should not ride.

Manta

SeaWorld's newest ride is opening at this writing and isn't available for review. Like most new attractions, it will almost certainly be popular when it opens and draw longer-than-average lines during its first year of operation. Manta looks both beautiful and powerful, much like the creature it is named for. Riders fly face down in a horizontal "superman" position, hanging beneath the wingspan of the manta. With a track that's over 3,000 feet, a variety or swooping dips and turns, and speeds of up to 60 mph, it's not surprising that the height requirement will be 54 inches. Probably too much for kids under 8.

SeaWorld also has some very simple kiddie rides inside Shamu's Happy Harbor, a play area across from Shamu Stadium. They include:

- Sea Carousel, a fish- and dolphin-theme merry-go-round

- Jazzy Jellies, swirling jellyfish that rise into the air

- Ocean Commotion, a spinning boat ride

- Swishy Fishies, a gentle teacup ride

- Flying Fiddler, a chair ride that rises and gently drops, a kiddie version of Dr. Doom at Islands of Adventure

- Shamu Express, a small coaster akin to Goofy's Barnstormer at the Magic Kingdom

Standing Exhibits

SeaWorld is also known for its fascinating standing exhibits, such as the Penguin Encounter, where you can observe the

Insider's Secret

At both the dolphin and sea lion exhibits you can buy fish and feed the animals. This is exciting for the kids and the ultimate photo op.

tuxedoed charmers both above and below the ice floe, and witness their startling transformation from awkward walkers to sleek swimmers. Check your map, which is also your entertainment schedule, for feeding times, when the trainers slip about on the iceberg with buckets of fish and the penguins waddle determinedly behind them.

If your kids are too cool to like cute, try the Terrors of the Deep exhibit, where you'll encounter sharks, moray eels, and barracudas up close.

The California sea lions live at Pacific Point Preserve, and in the Key West section, you can find the endangered manatee, as well as dolphins, stingrays, sea turtles, and other species indigenous to the Florida Keys. There are underwater viewing tanks where you can observe many of the animals from a different perspective. The newest exhibit houses the majestic mantas. These exhibits don't have special showtimes and can be visited at your leisure as you circle the park.

Wild Arctic is dedicated to polar bears. You can opt to ascend to the top of the exhibit either via a simulated helicopter ride or by walking. (Kids must be 42 inches tall to take the simulator ride.) The ride is a total snooze in comparison to the Disney and Universal simulator rides so you may as well save yourself the time and just walk to the top of the exhibit. The fun part is seeing the bears anyway, especially watching them from the underwater tanks.

Finally, the Budweiser Clydesdales are also part of the SeaWorld family, and everyone enjoys meeting these gentle creatures in their pretty stable. Children can get their pictures taken with a Clydesdale in one of the stalls during designated hours. The nearby Anheuser-Busch Hospitality Center is a quiet, cool escape from the rest of the park; there's free beer (you heard right) for adults, and the deli inside is never as crowded as other SeaWorld restaurants.

Insider's Secret

At certain times of the day, noted on your park map, one of the Clydesdales is taken out into a paddock and children are allowed to get close enough to have their pictures taken. The horses are so enormous that it makes a memorable snapshot.

Preschoolers and Toddlers

Small children at SeaWorld welcome the numerous chances to get close to the animals, so save plenty of time for the standing exhibits where you can feed a sea lion or reach over to touch a dolphin or stingray. At theme parks it's easy to get caught up in dashing from show to show but, especially with preschoolers, it's essential to slow down and savor the small moments of animal interaction.

Another kick for kids is Shamu's Happy Harbor, a play area that's not only happy but huge, with an elaborate web of climbing nets, a ship with water-firing muskets, a splashy climb-through fountain area, ball pits to sink into, and padded pyramids to climb. After a few hours spent in shows or exhibits, drop by and let the kids just play for a while. There's rarely a wait for any of the six kiddie rides. "Shamu's Happy Harbor is just that—happy," said one dad from Pennsylvania. "We have three kids under 6, and we just parked the strollers and let them play for awhile. They loved getting wet and splashing around, and there was absolutely no wait for the kiddie rides."

Helpful Hint

Appropriately, the crowd at SeaWorld moves in waves. The shows are timed so that you can move around the park in a circular fashion, taking in one show after another.

This also means, however, that if you want to visit standing exhibits, feed the animals, or play in Shamu's Happy Harbor, some times are far more crowded than others. For example, Shamu's Happy Harbor is virtually empty while the nearby Shamu show is going on, but the minute the show is over a flood of people head for the playground.

The solution? If you have young kids and would like to be able to play in the Harbor or interact with the animals in a calm, unrushed manner, make note of when the shows are in session and visit the play area or standing exhibits then.

Helpful Hint
The Baby Care and Lost Child Center, which has a shady porch and rockers, is also in Shamu's Happy Harbor—convenient, since this is the part of the park where you're most likely to lose track of your child.

A separate play area for smaller kids ensures that they don't get tangled up in the webs, whacked by an older kid on a tire swing, or, worst of all, lost. Because several of the play areas involve water, some parents let kids wear their bathing suits under their shorts and totally cool off. There's a midway and arcade next door where older kids can hang out while the younger ones play.

SeaWorld Adventure Camps

SeaWorld hosts educational camps for all age groups. Preschoolers (with a parent along) can participate in morning camps that explore how the animals are fed or how they play hide-and-seek in their environments. Grade-school-level children have lots of choices; there are weeklong camps that study dolphins, manatees, sharks, and other SeaWorld residents. Teenagers can participate in weeklong resident camps where they go behind the scenes of the park and assist the trainers in caring for the animals. Most of the day camps take place in summer, although some programs are offered periodically throughout the year. Prices begin at $280 per child.

Another neat option is the Family Sleepovers. Held in summer and on major holidays, these behind-the-scenes parties culminate in participants grabbing a sleeping bag and bedding down in the midst of one of SeaWorld's exhibits. (At present you're sleeping with the fishes, so to speak, in the manta exhibit.) Prices begin at $78 per person; if you'd like to include admission to SeaWorld for the day following the sleepover, the price rises to $113.

For information on all your options, call 800/406–2244 or visit www.seaworld.org.

Behind-the-Scenes Tours

There are plenty of ways to get an insider's look at SeaWorld. An exclusive 7-hour tour called Adventure Express gives guests a behind-the-scenes penguin encounter and a chance to feed dolphins, sea lions, and stingrays. The tour also includes front-of-the-line access for Kraken, Journey to Atlantis, Manta, Wild Arctic, reserve seating at shows, and a buffet meal backstage at Believe, the Shamu show. The price is $100 for adults, $80 for kids 3–9.

There are also several hour-long tours that venture behind the scenes. The most elaborate is the Dolphin Nursery Tour for guests 10 and up ($50 adults, $40 children), which allows you to meet a trainer during your backstage visit and interact with a dolphin family. Three other tours are less expensive ($12 adults, $8 children 3–9), such as the Polar Expedition, which takes you to the backstage areas of Wild Arctic and allows you to touch a penguin; Predators, where you visit backstage at Shamu Stadium and get to touch a small shark; and Saving a Species, where you visit rescue and rehabilitation facilities for manatees and sea turtles and get to hand-feed exotic birds.

These tours make great fodder for school projects, especially if you're feeling guilty about having your kids miss school to visit Orlando. You can reserve the tours in advance at 800/327–2244 or www.seaworldorlando.com. If you haven't made reservations, it's often possible to book a tour on the same day you're visiting. The tour booth, on the left as you enter the park, is easy to spot.

Discovery Cove

Discovery Cove offers you a chance to actually have up-close encounters with dolphins and other sea life. You get to swim and play with bottlenose dolphins, and snorkel through clouds of fish in a coral reef lagoon. Or you can just enjoy the tropical island ambience of beach chairs, hammocks, swaying palm trees, cooing birds—and hardly any people.

That's right. The most unique thing about Discovery Cove is what it doesn't have. Crowds. This is a reservations-only park that admits a mere 1,000 people per day. With such a low number of guests, you truly have the personal attention of the staff, which includes expert trainers (many of them drafted from SeaWorld, Discovery Cove's sister park).

Helpful Hint
Bring beach shoes. The pools are quite rocky.

You check in at a concierge desk (!) and from there a guide takes you on a walking tour of the park, explaining all the activities. A swim in the dolphin lagoon is the undeniable highlight of the day, but reserved for guests 6 or older. The trainers teach you about dolphin behaviors and then lead you out into the water where you play with the dolphin and learn how to communicate basic commands. Once you and the animal get used to each other, you can end the session by grasping onto his dorsal fin and going on a wild ride across the bay.

The saltwater coral lagoon offers a variety of experiences, including the chance to snorkel among tropical fish. Since the water is calm, clear, and warm, and there are thousands of fish, this is a great first snorkeling experience for young kids. In the ray lagoon, you can play with gentle stingrays, some as big as four feet in diameter, whose barbs have been removed, or you can swim alongside barracuda and sharks kept behind Plexiglas.

A freshwater tropical river meanders its way through the park. As you float along you pass through several different settings, including a tropical fishing village, an underwater cave, and an immense aviary that houses 300 birds from all over the world.

When you've explored to your heart's content, there's no better way to end the day than by snoozing in your hammock on a white-sand beach.

So what do you pay for this bliss? Prices are $289 per person if you opt for the dolphin swim. If you're willing to forgo the swim with the dolphins, the price is $189, but you'll be missing the major thrill of the park. (Since kids under 6 aren't allowed to participate in the dolphin program, the price is automatically $189 for children 3 to 5.) The price includes wet suits, beach umbrellas, lounge chairs, towels, a locker, swim and snorkel gear, and lunch. For details and reservations (remember, they're a must), call 877/434–7268 (877/4–DISCOVERY) or visit www.discoverycove.com.

Aquatica

Aquatica, SeaWorld's major new 60-acre water park, is just across I-Drive from SeaWorld. Positioned as a competitor to Disney's Typhoon Lagoon and Blizzard Beach water parks, Aquatica has been outfitted with all the slides and wave pools you'd expect from an Orlando water park and plenty of special SeaWorld touches as well.

   © *Dolphin Plunge.* In the park's signature ride, you zip 300 feet down a narrow tube into a lagoon holding two Commerson's dolphins. The plunge lives up to the hype—the dolphins, not so much. The bottom part of the tube is see-through, which means, theoretically, you can see the dolphins as you pass, but you move through in seconds, and there's water splashing your eyes the whole time. In other words, most people are zipping by so fast that they see zip. There are only two slides going on this ride, so expect to wait about an hour at peak times. Riders must be 48 inches tall.

Insider's Secret

From an animal standpoint, the Dolphin Plunge, prominently featured in Aquatica ads, is a bit of a letdown. "The Web site plays it up like you swim with dolphins," wrote one mother from Georgia. "The reality is that the clear tube that runs through the dolphin tank is only for a couple of seconds at the end of the ride—blink and you miss it totally. Fortunately, the rest of the park was great."

@ *Taumata Racer.* In the aquatic equivalent of a bobsled run, you climb into one of eight lanes and start your descent down 300 feet of slides, which includes a 360-degree turn at the top. The thrill as you crest the top of the slide is palpable (be sure to hold tightly to your blue mat) and the eight lanes mean that the line for this slide moves more quickly than Dolphin Plunge's. Riders must be 42 inches tall, and kids below 48 inches must wear a life vest.

@ *Roa's Rapids.* A flowing current is the highlight of this attraction that takes you along rapids and occasional waterfalls. Roa's is a lot of bang for the buck: There's no line (though the waters can get crowded with visitors at times), and, after strapping on your life jacket, you'll wade into the rapids via a wide entrance lane (and you exit the same way). You can hold on to your child as you bob around, and you're free to circle the rapids as many times as you wish. "Soooo much fun," wrote a teen from Ohio. "The current really challenges you, and we were pooped by the time we got out."

@ *Loggerhead Lane.* In contrast to Roa's Rapids, this is indeed a lazy river. A high point is that the lane leads to a 10,000 gallon grotto filled with thousands of colorful fish and a view of the Commerson's dolphins. There's next to no pull, so you might have to paddle a bit, especially if you want to choose the turn with the fish grotto.

@ *Tassie's Twisters.* This zippy little tube ride empties you into a large circular bowl, where you make a few wild revolutions before slipping down another tube, which leads you back into the Loggerhead Lane lazy river. (The resemblance to a toilet is impossible to overlook.) Fun and wild without being too scary, this is a good test to see if kids are up to handling the bigger flumes.

@ *Walkabout Waters.* Here, in one of the world's largest interactive water-play areas, a colorful 60-foot fortress provides 15,000 square feet of family slides, pools, water cannons, and two large buckets that periodically dump water on frolickers below. "A great option for families with preschoolers," said one mother. "Nothing scary at all and once my kids warmed up on the family slides, which let us all go together, they felt brave enough to do a few things in the general park."

@ *Wahalla Wave and Hoo Roo Run.* These family raft rides are side-by-side. Wahalla Wave is a winding descent from a six-story-high mountain, while Hoo Roo Run is more of a straight shot down with a couple of bumps along the way. Both are a lot of fun and, since riding together dilutes the intensity, they're another chance to break nervous kids in. "My twin 8-year-old sons weren't so keen at first," said a mom from London. "But all riding together made it a family adventure, and they got off with the giggles. Only trouble was, they liked it so well we had to do both slides again, and I almost never got them to move on and see more of the park." Riders must be 42 inches tall, and kids under 48 inches must wear a life vest.

- *Whanau Way.* You climb into tubes and have a choice of four descents, each winding with periods of darkness and a couple of steep drops along the way. You can also choose between one- and two-person tubes. Whanau Way is one of the most popular attractions in the park but because there are four points of descent, the line moves fairly rapidly.

- *Kate's Kookaburra Cove.* This play area has fountains and an array of small slides. Tucked away behind the cabanas that surround Big Surf Shores, Kate's never seems to be quite as crowded as Walkabout Waters. Note: Kids must be no taller than 48 inches to play.

- *Big Surf Shores and Cutback Cove.* Twin side-by-side lagoons provide different waves for different tastes. Since the pools are independent, one can generate crashing waves with five-foot swells while the other might provide gently rolling surf that laps the shore. A plus for parents is that it's easy to move from one pool to the other, and the park's white-sand beach faces the pools, providing a good base of operations if you're spending a lot of time in this area.

Insider's Secret

Aquatica draws large crowds, and after a certain capacity is reached, the park closes to ensure the safety of its guests. To avoid being shut out, come first thing in the morning or—if you're visiting in the summer with its extended evening hours—arrive in late afternoon, when people are beginning to drift out.

Aquatica admission is $42 for adults and $36 for children 3 to 9, excluding tax. The two-park combo tickets ($95 adult, $85 child) are a good deal if you're also planning to visit SeaWorld. Visit www.aquaticabyseaworld.com for more details.

Index

Notes

Notes

Notes

Notes

Write to Us

I love to hear from families about their trips to Walt Disney World, Universal Orlando, and SeaWorld. Stories and feedback from families like yours help me shape this book. If you'd like to share your travel experiences with me, please take a few minutes to respond to any or all of the questions below. I might quote your responses in the next edition. You can either fill out this survey online at www.fodors.com/disneysurvey, e-mail me at kwwiley@fodors.com or write to me at Fodor's, 1745 Broadway, New York, NY 10019. Thanks for your time!

— Kim Wright Wiley

1. When did you last visit Walt Disney World and/or Universal Orlando? How long did you stay?

   _____

   _____

2. What are the ages of your children?

   _____

   _____

3. Did your family travel alone or with friends and extended family? How many people were in your party?

   _____

   _____

4. Where did you stay? Were you pleased with the hotel? Did you feel it offered a fair level of services and amenities for the price?

   _____

   _____

5. Would you choose that hotel again?

   _____

   _____

6. Which park did your family most enjoy? (For questions 6–12 if there's a split of opinion among family members, please put the age of the respondent beside the choice.)

   _____

   _____

7. What was your family's favorite attraction in the Magic Kingdom?

_____

_____

8. What was your family's favorite attraction at Epcot?

_____

_____

9. What was your family's favorite attraction at Disney's Hollywood Studios?

_____

_____

10. What was your family's favorite attraction at the Animal Kingdom?

_____

_____

11. Were there any attractions that proved to be too frightening or too intense for your child? If so, please describe the situation.

_____

_____

12. Did you take part in any character meals? If so, did you enjoy it?

_____

_____

13. What advice would you give to other families traveling to Walt Disney World?

_____

_____

_____

_____